# THE
# IRISH
# IN
# PHILADELPHIA

# THE
# IRISH
# IN
# PHILADELPHIA

## TEN GENERATIONS OF URBAN EXPERIENCE

### DENNIS CLARK

Temple University Press

Philadelphia

Temple University Press, Philadelphia 19122
© 1973 by Temple University. All rights reserved
Published 1973
Second printing 1974
Third printing 1981
Fourth printing 1984
Printed in the United States of America

*Library of Congress Cataloging in Publication Data*
Clark, Dennis, 1927–
The Irish in Philadelphia.
Bibliography: p.
Includes index.
1. Irish Americans—Pennsylvania—Philadelphia—
History.  2. Philadelphia (Pa.)—History.  I. Title.
F158.9.I6C55   1981   974.8'110049162   81-18343
ISBN 0-87722-057-3   AACR2
ISBN 0-87722-227-4 (pbk.)

*To my wife, Josepha,*
*daughter of the O'Callaghans*

# CONTENTS

vii

# FOREWORD

Interest in urban history is steadily growing as America be-
comes overwhelmingly a nation of metropolitan complexes
with inner cities surrounded by a seemingly endless series of
suburbs. Can diverse people live together successfully in these
urban centers? Why are some cities quiet and conservative
communities and others unstable and conflict-prone? Is there
a relationship among economic growth, corrupt machine politics, and social integration?

The answers to these and other questions can only come
from detailed studies of actual city experience. Dennis Clark's
careful and incisive account of the Irish migration to Philadelphia and its consequences over the past century and a
quarter is an important addition to the small number of such
studies.

Superficially, Philadelphia is much like those other major
cities on the Atlantic seaboard to which the Irish fled after
the potato famine. Yet everyone knows that Philadelphia is
considerably different from Boston and New York and that
the experience of the Philadelphia Irish took a notably different course. The virtue of this book is that it goes far toward
explaining "what everyone knows" about Philadelphia but
finds hard to pin down.

Clark begins with basics. He points out, for example, the
simple fact of Philadelphia's much greater land area compared with that of Boston and Manhattan. Because land was
more available, land prices were considerably lower and the
population could become more widely dispersed. In one of his
best chapters, Clark analyzes Philadelphia's housing. Cheap,
available land made possible the low-density neighborhoods

in which ordinary working-class families were able to own a two-story brick row house. Low-cost, decent housing had many fascinating ramifications. For one thing, it meant the death rate in Philadelphia for the early Irish was dramatically lower than for the same group elsewhere: 12.2 per thousand, compared with 21.2 for New York and 37.7 for Boston. The city avoided the congestion and squalor of New York's tenements. "The owner-occupied row house fortified Philadelphians in a pattern of localism that gave the city's neighborhood life a settled quality and stability. Home ownership made neighborhoods less subject to turnover."

The industrial boom which Pennsylvania enjoyed in the middle and last decades of the nineteenth century enabled Philadelphia to absorb tens of thousands of impoverished Irish immigrants with very little overt friction. There were, of course, serious economic hardships for the immigrants, but the Irish rapidly penetrated the business community as building contractors, real estate brokers, saloonkeepers, and grocers. Many others entered the "aristocracy of labor" as skilled craftsmen. For the first generation of Irish, the contrast was vivid between this upward mobility and the stagnation and low economic horizons of rural Ireland. The record of the Irish in nineteenth-century Philadelphia suggests strongly that when an urban community has to accommodate large numbers of working-class newcomers, nothing helps social adjustment more than full employment and an expanding economy.

Philadelphia is unique among the older big cities in not developing a political machine controlled by the Irish. It had a machine, all right, and the Irish played prominent roles in running it, but they were never in exclusive control for long periods as they were in Boston, New York, and Chicago. The city did not have its first Irish Catholic mayor until 1962. Analyzing this deviation from the big-city norm, Clark shows how the Irish fractured their own potential strength. Many of them had the characteristic Irish affinity for the Democratic party, but the long-dominant Republican organization detached enough Irish to maintain unbroken primacy. The result was that the Irish exercised less political leadership in Philadelphia than elsewhere.

The Irish led the way in constructing that network of schools and churches, of fraternal societies and neighborhood alliances, and of Catholic prestige symbols and cultural totems which constitutes a flourishing ethnic subculture. The value of such subcultures in making big cities viable is only now being appreciated. Once they were objects of attack and ridicule as "clannish" and leading to "hyphenated loyalties." More recently, with the movement to the suburbs and the weakening of many of these ethnic subcultures, cities have seemed destabilized and less governable. Clark accurately observes that although these subcultures cushioned their members against misfortunes in the days before the welfare state and helped preserve a sense of identity, they had other more ambiguous results: "Within the social structure of the city, the Irish subculture acted in different ways, sometimes as a magnet, sometimes as a centrifuge, sometimes as a protective shell." What provided a wall of security could also be a barrier to adventure and risk taking; what preserved old and desirable values could also promote an excessive inwardness.

By American standards, Philadelphia is a very old city. It is a conservative city. The Irish are a volatile people; yet they have for a long time generated forces which have helped make the city operate in the way it has. For those interested in Philadelphia in particular and in cities in general, a reading of this book richly repays in fresh insights and deeper understanding.

WILLIAM V. SHANNON

# PREFACE

This is a book about one people in two countries. It is about an ancient people—the Irish—engaged with the tumultuous forces of modern city growth. Although it deals with only a portion of the great outpouring of population from Ireland that settled in American cities, it attempts to discern the process by which Irish countrymen became American urbanites.

For those of us who have had to cope with the recurring waves of city growth and distress in the twentieth century, the process by which our urban centers developed in the industrial age of the nineteenth century is of continuing interest. The technical and industrial expansion of our great cities in the last century took place within the vast panorama of trans-Atlantic migration. The ways in which harassed and struggling people from rural backgrounds learned to live amid the extraordinary new environment of industrial urbanism makes a fascinating drama of human endeavor and adjustment.

For the social historian, the flight of multitudes from Ireland to America is but one episode in the passage of modern man from ancient customs rooted in the soil to a new form of civilization founded upon the mastery of nature through science and technology. Since the eighteenth century, the gathering momentum of technological change has produced a "revolution of environment." [1] This transformation has, in turn, had profound effects upon human development and patterns of living throughout the world. From the point of view of American social historians only the most tentative inroads have been made into the study of this momentous change. [2] The same may be said of the study of the adjustment of immigrants to the urban environment. [3]

As an example of urban evolution involving immigrants, the city of Philadelphia has not been intensely studied. Indeed, the Irish community in the city has hardly been adverted to by professional historians, despite the fact that the city's Irish bear attributes that make them distinct as an urban ethnic group. First, their record of presence in the city is more extensive than that of any other urban group commonly considered an ethnic minority. Second, the Irish in their homeland have been and are, even today, singularly rural, and their transition from the Irish countryside to the vast complexity of American cities represents a journey from one edge of the continuum of social organization to the other. Third, the fact that the Irish were largely an English-speaking group when their huge migration to America began was to have broad implications for their adjustment to the dominant American culture. Finally, the Irish Roman Catholics, who were the great majority of the immigrants from Ireland, had a remarkable attachment to their church and in manifold ways used the extensive resources of this international organizational system to augment their group development.

Philadelphia, the setting for this study and my native city, has been ill-served by historians. Works on its past tend to deal at length with its distinguished colonial and Revolutionary periods, and the few histories dealing with the industrial and demographic changes that have produced its modern form are quite limited. In this sense, the history of the city is truncated. Books such as *The Philadelphia Gentlemen* and *The Perennial Philadelphians* give a good insight into some parts of the social structure of the city and should have prompted much further study. *The Private City: Philadelphia* is a much needed attempt to comprehend the scope of the city's evolution, but its limitations testify to the need for a large-scale effort to investigate and interpret the history of a city whose past in many respects differs conspicuously from those of other major American centers.[4]

I am readily aware of the shortcomings of this study. It is based upon diverse sources and lacks the consistency that the continuous exploration of a body of fully congruent materials might have provided; it concentrates upon the mid–nineteenth century, but there are absorbing topics to be pursued on both sides of that time period; and it gives inadequate attention to church history, labor history, and the analysis of various facets of social adjustment. I hope that time and resources will permit me to remedy such deficiencies in the future.

On several subjects this book offers revisionist interpretations. One is the ability of the Irish to adjust to urban life and the capacity of Philadelphia to facilitate this process. Another is the role of Philadelphians in the Irish-American nationalist movement dedicated to the liberation of the old country. These topics, and such matters as the significance of the anti-Catholic riots of 1844 and the role of the contractor-political boss, will remain subjects for historical debate. At least that debate should now contain additional references to the Philadelphia Irish experience.

In writing this book I have had recourse to the knowledge, memory, and skill of many people in both Ireland and the United States. It is with gratitude that I acknowledge this assistance and that of various institutions. In Ireland, the late Dr. James Scott of Queens University, Belfast; Dr. Thomas Wall of the Irish Folklore Commission, Dublin; and Miss Fidelma Clearkin of Trinity College Library, Dublin, were helpful in tracing important facts; and James McCann and Mr. and Mrs. Philip Burns of Shercock, County Cavan, were able interpreters of Irish rural traditions. In the United States, my gratitude is due Miss Kathleen Cohalan of the American Irish Historical Society in New York; the late Dr. Maire Condon of San Jose State College, California; Dr. Eoin McKiernan of the Irish American Cultural Institute, St. Paul, Minnesota; Mr. John Daly, archival examiner of the Archives of the City of Philadelphia; Father Edmund Halsey, curator of the Ar-

chives of the American Catholic Historical Society at Saint
Charles Seminary, Overbrook, Pennsylvania; and Dr. Raymond Schmandt and the late Dr. John J. Kane of Saint Joseph's College, Philadelphia. My special thanks go to Dr.
Allen Davis, Dr. Mark Haller, Dr. Philip Benjamin, and Dr.
Seth Scheiner, present and former members of the Department of History, Temple University. Without their assistance,
this book would not have emerged. To Dr. Paul Anderson,
former president of Temple University, my appreciation is extended for a travel grant in 1966 permitting me to complete
part of my investigations in Ireland.

Numerous skilled librarians have aided my searches for
materials in the fine collections of the National Library of
Ireland, Dublin; the libraries of Temple University, the University of Pennsylvania, and Villanova University; the Library Company of Philadelphia; and the Historical Society
of Pennsylvania. Two very able typists, each possessing a
lively sense of humor and history, worked to prepare the
manuscript: Mrs. Barbara Harley and Mrs. Ailis McInerney
Kumbhat.

Finally, I am grateful to all those Philadelphia Irish, including my parents and family, who imparted to me the lore,
memories, and enthusiasm required to complete this book.
They have retained and transmitted that sense of loyalty to
one's own without which no group and no man can survive.

In 1976 Philadelphia celebrates the bicentennial of the
founding, in that city, of the American nation. The problems
of the city will provide a grave reminder that the American
urban achievement is still a sphere for deep national concern.
How we have settled, built, used resources, and dealt with one
another raises trenchant questions about our integrity as a
people and our performance as citizens of a revolutionary
environment. It is my hope that this book will provide helpful
knowledge of our urban ways, and that this knowledge will help
to induce a greater understanding of the civic responsibility

needed if our cities are to be humane and ordered places for democratic life.

DENNIS CLARK

Philadelphia

# THE

# IRISH

# IN

# PHILADELPHIA

# ONE

## A TRADITION
## GROWS

On both sides of the Atlantic the Irish people have lived through the great transformations that have convulsed the modern era. Ten Irish generations over the last three centuries have experienced the reorganization of agricultural life, famine, and emigration. Political nationalism, guerrilla and civil war, and industrialization have swept through the life of this people. These movements have caused profound changes in their ancient island homeland and have scattered millions of Irishmen abroad. Beyond the seas the Irish concentrated in the cities of the new age, the centers of modernization with their novel patterns of human settlement and technical virtuosity. In these centers, especially the seaboard cities of America, the people of Ireland found a haven from the recurrent tragedies that plagued their native land.

The city of Philadelphia is one of the urban centers to which Irish people came steadily, beginning in the seventeenth century. It is a city in which the kind of urban development that has been a central experience for millions of men in the modern world has been enacted. Beginning as a religious refuge and utopia, the city moved on to mercantile eminence, democratic revolution, and industrial greatness. Through it all the Irish continued to come, and their experience in the city constitutes a fascinating study.

To explore the growth of the ethnic tradition of the Irish in the city, it is necessary to review the conditions in Ireland that first compelled their emigration. The migration of the Irish to the American cities has been more than a change of place; it has been one chapter in a global development that has presented modern man with one of the most difficult problems of his social experience—the transition from ancient folk cultures to the world of technology.

The Ireland from which a growing stream of emigrants parted for the New World in the seventeenth and eighteenth centuries was a deeply troubled country. Indeed, throughout most of the period during which the Irish have journeyed westward, the somber misfortunes and bitter struggles of Ireland have formed a grim background to the life of the immigrants in America. This is as true of the seventeenth and eighteenth centuries as of the nineteenth and twentieth. The history of national repression, poverty, and turbulence helps to explain the character of the Irish, their aspirations, and the stubborn idealism with which they defended themselves in the face of drastic challenges to their nationhood and to their very existence as a people. The characteristics of Irish society also conditioned the kind of adjustment emigrating Irishmen would make to other societies.

Few epochs of Irish history more morbidly illustrate human cruelty and distraction than the seventeenth and eighteenth centuries. At the end of the Elizabethan period England, after repeated attempts at conquest, was on the verge of establishing full suzerainty over the Gaelic population that had doggedly resisted English rule for so long. In 1607 the chiefs of the Gaelic clans fled their native land, and the ''Flight of the Earls'' signaled the decline of a Celtic social order that had been ancient when the Romans had first encountered the men of Ireland at the fringes of their empire. The price of conquest was still to be paid by the common people, however, and its exaction tore the island asunder for many lifetimes. In 1611 the English Crown began planting the province of Ulster with Scots to displace the diehard Irish clansmen, and in 1641 the Gaels of Ulster rose in rebellion under the great Eoghan Ruadh O'Neill. There followed a repression so savage that the name of Cromwell the oppressor achieved a status of odium it has maintained among the Irish to this day.[1]

Again, at the end of the seventeenth century, the attempts
of the Stuarts to regain the throne of England bred Irish
rebellion and left Ireland with a heritage of religious hatred
and a tortuous rack of penal laws that were a prodigious work
of persecution. Edmund Burke wrote of these laws as "a machine of wise and deliberate contrivance as well fitted for the
oppression, impoverishment and degradation of a people, and
the debasement in them of human nature itself, as ever proceeded from the perverted ingenuity of man."[2] All through
this period the forces of oppression moved across the land,
darkening the life of the country fearfully, and turning it, in
the words of the Gaelic poet Aodhagan O'Rathaille, into "a
land without stars."[3] In 1641 Catholics still held 59 percent
of the land; by 1688, 22 percent; by 1703, 14 percent.[4] Families with venerable ties to Europe and a sense of historic
power and prerogative were reduced to beggary and squalor
in the 1700s.

The religious rancor that infected Ireland had its counterpart in England, and the Society of Friends was one of the
groups upon which disfavor fell the most heavily. Harassed
and vilified in England, many Quakers sought refuge in Ireland, where their status, compared with that of the Roman
Catholics, was relatively sheltered.[5] But neither in England
nor in Ireland was there enduring security from the religious
passion against Friends; hence America beckoned when their
leader, William Penn, launched his "Holy Experiment" of
colonization.

William Penn himself had notable ties to Ireland. He was
converted to Quakerism there as a result of a sermon preached
in Cork. His view of the Catholic Gaels was distinctly critical
in contrast to his general benignity. Ironically, as a youth
landing at Carrickfergus, his first impulse was to follow a
military career in the turbulent island. Later, as an alien land-
holder occupying areas that had been expropriated from
Gaelic lords who had ruled them for ages, Penn found the
Irish somewhat less than respectful of his property rights.[6]

Penn's American enterprise bore marks of the English experience in Ireland. Even the Quaker reformer could not escape the influence of Irish struggles. Philadelphia itself was laid out by Thomas Holme, who planned the town of Waterford, and the original plan with its streets and squares all at right angles was very like the garrison towns planted in military regularity throughout the conquered Ireland that England occupied.[7] Although William Penn maintained a tolerant, even solicitous, view of the Indians, his successors and Pennsylvania non-Quakers took a harsher view that was similar to the prejudiced and bellicose English outlook on the Irish. The Indians practiced the same kind of implacable hit-and-run warfare as the Irish, and their cultural difference and hostility lent itself to prejudicial interpretation.[8]

The record of Irishman as Philadelphian begins almost at the inception of the city as a settlement poised on the edge of the unexplored continent. There were Irish Quakers and Quakers with Irish Catholic servants among the early colonists of Penn's enterprise. Trade restrictions, crop failures, and religious disabilities induced Quakers to venture to America from Ireland.[9] In 1729 the ship *George and Anne* made a grim passage from Dublin to Pennsylvania, with 100 of the passengers and crew dying on the voyage.[10] In 1736 an Irish captain complained of his ship's detention in Ireland prior to its passage to Pennsylvania; since destitute passengers owed their relentless landlords rent, the landlords had authorities detain the ship.[11] Not all the immigrants were Quakers, or even Protestants. There was in Ireland a brisk trade in the transportation overseas of convicts and other persons considered undesirable by the government. Sheriffs of Irish counties received five pounds for each person transported but paid only three pounds for his passage. They and other officials made a steady profit from this trade. In an early case, the Philadelphia Court of Quarter Sessions was persuaded to free a girl named Anne Dempsey from her indenture when she was proved to have been brought from Ireland illegally and against her consent and "Cruelly used on the Voyage." [12]

James Logan, the powerful agent of the Penn family, placed the following notice in the *Pennsylvania Gazette:*

> Run away from James Logan's Plantation near
> German Town the 28th Instant, an Irish Servant Lad,
> named Patrick, aged about 17 or 18 years, with
> straight dark hair, clothed with a double-breasted pea
> jacket, a brownish Kersey Coat, a pair of Leather
> briches, a good felt hat, but he had other clothes with
> him. Also a short Fowling Piece of a carbine length, or
> less. He went in the company with one Miles Mac
> Ward. [13]

This well-equipped young man roving forth toward adventure in America was not unique.

The first Irish Philadelphians—servants, freemen, and runaways—were the beginnings of a long immigrant tradition. The first 150 years of the city's life stimulated and shaped this tradition, moving it through several phases before it was vastly enlarged by the immigration of the mid–nineteenth century. The colonial period with its servitude and strict class distinctions cast the Irish in the role of menials of a not-too-trustworthy character. The period of the American Revolution, the building of the new nation, and the times of Jacksonian democracy would each make a particular contribution to the city's Irish tradition.

Philadelphia, with its reputation for religious tolerance, was attractive to many kinds of Irishmen. In the eighteenth century the influx increased, and the vessels from Ireland were usually crowded with passengers.[14] Among those entering Pennsylvania with alacrity were the so-called Scotch-Irish, a group that James Logan, administrator of the colony for the Penns, found very troublesome. He called them "bold and indigent strangers." [15] In the century and a half before 1850 most references to Irish people in Philadelphia refer to the "Scotch-Irish," that is, Protestant, largely Presbyterian, emigrants from the North of Ireland.[16] These extraordinary people exercised a strong influence on early American life, particularly on the frontier line from Pennsylvania south and westward. Having lived a garrison life in Ireland, they were militant and restless. Galvanized by a religious conviction that stamped their character with perseverance and certitude, they arrived in America whetted for the challenges of pioneering life, most of them entering the country through Philadelphia. Traduced by England into the perils of plantation existence in Ireland, they had little love for the Crown, and when the American Revolution occurred, they were quick to choose the rebel side. After the Revolution their exploits continued to be part of a record of intrepid pioneer deeds.[17]

The city that was to be the focus of much of the revolutionary activity that would separate England from the richest expanses of the New World was fairly large. Warner estimates that in 1776 the city and suburbs together contained 23,700 people.[18] Only a small percentage of these were servants, among whom Irish Catholics were most likely to be found. That the Irish Catholics were, however, a recognizable part of the city in pre–Revolutionary war years is indicated by the presence of Irish taverns and churches. The city contained a number of Irish taverns by 1758, including Isabella Barry's Faithful Irishman; the Jolly Irishman at Water and Race Streets; and the Lamb, at Second and Lombard Streets, owned by Francis O'Skullion.[19] In view of Carl Bridenbaugh's judgment that the tavern was probably the most important and flourishing institution in colonial towns, the early and lengthy role of the Irish as proprietors of taverns testifies to the homely but significant socializing influence they exerted.[20] Houses such as that of Elizabeth McGauley on Nicetown Road were used as informal chapels for itinerant priests, but the Catholic Irish soon opened churches tucked discreetly into the heart of the city. Saint Joseph's Church was opened in 1733 near Fourth and Walnut Streets; Saint Mary's, on South Fourth Street, in 1765.[21] Thus, the city of Benjamin Franklin contained its modicum of Irish Catholics.

With the growth of antagonism between England and the American colonies, the disaffected Irish would find a cause to champion that was close to their hearts. In Dublin the Protestant Ascendency class established a promising parliament between 1782 and 1800, and this body was an example of nationalist leadership and eloquence that was not lost on alert men in the Irish provinces. Beneath the Ascendency class was that "hidden Ireland," the landless, outcast Gaels. If Anglo-Irish Protestants had grievances against England, the Gaels had enormous ones. The American challenge to the Crown was a welcome inspiration to Irishmen in both Ireland and America, and Benjamin Franklin's visits to Dublin acquainted him with the widespread Irish enthusiasm for the American cause [22]

In Philadelphia the Revolution had its epicenter, and the Irish in the city, both Protestant and Catholic, largely chose the rebel side. It was not only the adventurous soldiers like Washington's young aide Colonel Jack Fitzgerald who responded, but businessmen like Thomas Fitz Simons and his brother-in-law, George Meade. General Stephen Moylan as quartermaster general of Washington's army would labor long and hard to keep the rebels supplied with the materials needed to make war, while the tough Wexford-born sailor John Barry took the war against England to the high seas. There has been considerable dispute about the part played by Irish Catholics in the Continental unit called the "Pennsylvania Line." What is clear is that Irishmen of various religious persuasions formed from one-fourth to one-third of this unit, which was one of the most reliable that Washington had. In addition to the local Irishmen, those from elsewhere were part of the Revolutionary ferment in Philadelphia. General John Sullivan, one of Washington's most intrepid fighters, but also one of the most difficult subordinates, participated in the battle of Germantown when Washington sought to harass the British during their occupation of the city. General Thomas Conway, whose name would long be associated with a suspected plot to oust Washington from command, was also at Germantown (Conway later had a brilliant record as a soldier in France). With such men, the Continentals held out until French assistance came, part of which consisted of contingents of the Irish Brigade under Berwick, Walsh, Fermoy, and Dillon.[23] The achievement of independence, and the role of Irishmen in attaining it, placed the Irish on a new footing in America. As time-tested foes of England, their traditional orientation against the interests of the Crown and colonialism endowed them with primary patriotic potential as citizens of the new republic.

The patriotism that later became such a strident characteristic of Irish-Americans owed much to the ardent deeds of the Irishmen of the Revolutionary war period. Almost alone among the groups that would later contribute multitudes of immigrants to the country, the Irish could count figures of their group in the dozens among the leaders of the Revolutionary period. This perhaps added to the distress they felt when in the nineteenth century they were accused of being subversive aliens or considered unwanted interlopers.

In the wake of the stunning success of the Americans, European notables came in growing numbers to view the marvel of the new republic. Some were unsympathetic. Thomas Moore, the once-liberal poet who became a Tory amid the flush of his success as a drawing room dandy, visited Philadelphia and penned,

> Alone by the Schuylkill the wanderer roved,
> And sweet were the flowery banks to his eye.

Moore, repelled by the raucous quality of life in the new nation, wrote,

> Take Christians, Mohawks, democrats and all
> From the rude wigwam to the congress-hall,

From the savage, whether slav'd or free,
To man the civilized, less tame then he,—
'Tis one dull chaos, one infertile strife
Betwixt half-polished and the half-barbarous life,
Where every ill the ancient world could brew
Is mixed with every grossness of the new.[24]

Another visitor was Theobold Wolfe Tone, who came to Philadelphia in 1796. Tone's visit permitted him to negotiate fur-
tively with French agents in behalf of his schemes for Irish
revolution, but he feared he was being shadowed constantly
in the city by English spies. Tone, whose passionate devotion
to Irish liberty and the ideals of the French Revolution would
lead to his sacrifice of himself after a futile struggle against
his country's English overlords, could not help being inspired
by the implications of the American achievement.[25]

If there were famous men who viewed America and left it,
there were other men who stayed. The new conditions of the
busy city were expanding the aspirations of Philadelphians,
and the opportunities of the country were bringing Irishmen
of talent and conviction to the city. These men were self-as-
sured and competent; and, though contentious, they had considerable dignity.

Outstanding in early nineteenth-century Philadelphia was
Mathew Carey, a publisher, a pioneer political economist,
and an admirable person whose human sympathy was deeply
aroused by the sufferings of the immigrant poor of the slums.
Born in Dublin, the son of a well-to-do businessman, Carey
early became involved in the radical republican plots of the
1780s. He had to flee Ireland because of his writings against
the government.[26] Coming to Philadelphia, he began a long
career of writing and publishing that addressed the foremost
problems of his day. His writings on economic policy helped
to shape the commercial and industrial growth of the Commonwealth of Pennsylvania. His *Essays on Political Economy*
set forth a detailed analysis of trade and argued for tariff

protection of American manufacturing. In his *Emigration from Ireland and Immigration to the United States* he warned the Irish against dreams of an easy life in America. His report "A Plea for the Poor," written in 1837, denounced the cruel conditions under which poor workers lived in the city.[27] One critic denounced his democratic sympathy, saying, "The people, the people, the people, the people. I am tired of this unceasing and nauseating repetition. If we are to have nothing but Paddy Carey played to us . . . let us have some variations."[28] In addition to economics and politics, Carey was interested in the promotion of public schools. His love of Ireland was memorialized in his book *Vindiciae Hibernicae; or, Ireland Defended,* a work written to refute the distortions of English historians dealing with his native country. It is a furious, polemical book, fired with all the ardor of Carey's patriotism and learning.[29] For all the force of his criticism and argument, Carey attained a stature that elevated him above the eccentric "agitators" of the time. Such men, one of whom was Thomas Brannagan, were shrill figures well known in the city. Born a Catholic, Brannagan was converted to evangelical Protestantism. While a seaman he had seen the horrors of the slave trade, and he became one of Philadelphia's earliest abolitionists. John Dougherty, a canal promoter and inventor, was the first to devise a scheme for transporting canal boats across the Allegheny Mountains. Interested in many of the same questions as Mathew Carey, he became stigmatized as "Agitator Dougherty," an erratic rhetorician and disputant.[30]

Robert Walsh, son of Baron Shannon, became an admired figure among the educated elite of the city. Walsh had French connections and a brilliant pen. In 1820 he founded the *American Review of History and Politics,* one of the first learned journals in the country. He also edited the *National Gazette,* a paper expressing strong abolitionist views. Walsh served as professor of English and later as trustee of the University of Pennsylvania. From 1844 to 1851 he was United States consul in Paris. As a writer and literateur he added considerable cultural distinction to Philadelphia.[31]

Another scholar, but a different kind, was Matthias O'Conway, a native of Galway City who had received some of his education in Spain. O'Conway was a linguist and a translator, whose knowledge of French and Spanish took him to Havana and New Orleans. After an unsuccessful attempt at Indian trading on the frontier, during which he learned Indian dialects, he settled in Philadelphia and worked as a poorly paid translator. For years toward the end of his life O'Conway labored on a Gaelic dictionary, his chief interest, into which he poured his knowledge of Gaelic and seven other languages; it was the work of a scholar still linked to the splendid music of Gaelic poetry despite years of exile.[32]

In business some Irishmen managed to create rewarding careers for themselves. One of these was Dennis Kelly, founder of Kellyville, Delaware County, six miles from the center of Philadelphia. Arriving in America with the intention of going West, Kelly alighted with his wife from the westward-bound wagon because of the blaspheming of the driver. He settled beside Darby Creek and after a period as a day laborer set up a weaving business. His sales of bagging to the army in the War of 1812 enabled him to expand, and eventually he built a five-story mill and collected a whole village of weavers, spinners, and dyers around him. The village of Kellyville was one of those mill villages in which the industrial revolution was enacted in miniature. In the 1840s and 1850s Dennis Kelly and his son-in-law, Charles Kelly, conducted a thriving textile enterprise with a heavily Irish work force. Both proprietors were great horse and cattle fanciers and breeders. Living in their large houses, helping immigrants by the score with money and jobs, they were admired and respected. They were more like easygoing landed gentlemen then capitalist manufacturers. Each of the Kellys founded a Catholic parish in the area near his mill.[33] From the poverty of their boyhood homes in Donegal, they rose to wealth in Pennsylvania. With other successful Philadelphia Irishmen such as Christopher O'Fallon, who had been born in Spain and had an estate in Delaware County, and Bernard McCredy, another cotton manufacturer, they made up a network of some affluence.

Some of the well-to-do Irish lived in the fashionable central area of the city. One of these was Baron John Keating, a veteran of the Irish Brigade, which had served the kings of France. The Keating family lived on South Fourth Street and had a large estate in Roxborough. John Keating was a confrere in banking with members of the Biddle family. Men like Keating were participants in the economic and cultural life of a city that was humming with activity as it moved toward industrialization. They were Irishmen quite capable of dealing with the wealthy and prestigious families of the Philadelphia upper class. They commanded the respect of the community, but their abilities and good fortune raised them above the difficulties confronting most of the immigrants. They formed their own circles for such occasions as the first reading in America, in 1806, of Robert Emmett's famous trial speech; they raised subscriptions for their Society for the Defense of the Catholic Religion from Calumny and Abuse.[34] The Keatings, Meades, Careys, McGills, and Kellys lived the good life of Philadelphia in the Federalist years.

The political life of the city was quickened by the assertiveness of Irishmen exploring and testing the limits of democracy for the first time. The ideals of the American Revolution, the ambitions of able men, and the grievances of those less able all contributed to Irish political involvement. The Irish of the city were generally allied with the Jeffersonian Republicans. Their disputes among themselves and with the Federalists produced fiery episodes. A riot occurred outside Saint Mary's Church in 1799 when Protestant Irishmen tried to get Catholics to sign a petition against the xenophobic Alien Act of 1798. This act and its companion, the Sedition Act, were passed by the Federalists, who were frightened by the French Revolution and the Irish sympathy for its ideals.

Harrison Gray Otis, a Federalist champion, gave what was known as his "Wild Irish Speech," urging that America reject the entry of "the mass of vicious and disorganizing characters who cannot live peaceably at home," and warned of "hordes of wild Irishmen." The term "Wild Irish" was usually applied to the Catholic Gaels, but Otis also feared the Protestant revolutionaries inspired by Wolfe Tone. Uriah Tracy, a Federalist senator from Connecticut, found plenty of these in Pennsylvania; he called them "the most God-provoking democrats this side of hell." [35]

There ensued the Federalist prosecution of such tempestuous characters as New York editor John Daly Burk and the Vermont congressman Matthew Lyon, whose utterances in Philadelphia were inflammatory even in the context of the furious diatribes that passed for political commentary in those days. There was also the trial of Patrick Lyon, no relative of the congressman, who was convicted under the Sedition Act. Lyon, a blacksmith, sued for redress and won reversal of his conviction and damages. With a part of the compensation he eventually had John Neagle paint a full-length portrait of him in his smithy against the background of the Walnut Street prison where he had been unjustly incarcerated. Such was the revenge of one civil libertarian.[36] These episodes etched deeply the agitated image of the "Wild Irishman"; upper-class Philadelphians could agree with Sir Augustus Foster, a resident British diplomat, who wrote of "a motley set of imported grumblers from Dublin which is disgusting." But in Philadelphia, "the insolence of the Boors" was restrained by the justices of the peace, "who never spared them when they were to be fined for some act of Brutality." [37]

Despite the misgivings of such patronizing British visitors, the Irish responded with order when order was demanded. When the city was threatened by the British during the War of 1812, contingents of Irishmen numbering over two thousand assembled at five in the morning to march to Blockley Township across the Schuylkill where they labored without pay to build the fortifications erected there for the city by the Committee of Defense.[38]

The impact of the Irish on the politics of the city during the early nineteenth century extended beyond alarms and agitation. They were adding a new dimension to politics, a dimension that was to help in the evolution of the party system. By 1800 there were over five thousand Irish-born in the city.[39] Many of these were veterans of the Irish Volunteers, a group that had led the rising in Ireland in 1798. With the failure of this insurrection, many of them had fled to the United States. John Binns was representative of this group. Born in Dublin, he had been arrested as a young man for revolutionary activity, and after two years' imprisonment, he came to the United States in 1801. He first edited the *Republican Argus*, then the *Democratic Press*. Although a Protestant, his paper spoke to and for Irishmen of all backgrounds in its campaigns for the extension of democratic rights.[40] As another editor and publisher, Catholic Mathew Carey, wrote, concerning the case to be made for political liberty in Ireland and the United States, "There are in the United States thousands and tens of thousands of liberal and enlightened men, who only require to have the fair and holy form of truth placed before their eyes, properly authenticated, to have them clasp it to their bosoms."[41] But this elevated doctrine was constantly being challenged by men whose sufferings or partisan interests drove them to frantic protests. Wolfe Tone had found the poorer Irish of the city "actively troublesome." Their political penchant and factious energy drew sharp criticism. As early as 1792 one H. H. Breckenridge felt compelled to place in his novel *Modern Chivalry* a passage headed "How the Bog-Trotter Is Nearly Elected to the Legislature." The satire tells of Teague O'Regan, an illiterate servant overly fond of whiskey, who confounds his master by being nominated for public office, and also by being invited to join the American Philosophical Society. The *Erin*, a well-edited Philadelphia newspaper, belied the illiterate image assigned to the Irish.

It sought in 1832 to expose "the machinations of those who have degraded the name and trampled the liberties of Ireland." [42]

The republic was building, and the work to be done strained the backs of immigrant and native alike. Frederick Marryat noted that the Irish might have been the most troublesome immigrants, but they were also the most valuable, providing the labor for those enterprises, called "internal improvements," that were extending the communications and gathering the resources of the new nation. He noted also of the Irish workers that they "hold themselves completely apart and distinct, living with their families in the same quarter of the city and adhering to their own manners and customs." [43] He found them a formidable group—clannish, politically sensitive, and intolerant of interference. In the alleys where they lived, conditions did not breed tolerance. In 1832 a citizens' committee found in a workers' area near the Delaware River fifty-five families without a single privy for their use. Mathew Carey wrote in 1829 that the hardest working among the city's poor earned only $58 a year and had to spend $39 of this for rent and fuel. [44] As early as 1818 Irish societies in the city had asked for land on which to settle immigrants, but the call went unheeded. [45] Crowding and misery increased as the tidy Quaker town changed into a raucous city.

The pressures brought to bear upon the Irish minority by the primitive industrialization of the city produced an acute crisis for them, and they responded with a rising turbulence that focused on religious, economic, and political issues. The disturbances began with a bitter religious dispute in the 1820s at Saint Mary's Church. The "Hogan Schism," as it was called, was led by Father William Hogan, who induced a group of parishioners to oust their bishop and install a lay-dominated trustee system for parish control. This was in part an attempt by Catholics to imitate the lay influence common among Protestant congregations. "Trusteeism" flamed into a major issue in the young American Catholic church, and its outbreak caused a stern conservative reaction among prelates that long affected the Catholic life in Philadelphia.[46]

Economic grievances were also a ready source of disruption. The struggling hand-loom weavers of the city, a heavily Irish group, rioted often. In 1835 the Irish coal heavers along the docks of the Schuylkill River made one of the first recorded attempts in the nation to organize unskilled labor. Race riots between Blacks and Irishmen occurred in 1832 and 1842 in Southwark and Schuylkill, for Blacks were competitive with the immigrants for menial jobs.[47]

Because of their economic vulnerability, the Irish often made unsteady allies in politics. Andrew Jackson's popularity as the symbol of the common man drew many of the Irish to his standard. Between 1827 and 1833 the *Irish Republican Shield and Literary Observer* upheld Jacksonian democracy with fiery zeal. But in 1832, despite a raging cholera epidemic, a mass meeting was held in Independence Hall to denounce Jackson. The invitation proclaimed, "Irishmen! You cannot support Andrew Jackson." The large Irish crowd vowed to vote against Jackson, largely because he was reluctant to permit the national government to build the "internal improvements" that gave the Irish work in constructing canals and roads.[48]

An example of the factionalism and roaring disputes in the Irish community is provided by the behavior of the Philadelphia branch of the Repeal Association in 1843. The leadership of Daniel O'Connell in Ireland inspired a new movement of Irish nationalism. His achievement of partial Catholic emancipation and his drive to repeal the Act of Union (1800) joining England and Ireland under the Crown generated support from Irish and non-Irish liberals in the United States. In Philadelphia the local Repeal Association collected $2,000 in one week for the cause. The *Public Ledger* stated, "The spirit which has been shown in this matter, the money which has been sent and the interest manifested in the success of their efforts, prove that the Repealers of this country are hand and heart with their friends abroad.''[49]

The Repeal Association, however, blew up in a bitter dispute over remarks O'Connell made in Parliament favoring the abolition of slavery. The majority of the Irish feared Black competition for jobs and were against the antislavery movement. They were skeptical, as well, of the Protestant leaders of abolitionism, since they saw little evidence among them of a parallel sympathy for the plight of the Irish poor. At least one participant in the tumultuous Repeal Association debates on the subject felt that the antislavery issue had been introduced by Orangemen, that is, Irish Protestants loyal to England, to wreck American support for O'Connell.[50]

Through such disputes, the Irish community moved in a constant search for unifying ties and social positions. It was an uneasy search by combinations of leaders and factions seeking direction with respect to Ireland, America, and the new life of the city. The Catholic Irish, steadily growing in numbers, bound by the memory of Ireland and by religious allegiance, were keenly aware of their unstable position in the city. This prompted a superpatriotism that sought to offset suspicions about the loyalty and the alien character of the group. In 1837 Joseph M. Doran, at a Saint Patrick's Day celebration at the Hall of the Franklin Institute, declaimed,

> Irishmen, naturalized citizens of America! Driven by tyranny and oppression from your own beloved and much injured country, you have come here to enjoy the blessings of civil and religious liberty. . . . A new existence awaits you here, and though the green fields of Erin cover with their verdure the graves of your fathers . . . yet this is now your country—here is all that is dear to you; here are your families, your friends, here are your homes and property. Call forth then your powers, and assist your fellow citizens in preserving those

> liberties which you are permitted to enjoy . . . cherish,
> promote and protect the great interests of the country,
> and show by your conduct that you are worthy of being
> naturalized citizens of a prosperous Republic.[51]

Such exhortations betray the Irish background, and the desire
to prove worthy of the adopted country's opportunities. They
also betray an ambiguity, a sense of confidence flawed by a
consciousness of inferiority. How grave the feelings against
the Irish Catholics were was to be revealed in appalling fury
in the year 1844.

As the Irish population grew, a grim reaction began to
take place in the city. The feeling against the Irish Catholics
coincided with a rising wave of Protestant evangelism. Interreligious violence loomed. The anti-Catholic riots which occurred in Philadelphia in May and July of 1844 provided a
bitter example of the violence inherent in the confrontation between the Irish Catholics and other elements of the city's population. Riots and violence were not uncommon in the city, for
labor troubles, racial antagonism, and boisterous political factions intermittently caused outbreaks.[52] The riots of 1844, however, had two aspects that invested them with a particular
potency. First, they involved the highly emotional issue of religion. Second, the two riots, occurring at separate times and at
different locations, were sufficiently extensive to reveal the
shortcomings of the police and the civil forces available to quell
disorder.

The rioting grew out of a convergence of tension-producing
influences. The American Protestant Association was formed
in Philadelphia in 1842 with 100 charter ministers at its head.
It carried out a campaign of pulpit fulminations against
Catholicism. It served as one of the inspirations for the Native
American (Nativist), or "Know Nothing," party, which
sought to give expression to militant Protestantism. In 1842,
Archbishop Francis P. Kenrick precipitated further controversy by efforts to prevent public schools from requiring

Catholic children to read the Protestant King James Version
of the Bible. These religious disputes continued until 1844,
fueling the passions of combative elements on both sides.

On 6 May 1844, a Protestant meeting in Kensington provoked a riot and bloodshed that lasted for three days and only
terminated after the militia and been mobilized. These disorders resulted in the burning of two Catholic churches, Saint
Michael's at Second and Jefferson Streets and Saint Augustine's at Fourth and Vine Streets; the destruction of dozens
of Catholic homes; and sixteen deaths. Refugees streamed out
of the riot-torn Kensington area. In July the Southwark area
was plagued by similar outbreaks.[53] These events caused a
crisis of confidence in the city that was to have notable political repercussions.

The riots were deplored by city authorities. Most Philadelphians were disturbed at the scale and the portents of these
religious clashes.[54] The riots had flagrantly stained the city's
reputation and frightened a great many citizens. Even while
they were in progress, some citizens were expressing sympathy
for the victims. Although the Know-Nothing movement gained
recruits rapidly, reasonable men were troubled.[55] In the
decade following the riots, one of the strongest motives behind
the consolidation of the disparate communities in the county
into one enlarged municipality was the desire to obtain the
basis for a strong and unified police force capable of prevent-
ing recurrences of such rioting.

The nature of these riots is important for the subsequent
history of the Irish in the city. There is convincing evidence
that they were essentially a clash between Irish Protestants
and Irish Catholics, at least at their inception. Contemporary
sources and later investigators such as Ray Allen Billington
and Elizabeth Geffen note North of Ireland "Orange" elements as initiators.[56] Kensington was an area inhabited by
numerous "Scotch-Irish" Protestants who worked in the textile trades. The call for the Protestant meeting that broke up
in disorder and brutal fighting on 6 May 1844, was signed by

William Craig and John McManus, two names suggesting North of Ireland ties, and one of the first men killed was Patrick Fisher, a Protestant of Irish background. Digby Baltzell concludes that the riots were more anti-Irish Catholic than anti-Catholic as such, because German Catholic churches near the riot areas were unmolested.[57] If this interpretation is valid, the long-range significance of the riots can be placed in perspective. While anti-Catholic hostility was certainly widespread in the city, the violent eruptions of 1844 were basically an intra-Irish phenomenon. The majority of Philadelphians did not provoke them. They were launched by an agitated Protestant group of a particular background against what it perceived to be its ancient foes. This militant Protestant cadre represented a problem for the Irish Catholics, but it did not reflect the views of more temperate Philadelphia Protestants. "Know-Nothingism" with its frenetic attacks on Catholicism was still strong enough to elect a mayor, Richard Conrad, in 1854, but it was a negative movement that in the long run could not repress Irish Catholic mobility amid the complexity of the city.[58] But the riots deeply disturbed Bishop Kenrick and other Catholic leaders, confirmed them in their fear of assimilation, and convinced them that the public schools could not properly serve Catholic children.[59] The riots led to a more devious course of containment devised by non-Catholics to deal with the immigrants. A labyrinth of social and class barriers was henceforth used to baffle Irish bids for leadership in the city.

The minority history of the Irish in the city prior to the famine immigration of 1846 can be seen as a sequence of four periods, each contributing toward a general image of the group. The colonial period saw the Irish as servitors and as an alien element. The period of the American Revolution endowed them with a claim to patriotic distinction. The early period of the nineteenth century brought a convergence of talented men—articulate, scholarly, and able to provide exemplary leadership in the community in a variety of roles. The period of Jacksonian development shifted the emphasis back to the mass of immigrants whose exploited labor and inflamed social condition produced outbursts of factionalism and strife that hardened old prejudices against the Irish as a whole. By the mid-1840s the Irish in the city were in an unenviable position. They had contributed many outstanding citizens to the economic, cultural, and political life of the city; they had demonstrated and proclaimed their patriotism. Still they were suspect. A besieged minority, nagged by the persistence of poverty and distress, they unleashed a violent force that challenged any leadership. The perturbation the city's leaders felt, however, was but a prelude to the gloom that was to descend when the refugees from the Great Famine poured into the city.

# TWO

## THE FAMINE
## GENERATION

Sundering modern Irish history is the cataclysm of the Great Famine of 1846–47. Its effect upon the thousands of its victims forced to flee Ireland can only be fully comprehended if their passage to America is analyzed. The transfer of a host of people from one place to another cannot fail to produce powerful social changes, and the arrival of the famine refugees in a city such as Philadelphia would deeply affect its life and institutions. By 1846 the city had received Irish immigrants for six generations, but it was the seventh generation that was to greatly change Philadelphia's composition and its posture with respect to immigrants. Despite the contention with the Irish prior to 1846, the city had accommodated the immigrants on a manageable scale. The increase of Irish immigrants in the postfamine years introduced a ghetto system and an elaborate pattern of reaction that was to buttress the city's response to a long period of immigration. Of equal moment was the reaction of the immigrants themselves to the novel experience of urban life. It is this adjustment of the Irish to urban living that will be the subject of the succeeding chapters.

It is important for an understanding of the transition involved in the Irish entry into urban condition to review the social background from which the immigrants emerged. The fabric of that vulnerable society provides many insights into the disastrous effects of the famine and the capacity of the Irish to cope with the ensuing emigration and urban experience.

At the heart of the economic instability of Ireland was the land problem. Ownership of the land was vested in a landlord class composed largely of parasitic absentees. The bulk of the people was sunk in poverty and depended for sustenance upon the potato, the staple crop. This system, deeply exploitive and inefficient, was subjected to critical pressure as the population of the island began to increase steadily after 1750. In the first half of the nineteenth century, the majority of the Irish people lived a truly marginal existence. Whether they were owners of cabins and tiny plots themselves, cottiers paying rent as tenants, or laborers with no fixed employment, their plight has become legendary.[1] In Ireland, as one writer says, "The poor may be said to have been without a standard of living."[2]

The famine of 1846–47 was the culmination of generations of neglect, misrule, and repression. It was an epic of English colonial cruelty and inadequacy. For the landless cabin dwellers it meant emigration or extinction. Between 1841 and 1861 the number of cottier holdings in Ireland decreased from 310,375 to 88,083.[3] The laboring classes and small tenant farmers were swept from the land in multitudes, stalked by starvation and disease. Emigration possessed the people, and they fled headlong to whatever refuge was accessible to them. The population of Ireland fell from above eight million in 1841 to six and a half million in 1851, and the decline would not cease for a century.

The dimensions of the calamity can hardly be delineated by simple statistics. England had presided over an epochal disaster "too monstrous and too impersonal to be a mere product of individual ill-will or the fiendish outcome of a well-planned conspiracy."[4] It was something worse: the cumulative antagonism and corruption of the English ruling class was visited with crushing intensity upon a long-enfeebled foe. It was as close to genocide as colonialism would come in the nineteenth century.

Aside from the demographic decimation of Ireland, the chief internal results of the famine were the further consolidation of the land and the virtual suffocation of that folk culture that had been the great resource of the Irish through the ages.[5] The cultural divestment of the Irish countryman is especially important in view of the adaptation that he was to undergo in American life, for the flaying Irish experience of the 1840s would confer upon him a keen sense of survival and accommodation.

A folk culture is learned at the hearth, transmitted subtly by grammar and phrase, gesture and intimation. Food, clothing, shelter, work, and leisure are patterned according to a style felt in the bones. The whole flows between generations through communal teaching and complex motivation. The folk life of the Gael, ravaged before the famine, was shattered by that great event. The Gaelic language, the music, the crafts, the patrimony of a people—indeed, the people themselves— were dispersed.[6] Driven outward in a vast diaspora, the main expositors of the culture were set adrift. This subverting process sent the Irish to American shores ready for innovation. The conservatism of the folk culture was diluted. The new patterns of life and work in the city were readily accepted. Only the memory of the Irish patrimony remained, a memory that seethed with bitterness.[7]

One of the most important features of the social background of the emigrating Irish was its singularly rural character. Some knowledge of this ruralism is important to gaining an understanding of the significance of the Irish encounter with American cities. So deep was the rural heritage that Sean O'Faolain says with sardonic brevity, "The Irish never founded a town."[8] The reasons for this were both economic and historical. As clansmen the Gaels had followed a hereditary chief. Loyalty was to the man and a group, not to a place or a government.

In a fundamentally poor country under sustained pressure from foreigners, the resources and stability required for urban development were not readily attainable. Equally important, however, was the fact that the city was introduced into Ireland as an agency of conquest, an admininistrative seat **for** the foreigner—the Dane, the Norman, the Englishman. It was the foreign trader, merchant, exploiter, and interloper who built the city.[9]

Between Norman and Tudor times, the towns became the area of clearly English jurisdiction. As early as 1439 English law had ordained that no man of Irish blood was to be received into the city of Waterford. By Elizabethan times there were forty-three fortified garrison towns. The wars of the seventeenth century destroyed many of these centers.[10] In the eighteenth century they were somewhat revived, but there was no great movement such as the industrial revolution to stimulate them. Even at this time the Catholic Irish were excluded from municipal functions and rights and the native Irish could join the town guilds only as "quarter brothers."[11]

In 1841 only one-fifth of the Irish population lived in communities that could be termed towns or villages.[12] After the Census of 1841, the boundaries of the chief towns were enlarged to take in adjacent areas. Montgomery-Martin in a statistical view of Ireland lists only four cities of over 25,000 in 1841: Dublin, Cork, Limerick, and Belfast. Thirteen other towns exceeded 10,000: Wexford, Carlow, Kilkenny, Dundalk, Drogheda, Armagh, Newry, Derry, Tralee, Waterford, Galway, and Sligo. These towns and sixteen others embraced 687,514 people, or 8 percent of the 1841 total of 8,175,124.[13] "City" or "town" is an anomalous term in the Irish context, for the populous areas were largely English cores with barely organized Irish agglomerations. McDowell describes the municipal corporations as "antiquated, inefficient, cliquish and riddled with petty jobbery," unfit to survive in a reforming age.[14] Halévy proffers an unflattering judgment of their inhabitants: "A vast proletariat, ignorant, miserably poor, superstitious and disorderly."[15] This excessively critical picture is contradicted, however, by the shops, institutions, and native Irish craftsmen, at least of Dublin, which evinced a notable degree of skill and urban pride.[16]

Beyond these larger centers, there were ancient market sites, pilgrimage shrines, and geographical crossroads that gathered population, but they could hardly be classified as towns. A London *Times* correspondent described a settlement in Galway in 1845: "As this is the largest village I ever saw, so it is the poorest, the worst built, the most strangely irregular and the most completely without head, or center, or market, or church, or school of any village I ever was in. It is an overgrown democracy. No man is better or richer or poorer than his neighbour in it." [17]

The natural result of this deep-rooted ruralism among the Irish was the lack of a tradition of local town government. Daniel O'Connell's distrust of the Municipal Corporations Act of 1840 was seen to be justified when franchises for local voters were restricted to ten pound householders to undercut Catholic political aspirations.[18]

By the time of the famine, it was hard for anyone to imagine the Irish as urban dwellers, and well-meaning counselors strongly warned emigrants against city life. The marquis of Clanrickard firmly believed that emigrants heading for America would go to the land, Adams describes the America-bound emigrants as "almost as ignorant . . . as an insect released from the chrysallis," and Handlin sees them "escaped into a way of life completely foreign and completely unfavorable to them." [19] Still, when the famine struck, they left their land. Lacking a livelihood, the community ways of the past, and any real alternative, the people crowded into steerage and came to the American cities.

The flight took many forms. There was the "selling up" of land to gain the three or four pounds needed for passage; there was a minimum of assisted emigration by landlords or the government; there was prepaid emigration, whereby a relative or friend who had previously departed for America would pay passage for the emigrant. The last-named method, with agents in American cities to facilitate it, was common. The details of the Atlantic passage have been extensively recounted in other studies, and their repetition here would be superfluous, since this book seeks to concentrate on the urban conditions that were the lot of the immigrants after arrival.[20]

Philadelphia, the premier industrial city of America in the mid–nineteenth century, was reaching its peak rate of urbanization in the 1850s. It was during this period of the city's dynamic growth that the proportion of immigrants to the total population of the United States was at its largest. Internal developments in the city, including political consolidation, industrial expansion, railroad growth, and street railways, combined to promote its eminence. As the economic base grew and diversified, the residential and institutional life of the city became more elaborate. Philadelphia during this vital period of its history constituted one of the greatest conceivable contrasts to the fields and villages of the Irish countryside.[21]

In 1850 there were 72,312 Irish-born in the County of Philadelphia, or 18 percent of its total population; by 1860 there were 95,458, or 17 percent. Although the Irish would remain the largest foreign-born group in the city until 1910, they constituted only 4 percent of the population of Pennsylvania. On the other hand, in 1860 the Irish-born populations of New York and Massachusetts constituted 12 percent of the totals; of New York City and Boston, 23 percent.[22] That both in the city of Philadelphia and in Pennsylvania the proportion of Irish-born to total population was lower than in the two other major seaboard areas of immigrant concentration may explain why the history of Irish immigration in the United States has been dominated by studies of New York and the New England area.[23]

During the famine, the Society of Friends in Philadelphia distinguished itself by its dedication to the relief of the suffering in Ireland. Although Quaker families had found hospitality and refuge in Ireland in the seventeenth century, they had also found hostility. It is a mark of the high principles of these families that many of the descendents of the earlier Quaker emigrants contributed heavily in the 1840s to the stricken Irish people. While Queen Victoria gave a niggardly sum to famine relief, the Philadelphia Quakers contributed over £4,000 in 1846–47. Thomas Pim Cope, James Martin, and John B. Gibson gave heavily. The Central Relief Committee of the Society of Friends in Dublin received clothing, food, seed, and medical aid from Philadelphia. The bark *John Walsh* was sent to Derry from Philadelphia with $10,000 worth of food.[24] The merchant John Wanamaker headed the Famine Relief Committee and also contributed to the Friends' effort. To Irishmen whose families were dying of hunger before their eyes, the name "Philadelphia" must have seemed synonymous with "kindness."

John Francis Maguire, a member of Parliament, wrote after an American tour that it was not within the power of language to describe the evil consequences of American city life for the immigrants. But for the immigrants in their thousands, the contrast between the decaying Ireland they had left and the dynamic cities they now entered was eloquent. They viewed America as a hard-driving business country, a place where work and enterprise were mandatory. Americans were a "go-ahead" people.[25] The vitality of the city affected even those who existed at the margin of its influence. The brilliant architect Louis Sullivan, the son of one Irish immigrant, saw the city as a challenge to those who entered it: "This is the Great City. It is the crux of things. Men are crowded here, hence they must be put to the test. We see them better here than scattered sparsely over the land. We shall see better what they create. . . . And we shall see the iron truth of it."[26]

The Philadelphia into which thousands of the immigrants were thrust was a growing industrial center. It was approximately five miles long and extended for two miles between the Delaware and Schuylkill Rivers. In the 1840s it had begun a remarkable period of new growth. "The city is extending with wondrous strides," said one local observer.[27] The areas between the rivers, especially the section west of Broad Street, which had till then been open land with reed-rimmed duck ponds, were being built up. Along the northern edge, the fields above Poplar Street were undergoing similar development. Thirty-five hundred buildings a year were constructed in 1849, 1850, and 1851. The population of the County and City of Philadelphia combined rose from 258,037 in 1840 to 408,762 in 1850, and then to 565,529 in 1860.[28] Philadelphia was indeed a city pulsing with the energy of industrialization and rapid growth.

The city was a broad-based industrial center in addition to being eminent in finance and mercantilism. Huge heavy-metals manufacturing firms such as the Norris works and the Baldwin locomotive factories paced its industrial production. The Paschall Iron Works and the Morris Iron Foundry contributed to the ore-smelting industry. The Southwark foundries of Merrick and Sons alone employed 300–350 men. In the "Age of Iron," the city's foundries, forges, and rolling mills employed over 10,000 of its workers. This was the core of its construction and productive system. With this metals production went the machine-tool fabrication for which the city was famous and which was a key element in the technology of industrialization. The Alfred Jenks firm in Bridesburg and the Bement and Dougherty Company were noted for their machinery construction. Pig iron, structural iron, piping, boilers, and ornamental iron rolled from the mills, as well as forges and machines to make more. By 1850 the city was dotted with smoking metal plants.

Fifty brickyards produced the building materials to extend Penn's "red brick town." The residents of its 100,000 dwellings were served by eleven markets and 7,400 stores. Its streets were lined with over 5,600 gas and fluid lamps. Its workers rode on street railways to jobs where they moved 28 million tons of coal a year to fuel its power system.

If any one field of manufacture was characteristic of Philadelphia, it was textiles. The processing of fibers, carding, spinning, weaving, dyeing, and tailoring were carried on in most districts, but especially in the mills and lofts of Kensington and Southwark. The city had long been a weaving and textile center, its skills having been augmented by those of English, Scotch, and Irish craftsmen early in the nineteenth century. Hand-loom production dominated until the 1840s, when new textile mills with power looms surpassed the production by handicraft methods. Still, the hand-loom weavers did not disappear but hung on in great numbers, working in their homes and in small shops thoughout the various neighborhoods. One commentator notes the racketing sound of the hand looms that filled the streets of Kensington. Over 4,700 hand looms competed with the new factories, one of which contained 900 looms. The city, according to one authority, had more textile factories than any other in the world. Their production provided the basis for a truly mass industry, which steadily changed its output to meet the needs of a spreading market.

As a port the city was entrepôt for a far-flung commerce. In 1851, 30,000 vessels, large and small, cleared its docks. One steamship line and four lines of sailing packets linked it to Liverpool on a regular basis, and dozens of other ship lines in both foreign and coasting trade called. The Delaware River was the site of a number of shipyards, including the big U.S. Navy Yard at the foot of Washington Avenue. The Schuylkill River in the vicinity of Grays Ferry was a thriving wharf area where huge tonnages of coal, lumber, and cargo from upstate Pennsylvania were handled. Here the barge traffic of the Schuylkill Navigation Company terminated. This was one of the various canal port districts for the city.[29]

In an age when railroads were becoming the largest business enterprises in the nation, Philadelphia was the hub of a wide-ranging rail network. Seven major railroads fed into the city, including the vast Philadelphia and Reading Company; the Pennsylvania; and the Philadelphia, Wilmington, and Baltimore roads. The amount of trade and employment generated by these lines alone was sufficient to sustain a good-sized city. Within Philadelphia the street railways, or horsecar lines, boomed during the 1850s with furious competitive and speculative activity. Three major lines—the Northern Liberties and

Spring Garden, the City Line, and the Southwark Railroad—
served passengers for inner-city transportation.

Financing this great and enlarging hive of enterprise was a
financial establishment with strongly developed capital resources. There were twelve major banks, including the famous
Bank of the United States, and a number of venerable savings
banks. Some of the nation's leading insurance companies,
among them the Insurance Company of North America, were
located in the city. All these fonts of investment and brokerage
took part in the city's rising growth.

The services and amenities of the city were renowned. The
Fairmount and Spring Garden Water Works were something
of a marvel of the age, having almost freed the city of the
periodic epidemics that had marked its early history. There
were eight medical schools, including one for women, making
Philadelphia the center of American medical education. Institutions for the blind, the insane, orphans, and paupers had
been established decades earlier through the initiative and
charity of the city's well-to-do. Theaters, lecture halls, and
libraries, including the renowned Library Company of Philadelphia, were easily accessible.

The city also had its squalid slums, its shantytowns, and a
notorious red-light district. Overbuilding and overcrowding
had created ugly and fetid court and alley quarters in Southwark, Schuylkill, Moyamensing, Kensington, and Port Richmond. These areas were a threat to the health, the stability,
and the reputation of the city, but they were far from being its
most prominent feature. Visitors constantly remarked on
Philadelphia's cleanliness and on the impressive solidity of its
institutions.[30]

To the upper class and the comfortable middle class of the
city, what had been created was good. They looked askance at
New York and accorded Boston grudging recognition.[31] The
exciting and profitable economic development of Philadelphia
was a source of pride. It was sufficiently rewarding and divert-
ing that the Irish immigration, though at first considered

menacing, did not on second thought appear to pose a major threat. Indeed, the labor supplied by the immigrants was essential. They were a valuable pool of laborers and servants for a city intent upon industrial greatness and residential enjoyment.

Besides the great numbers arriving in Philadelphia from New York during the 1840s, there was a smaller direct emigration from Ireland. Three ships a month left Derry for Philadelphia in the summer, and additional vessels brought Irish people from teeming Liverpool to the city.[32] The representation of common Ulster names in Philadelphia was notable, as can be seen in *McElroy's Philadelphia Directory* for 1850–65. Dougherty, Duffy, Maguire, O'Donnell, Devlin, and Sweeney are North of Ireland names, indigenous to the area and rich with the history of the great clans of Ulster. The immigrants came from both the North and the West of Ireland and were mostly young and single.[33]

The Know-Nothing riots and church burnings in 1844 had placed the Irish vividly before the eyes of the city as a troubling force. For much of the public the violent events of the 1840s helped to brand the Irish Catholics as a source of disorder and distress.[34] The antipathy toward them rested not only on their reputation for violence and their religous difference from the bulk of the city's natives, but also upon their competition for jobs at the lower occupational levels, their menial status, their foreign aspect and clannishness, and their notorious intemperance.[35] No white men in America were so thoroughly stigmatized. To the grievous sufferings of the famine generation were added the cultural and class indictments of a largely hostile public opinion in the country to which they had fled.

The Philadelphia newspapers reflected the ethnic prejudices of the time. The Irish were seen as foreigners whose feelings against England could be easily and dangerously manipulated. "Foreign pauperism" in the city prompted memorials to the state legislature, and conflicts among charitable groups over

methods of handling the problem.[36] The immigrants were
"motley multitudes." Emigrant aid groups performed some
services for the newcomers, but the Irish immigrants benefited
less from this kind of service than the arrivals from other
countries.[37]

This image of social disability became an enduring part
of the city's view of the Irish Catholics. It lasted for several
generations. Prominent upper-class reformers penned pseud-
onymous satires of the Irish in politics, and one such effort
popularized "Mulhooleyism" as a synonym for ignorance, corruption, and crudity. Ellis Paxson Oberholtzer of the University of Pennsylvania, a historian of the city and a partisan of
the city's upper-class traditions, wrote of the immigrants
that they had "revolting and vicious habits. Being of the
lower order of mankind, they were repellent to those who were
further advanced in the social scale." The result of this antagonism was to prompt in Philadelphia a response among the
immigrants not unlike that in Boston discerned by Handlin :
"Unable to participate in the normal associational affairs of
the community, the Irish felt obliged to erect a society within
a society, to act together in their own way. In every contact
therefore the group, acting apart from other sections of the
community became intensely aware of its particular and exclusive identity." [38]

The Irish in Philadelphia organized their own separate organizations. The Friendly Sons of Saint Patrick and the Hibernian Society continued from 1771 onward.[39] In 1842 the
Friends of Ireland held a national convention in Philadelphia,
marked by agitation for Daniel O'Connell's drive to repeal the
Act of Union, and also by a wrangling debate on slavery. In
the 1840s the Irish organized their own militia units. Their
group affinity and growing church and political activities, as
well as the economic and social position they shared, bound
them together. They developed a vainglorious view of themselves, and a tendency toward strident patriotic declamation.
They defended themselves as a vital new element bestowed

upon America, bringing a love of liberty and a dedication to democratic principles.[40]

But if there was a consciousness of separateness, there was also a consciousness of being part of the strenuous experience of the urban life of Philadelphia. The new life in America was hard and beyond previous experience. As one Michael Carr wrote to his sisters from the city in 1855, ''You know how things is with you in Ireland but what do you know how they are with me—they are not by a long way what you perhaps think the[y] are.'' [41] Thus was expressed the gulf between the old country and the new.

What Philadelphia was undergoing was part of a great upheaval that was resettling the peoples of the countries bordering the North Atlantic. The social impact of the immigrants on their host countries was far-reaching. Friedrich Engels described the outrageous conditions under which they lived in England.[42] Over half a million Irish-born refugees —an afflicted, struggling, disaffected mass—were crammed into English and Scottish cities by 1851.[43] In the United States, the seabord cities were shaken by the impoverished influx. Between 1845 and 1851, 750,000 entered the country, most concentrating in the eastern urban areas.[44] Their presence served to simultaneously stimulate and compromise the cities they entered. Their impact was one of those fundamental changes that shift the axis of the social, and especially the political, order. As Kitson-Clark puts it, ''What probably in the long run determines the shape of politics are the social movements, the groupings and regroupings in the mass of the community, which are beyond the reach of politicians.'' [45]

It is against this larger background that the involvement of the Irish with the city of Philadelphia must be viewed. Their economic and social history in Ireland did little to prepare them to cope with an industrial city. The conditions prompting their emigration left them afflicted in the extreme. The city into which they were transported was in the throes of extraordinary changes. The record of how immigrants in such a situation responded to the urban environment and its problems may provide significant insight into the nature of urban society and the adaptation of newcomers to it. It is for this reason that the famine generation demands the special attention devoted to it in the following chapters that deal with development in housing, work life, education, religion, and civic activity.

# THREE

## CITY SHELTER

One of the fundamental factors determining the social condition of people anywhere is the kind of shelter available to them. The house is the setting for the intimate experience and daily ritual of family life. As such, it subtly influences the psychology and outlook of its inhabitants, as well as helps determine their safety, health, recreation, and relationship to the surrounding community.

The movement of Irish people from the rural countryside of their native island to the neighborhoods of an American urban center resulted in a marked change in housing conditions. The shelter in rural Ireland was notoriously inadequate in the mid-nineteenth century. William Carleton described one of the villages in his novel *Valentine McClutchy: The Irish Agent:* "The village was indeed a miserable and frightful scene. There it stood, between twenty and thirty small and humble habitations, from which, with the exception of about five or six, all the inmates had been dispossessed without any consideration for age, sex, poverty or sickness." [1] Half-abandoned, the villages were a jumble of ill-repaired, tiny houses, and in the mountains and fields where dwellings stood alone, they were usually of the most forlorn construction.

In Ireland the housing for the vast majority of the people who emigrated to America generally consisted of a structure with walls made of stone, clay, sod, or turf. The houses were of varying length, but usually twelve to fifteen feet wide, with the hearth either at the center or at a gable end. The roof was of thatch secured with ropes and pegs, sometimes masterfully woven, sometimes woefully bedraggled. In most cases, the house, or cabin, as it was commonly called, blended well with the landscape. Providing only one or two rooms with a scanty loft inside, these houses were simple at best, but dank, dirty, and bestially overcrowded at their worst. As E. Estyn Evans remarks, "Cows, and calves, men, women and children, horse and poultry were herded together in one apartment on occasion." [2] It was not unusual for one end of the house to be partitioned off for stock. Poverty and the rack-rent system partially explain the rudimentary character of these dwellings, but Evans suggests ethnic traditions as another explanation. [3] The Irish Census of 1841 counted 491,278 one-room, mud-walled cabins. By 1851 these had decreased to 135,589, so great had been the emigration of the poor. [4]

In the first half of the nineteenth century there were still places in Ireland where the ancient custom of *Buailteachas,* or transhumance, was practiced, particularly in Donegal. In this practice, a man might have three dwellings—one in the mountains, where youths would care for cattle in the summer months; one upon the shore; and the third on an island, for the fishing season. [5] These dwellings, used seasonally, must have given the families a rather casual attitude toward housing. In addition, the simple facts of rural orientation and of lack of an economic stake in the dwelling reflected a certain view of life and the world. As Sir Horace Plunkett, who worked diligently to promote the rural self-help movements in Ireland, wrote of the Irishman of his time, "If he loves the place of his habitation he does not attempt to improve or adorn it, or indeed to make it in any sense a reflection of his own mind or taste. . . . What the Irishman is really attached to in Ireland is not a home but a social order. The pleasant amenities, the courtesies, the leisureliness, the associations of religion and the friendly faces of neighbors." [6] Another writer sees the Irishman as a "communist socially," so that the tenement life of the American cities accorded with a supposed lack of individuality and a preference for neighborliness. [7] According to these views, which are those of men separated by education, class, and language from the kind of people who made up the immigrant population, the Irish countryman's house with its dirt floor, one window covered with sheepskin, and rude appointments represented a preferred way of life. The limitations of a harsh life do curtail human wants and aspirations, and custom does ratify the inevitable, but that ordinary men prefer the crude and the inadequate to betterment is at least debatable.

If we turn to the housing in Philadelphia, a different residential tradition is apparent. Even in the 1850s Philadelphia was proud of itself as a "city of homes." The residential building formula of the city was fortunate. Its expanding gridiron pattern of streets permitted the orderly plotting of land, and the brick construction of its ubiquitous row houses was relatively simple and economical. If the rows were somewhat relieved by white marble corbels and white front steps, the effect was still one of unexciting, homely solidity. The city, of course, had its spacious mansions and town houses, representing the grand tradition of its genteel class, but, for most Philadelphians and for visitors to the city, it was the row house that characterized its mass residential prospect.[8]

In 1851 the *Philadelphia North American* editorialized on the relative good fortune of the city with respect to housing. Citing New York's 515,000 residents and 37,730 houses and Philadelphia County's 490,000 inhabitants and 61,202 houses, the paper gloated over the favorable contrast. The New York density of 13.66 persons per house was set against Philadelphia's average density of 6.68. Even in the city's Nineteenth Ward in Port Richmond, where the Irish were numerous and there were 18,463 persons and only 1,772 houses, the density was 10.42 persons per dwelling—still lower than the New York average.[9] The British traveler William Baxter and others found less of the perilous cellar dwelling and fewer "small, low-class houses" than in other cities. Philadelphia did not appear to suffer as greatly as Boston, either, under the impact of the overcrowding produced by the immigrant influx. Handlin's description of Irish housing conditions in Boston's Fort

Hill and South Boston districts provides a grim picture of land scarcity, intense competition for housing, and dreadful overcrowding.[10]

This relative housing adequacy in Philadelphia should not obscure the fact that the city also contained its quotient of miserable slums. Behind the prospect of large gracious homes and neat row dwellings, there was another world in Philadelphia. As in most large cities, housing neglect, poor building practices, overcrowding, and exploitation produced areas of wretched deterioration and disorder. These coincided with the areas of heaviest Irish concentration, the districts of Southwark, Moyamensing, Grays Ferry, Kensington, and Port Richmond.[11]

In 1850, the Second Ward of Moyamensing had 2,318 Irish-born inhabitants, who constituted 28.6 percent of the total population of 8,097.[12] The ward, included a number of the older streets in the southern part of the city. The First Ward of Moyamensing included the shantytown districts at the edge of the built-up areas and extended to the Schuylkill River banks, where the Irish riverboatmen, stevedores, coal heavers, and laborers were crowded along the waterfront. Port Richmond on the Delaware River was similar to the Schuylkill area, while Kensington's Irish population worked in the mills, on the railroads, and on the docks of the Delaware (see fig. 1). There is evidence that those from the same area in Ireland concentrated in the same city neighborhood. Bradys, O'Donnells, and Gallaghers, for example, would cluster together; owing to the legacy of the clan system, many families unrelated by blood carried the same surname.[13]

In Moyamensing, the records of the tax assessor show slightly more than half the property owners were Irish by name in 1851. In a sample of blocks from Cedar Street (now South Street), Passyunk Road, Sixth Street, and Seventh Street both owners and tenants are predominately Irish. The acquisition of such a considerable amount of property by Irish people by 1851 suggests that the Irish community in

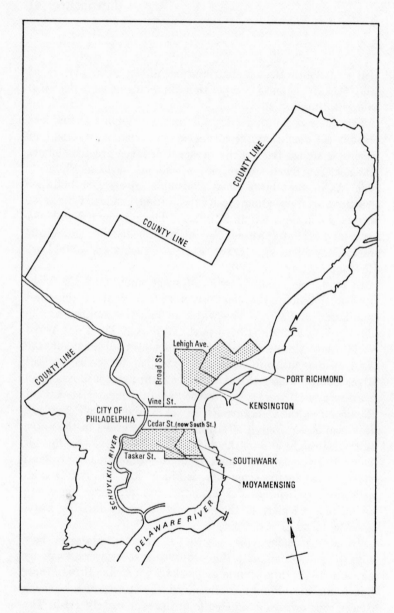

Figure 1   *Map of Philadelphia County, 1850.   Dotted sections show areas of heavily Irish residence.*

Philadelphia began its property-owning tradition relatively early, probably before the postfamine influx of immigrants, for it is not likely that so many Moyamensing properties could have been acquired between 1846 and 1851.[14]

In the Moyamensing area around Baker, Bedford, and Spofford Streets was a neighborhood of extreme privation.[15] In 1849 visitors for the Board of Health found "contracted and badly located houses, crowded by occupants, filthy and poor, without ventilation or drainage, or receptacles for refuse, or supply of water, or the common comforts of life."[16] Tax assessors' ledgers listing Moyamensing residents enumerate an almost completely Irish population of laborers and weavers in Baker, Bedford, and Spofford Streets in the neighborhood around Seventh and Fitzwater Streets; and in such squalid rookeries as Black Horse Alley, McAfee Court, and the ironically named Prosperous Alley. It is notable also that not only were the majority of the tenants Irish, but the slum property owners as well. Owners and estates bore such names as Patrick Boyle, Mary Cassiday, John McAfee, Gaffney, Quinn, and McMahon.[17] In the mid–nineteenth century, the Irish, at least in some locations, were their own slumlords. Some of the Irish were garnering incomes from property, and this may have provided upward mobility for men without much capital or skill. The pattern of exploitation of later immigrants by those who had arrived earlier is suggested by these data.

At the western end of South Philadelphia, along the banks of the Schuylkill River in an area known as Schuylkill, or Grays Ferry, fewer property owners were Irish—on Grays Ferry Road and Irish Lane, for instance, only between one-fourth and one-third of the owners. On Christian and Brazier Streets, however, the owners were heavily Irish.[18]

In Kensington, although the living conditions were little better, the landlords were almost all non-Irish. This area had been settled originally by English, Scottish, and German textile workers and skilled craftsmen, and there were few lots left

for Irish immigrants. The residents had become embroiled
with the Irish in the riots of the 1840s, when the Irish filtered
into the little streets, occupying housing that was too old or
undesirable for the more fortunate workers. On Beach Street
above Marsh Street, for instance, twenty of the forty residents
in 1853 had recognizable Irish names. The tax ledgers list
only nominal assessments for the twenty, who were laborers
and unskilled workers.[19]

The Irish neighborhoods had notorious reputations. The area
around Fourth and Plum Streets in Southwark contained a
number of bawdy houses and other unsavory haunts. Both
Moyamensing and Southwark were seen to be infested with a
picaresque population of loafers and low characters.[20] In
1863, Ninth Street between Federal Street and Washington
Avenue was the scene of a devastating fire that consumed four
blocks of dwellings, many of which housed Irish families.[21] In
1867, the *Evening Star*, in one of the city's earliest pleas for
urban renewal, bade the city tear down the rancid slums from
Fifth to Seventh Streets between Lombard and Fitzwater.
The same area was seen by one charitable group as full of
"ill-built, unventilated tenements, often no better in any respect than pens for cattle." [22]

The influx of immigrants washed into the city a wave of
human distress of the most stark and troubling character.
George Lippard in his novel *The Quaker City* caught the grim
contrast between the famine survivors and the secure native
Philadelphians in the portrayal of a scene on Chestnut Street:

> The State House clock had just struck eight, when amid
> the gay crowds who thronged Chestnut Street, might
> be discerned one poor wan-faced man, who strode sadly
> up and down the pavement in front of a jeweller's
> window.The night was bitter cold, but a tattered
> round-about and patched trousers constituted his scanty
> apparel. He had not been shaven for several days, and
> a thick beard gave a wild appearance to his lank jaws

and compressed lips. His face was pale as a mort-cloth, but his eye shone with that clear wild light that once seen, can never be forgotten. There was Famine in the unnatural gleam of that eye. His much-worn hat was thrown back from his pale forehead, and there, in the lines of that frowning brow you might read the full volume of wrong and want, which the oppressors of this world write on the faces of the poor.

Up and down the cold pavement he strode. He looked from side to side for a glance of pity. There was no humanity in the eyes that met his gaze. Fashionable Dames going to the Opera, Merchants in broad-cloth returning from the counting-house, Bank Directors hurrying to their homes, godly preachers wending to their churches, their faces full of sobriety and their hearts burning with enmity to the Pope of Rome: These all were there, on that crowded pavement. But pity for the Poor man, who with Famine written on his forehead and blazing from his eyes, strode up and down in front of the jeweller's gaudy window? Not one solitary throb! [23]

The indictment of smug unconcern may be overdrawn. Although Philadelphia had long had strictures against the importation of indigent immigrants, and although those had been strengthened in 1849, the city did have an extensive network of facilities for caring for the poor according to the precepts of the time.[24]

There were ten hospitals, one of them Saint Joseph's Hospital, was under Catholic auspices, plus a number of clinics; there were asylums for widows, orphans, the blind, and the insane. In addition, soup societies, almshouses, various immigrant-aid and benevolent societies, and the churches contributed to the alleviation of the lot of the poor and the afflicted.[25] One of the groups, the American Emigrants Friend Society, which in 1848 had been aiding a clientele that was

63 percent Irish, caustically cited English policy as the reason for the society's work, noting that England "starved out" people and "sends them to their graves."[26]

The annual reports of such organizations give ample evidence of the mounting problem of poverty as immigrants flowed into a city that already had its reservoirs of despondency and unemployment. The Society for the Employment and Instruction of the Poor was organized in 1847 on the heels of the famine influx. It opened Houses of Industry at Fifth and Pine and at Tenth and Shippen, the latter adjacent to one of the worst slums. Inmates made rugs, baskets, mats, and brushes for nominal wages. A "Ragged School" was opened for the children of the poor, and another House of Industry was opened in 1849, at Seventh and Catherine Streets. In the area from Fifth to Eighth Street on Saint Mary (now Rodman) Street lived "the discharged convict, the gatherer of bones and offal, the rag picker, dog catcher and river thief," the society reported. The expenditures of the society increased from $351 in 1847 to $4,987 in 1853.[27] In 1854 unemployment increased, but direct donations of money to the poor were withheld because of the fear that they would go to "grog shops and brothel keepers."[28] In 1854 three-fourths of the inmates of the Houses of Industry were foreign-born, which, the annual report noted, "indicates the true source of the great mass of pauperism which affects the community."[29] The 1855 report mentions that over half the inmates were Irish.[30] In a 750-member sample, stratified by year and selected at random from the 6,800 registered as receiving food and lodging at one of the Houses of Industry in the period 1861–69, 46 percent of the males were Irish and two out of five of those were laborers. The average age of these men was thirty-five years, and though the largest group was composed of laborers, the sample represented thirty-five different occupations.[31]

Such agencies were voluntarily supported. In 1853 the appeal letter of the Moyamensing Soup Society asked aid for "thousands of hungry, starving poor who apply daily for food."[32] Institutions supported by the government, among them the Almshouse at Blockley, in West Philadelphia, and the Board of Guardians of the Poor, also housed and fed paupers. If the societies sponsored by Protestant evangelical groups were suspect by the Irish as proselytizing groups, the Board of Guardians supervising the public almshouses was known as "The Board of Buzzards." The characterization drew venom from incidents such as the scandal in the 1840s when an almshouse guard, Captain Kelly, exposed the superintendent, Mr. A. B. Hutchinson, for stealing potatoes from the almshouse supply. Having escaped a potato famine only to have one's "pauper spuds" purloined was a circumstance laced with the sharpest irony.[33]

Those who availed themselves of the almshouse were truly destitute. Entering paupers, almost all Irish, were pathetically bereft of money or clothes.[34] Some would even have sought to return to Ireland in the desperate hope that there conditions might be better. One old woman, hoping to die in her native place, petitioned the Board of Guardians for such passage but was refused. The *Evening Bulletin* editorialized in the cold month of December 1855 about an "army of paupers," observing that, of the 2,070 in Blockley Almshouse, only a small proportion were Americans by birth: "The Irish generally compose more than two-thirds of the population of the house." The paper also commented at a later date on the Irish women who begged in the streets, aggressively pleading their cases with pronounced brogues.[35]

The depression of 1857 struck hard at Philadelphia, forcing the municipality to consider public works to aid the unemployed. The suffering was intense. The toll among the poor included suicide and death from too much whiskey and not enough food.[36] For those who had suffered through the famine, there was now the possibility of starvation even in wealthy America. The *Catholic Herald* protested against the practice of dragooning those in almshouses and other institutions and lending them to influential contractors as laborers.[37] It was not unusual for the Irish to feel victimized by those in charge of charitable institutions.[38]

Jammed into the slums in the least desirable dwellings of the city, the Irish were easy prey to the ravages of disease. In 1848 the Sanitary Committee of the Board of Health, recalling the terrible cholera epidemic of 1832, warned of the dirt and overcrowding in the city. It asked better drainage; sewerage; and inspection of piggeries, pigsties, and cellars.[39] In the summer of 1849 the committee's forebodings were borne out. A terrifying cholera epidemic struck the city, especially the Irish districts in Southwark, Moyamensing, and Port Richmond. In Moyamensing the Board of Health blamed the ''depraved condition of hundreds of its inhabitants, filthy and crowded conditions of many of its small houses, inhabitated cellars.'' In Port Richmond it blamed the want of proper drainage along the river front, and the ''character, habits, and occupation of a large portion of its population, viz., canal and river boatmen, coal heavers and laborers.''[40] Reports tell of ''extremes of filth and misery and loathsome disease . . . putrefying garbage and refuse of every kind, carcasses in disgusting decomposition; filthy rooms and damp, dirty, mouldy cellars, full and foul privies in close and illy ventilated locations.''[41]

The dead from the scourging epidemic of 1849 numbered 386, with the highest mortality rates in the areas of Irish concentration.[42] Besides devastating epidemics, the slum dwellers faced a greater danger from the other leading causes of death —scarlet fever, cholera infantum, ''convulsions,'' and consumption[43] The Irish were particularly ravaged by tuberculosis; whole families were infected with it.

The cholera epidemic was seen by many to be a retribution by God for ''filth, intemperance and vice,'' and the outbreak was blamed directly on the Irish by some.[44] The attribution of spiritual degeneration to the Irish was not unusual. That the avenging Almighty would smite them seemed reasonable.

Their reputation for alcoholic intake was widespread and damaging. As John F. Maguire wrote in his work *The Irish in America* after visiting the country, "Drink, accursed drink is the cause why so many Irish in America fail."[45] The Committee on Vice and Immorality of the Pennsylvania Senate widely circulated its plea that the "grogshops" of Philadelphia be closed.[46] Even one of the foremost of modern historians of the Irish emigration sees "insobriety" as the factor most affecting the success of the Irish.[47]

For many, the relentless cycle of poverty and affliction was overwhelming. They appeared occasionally in newspaper references as persons in a "state of mental aberration." In 1856, two-thirds of the insane in the state hospital in Philadelphia were Irish-born.[48] The refugees of the famine generation were pursued even in America by unemployment, disease, and privation.

If there were terrible conditions in Philadelphia, they were not so outrageous and widespread as in the other big cities. The death rates of New York, Boston, and Philadelphia were 35, 26.5, and 20.9 per 1000, respectively. Among the Irish-born in the same cities, the death rates per thousand were: 21.2 (New York), 37.7 (Boston), and 12.2 (Philadelphia). These figures indicate that, despite the hazards of its slum life, Philadelphia was less perilous than the other major eastern cities.[49]

More important, the city offered better housing opportunities to the immigrants once they began to make their way as workers and upwardly mobile citizens in the industrial environment. They had to survive the fetid slums and the impersonal economic pressures of the city, but if they could do so, and obtain jobs and savings, a way was open to housing improvement for them. For in Philadelphia, because of its distinct residential characteristics, better housing was available to a greater proportion of its working people than in any of the other major cities.

Philadelphia, even after it was consolidated in 1854, consisted of a fairly scattered constellation of smaller communities. If the central area was built up, and pocketed and fringed with slum alleys and shantytowns, there were other areas where neighborhoods provided open space and other amenities. Such districts are described by Wiebe: "Within the city limits yet detached from its core, neighborhoods provided fairly cloistered way stations between urban and rural living. In these years garden plots and a smattering of livestock came as standard accouterment to the city scene." [50] These became the goal of immigrants who had survived the physical and moral rigors of the noisome slums. There are numerous examples of Irish property purchases in such areas even in the early 1850s.[51]

The Philadelphia phenomenon of "ground rent," a survival of colonial proprietary days, was part of the city's advantage. This legal device obviated the need to purchase a building lot for a house; instead, the lot could be rented for a nominal sum for a long period. The custom lowered the immediate cost of housing. The row house was another boon. It had been adapted from the fashionable eighteenth-century English town-house rows, and during the nineteenth century, in a cheapened and smaller version, it became popular in Philadelphia. Early in the century it was already in common construction. The most popular type built between 1850 and 1870 was the sixteen-by-thirty-one-foot brick structure of two stories, with two bedrooms and a bathroom on the second floor and a living room and kitchen on the first. With a cellar and gas service, such a house sold new for $1,000–$2,500 according to location. It could be rented for $8–$15 a month. Old houses could sometimes be bought for as little as $300.[52]

There was advantage also in the fact that Philadelphia was not so compressed as Manhattan and Boston. Land was more available and less expensive. If Philadelphia was narrowed at the center by the Delaware and Schuylkill Rivers, on both the north and the south it expanded broadly. Manhattan's 22 square miles and Boston's 4 square miles could not compare with its 130.[53]

In the eleven years from 1840 to 1851 over 5,000 buildings were added to the city of Philadelphia proper. In 1850 Philadelphia County added 3,815 new structures.[54] The housing output of the Civil War years was somewhat irregular. Because of the unsettling effect of the early months of the war, only 1,535 houses were erected in 1861, whereas in 1860, a fairly good building year, 2,148 had been built. There was an upturn in 1862 and 1863, with 2,154 and 2,462 houses built, respectively, but the number declined to 1,166 by 1864. This reduced construction pattern continued until 1867.[55]

Lorin Blodgett, an astute and skillful statistician, compiled reports for various types of Philadelphia organizations in the nineteenth century. One of his reports comments upon the housing expansion of the city in the last half of the 1800s. Blodgett was a confirmed Philadelphian, and he decried the tenement housing patterns of New York City. He stated that the mass building of brick row houses began to come into vogue in the 1860s. The ability of Philadelphians to own houses was probably the most notable factor in the growth of the city in the second half of the last century. The brick row house, long a trademark of the city, had a profound impact upon its social character. This fact did not escape Blodgett. He discoursed at length on the differences between New York and Philadelphia, to the credit of his native city.[56] The owner-occupied row house fortified Philadelphians in a pattern of localism that gave the city's neighborhood life a settled quality and stability. It also gave the city a visual aspect of low-density development that matched the image of home-owning solidity. The Civil War years extended the gridiron, row-house pattern of modest, economically accessible dwellings, and by 1867 each year saw an average of 4,500 such houses added to the dwelling supply.[57]

The row house was not the only kind of construction, of

course, for we can read of the erection of large Victorian mansions on South Broad Street as well. Where the building of houses took place there were accompanying installations of water and gas service, street lamps, paving, and a wide variety of amenities that the public had come to expect as part of good nineteenth-century city living. In 1864 the *Philadelphia Inquirer* reported that seven churches, four schools, eight firehouses, and numerous stores and offices had been constructed during the year 1863.[58] Emerson Fite, in his work on conditions in the North during the Civil War, wrote of Philadelphia: "In this healthful manufacturing city the number of gas consumers increased by 6000, the consumption of gas 33½ per cent, that of water 50 per cent, while 45 miles of water mains and 92 miles of gas mains were laid, 1000 new street lamps set up. . . . There is contemporary evidence that in any particular section of the city the extension of the public services and building operations went together."[59] Such contemporary evidence is contained in the *Philadelphia North American*. An account of new building early in 1864 states that "in the Fifteenth and Twenty-Fifth Wards buildings are going up in numbers too tedious to mention," and later in 1864 an account of expansion of the gas system cites "a vast amount of building operation in constant progress." The areas of Vine Street to Montgomery Avenue, Eleventh Street to Susquehanna Avenue, and the Twenty-First Ward are cited.[60] These areas were adjacent to the older districts where the Irish were located in North Philadelphia.

Some mention should be made of the extraordinary growth of railway transportation as part of the city's extension during the Civil War. Beginning in 1857, street railways were first laid through the city's thoroughfares. Despite opposition from residents who resented the rattling innovations, by 1859 there were eighteen companies chartered for "horse trolleys." The swift construction of these lines proceeded until 1864, when some 129 miles of track were in service in Philadelphia, and stock in the transit companies was paying 9.9 percent dividends to investors.[61] Citing the number of charter bills presented to the Pennsylvania Assembly for street railway companies, the *Philadelphia Press* noted, "If this and a half dozen other railway schemes of the present Assembly session culminate into laws, the city of Philadelphia will be so thoroughly gridironed that public conveyances and private vehicles drawn by horsepower will be unable to traverse the streets without the risk of being upset or having their springs broken." [62] The proliferation of street railway lines in all directions was certainly one of the key developments of the mid–nineteenth century for the city. It made large-scale building in outlying areas feasible and made it possible for workers to move farther from their jobs. For the urban worker it provided a new mobility that broadened job opportunities and general experience.

Some idea of housing costs in Philadelphia in relation to those in other cities can be gathered from available figures on the subject. Lorin Blodgett, in a study of living costs in 1870, said that houses could be rented in Philadelphia by skilled workers for $15–$20 a month. Martin gives a family budget for 1851 showing a Philadelphia workingman's expenditure of $13 a month for rent but concedes that this expenditure was probably beyond the reach for most workers.[63] These figures indicate that the inflation accompanying the growth during the years 1851–70 was not acute.

A contemporary source, Edward Young, in a booklet of information for immigrants published by the U.S. Bureau of statistics, gives figures for rentals per mouth in the States in 1869 ranging from $4.40 in Pennsylvania to $9.70 in Massachusetts for four-room tenements, with New York's rate $8.40. The range for six-room tenements is similar, with Pennsylvania again having the advantage.[64] The testimony of contemporary sources concerning the better housing quality and the greater access to home ownership in Philadelphia, however, leaves some conjecture about the rental market. Certainly the Irish, largely unskilled and earning as little as $5 a week as laborers, were frequently in no position to pay even $5–$10 a month for rent.

Stephan Thernstrom shows that laborers in Newburyport, Massachusetts, were paying between $60 and $100 a year in rent in 1850. This surpasses the average Philadelphia rent of $53–$68 suggested by Martin and Young. Handlin cites rentals in the Fort Hill area in Boston of $1.50 per room per week, and equally exorbitant rents for attics and cellars.[65] While the unskilled immigrants to Philadelphia no doubt faced similar gouging, the fact that the city was able to expand its housing supply and make more working-class houses available was some relief. In addition, rental housing simply was not as large a portion of the Philadelphia housing market as it was in Boston and New York.

As early as 1851 Patrick McKeown was writing home to his sisters in Ireland that "almost every family has a house to themselves let it be large or small and a great many working people own the houses the[y] live in." [66] The opportunity for a workingman to obtain a home of his own was really there. Advertisements in the *Evening Bulletin* proclaimed, "There is not a Man in the Consolidated City of Philadelphia but Can Avail Himself of a Home If He Desires," and James Tagert of the Plank Road and Harrowgate Land Company offered to sell the houses desired.[67] At the edge of the city sizable lots were for sale, and builders were invited.[68]

A good many of the Irish were in a position to take advantage of these opportunities. Whereas a two-story house in Ireland was a mark of notable affluence, in Philadelphia such a structure could be had by a thrifty workingman. Few would be so fortunate as Bernard McCredy, who in 1855 willed his daughters $33,000 worth of property.[69] But an examination of bequests of Philadelphia Irishmen of the 1850s indicates that it was not uncommon for members of the city's Irish community to own houses and real property.[70] True, some of the property was in slum areas, but some was in other areas as well; a skilled tradesman like the Kensington wheelwright

John W. Kelly was able to own two three-story brick houses, and one frame house worth $5,000 at Germantown Road and Franklin Street, and a man of lesser means like Barney Murphy of Front and Otter Streets had a small two-story frame house worth $500.[71]

An examination of a typical deed book, selected at random from among those in the Archives of the City of Philadelphia, shows several hundred property purchases recorded in 1853, with eighteen by Irishmen in Moyamensing, Schuylkill, Port Richmond, and Kensington. For example, John McGinty bought a house for $567.67 in North Philadelphia and had to sign the deed with an "X"; Catherine Cline and John Killan bought houses in Schuylkill, Killan's on Brazier Street, for $600 and $413, respectively; William McKnight sold a three-story tenement in Schuylkill on Fifth Street to Terrence Mellon, for $1,400; builder Thomas Dugan sold three new three-story brick houses in Kensington to a carpenter for $1,200 each; while John Burke purchased a house at Jefferson and Marvine Streets for $1,100. It is clear that home buying among the Irish was not unusual, and that the purchases ranged from older, less expensive houses in such areas as Schuylkill to new dwellings at the expanding edge of Kensington.[72]

The process of property acquisition often took a long time. John McDermott came to the city from County Clare in the 1840s. He first lived in South Philadelphia but, being a weaver, moved to the Kensington textile area, where he bought a house at 448 North Washington Street (now American Street) near Jefferson. The house looked out on the turbulent Nanny Goat Market that occupied the street before it. In a shed in the rear of the house, John McDermott set up his loom. He helped other Clare men, and they helped him. He prospered, purchased a metal-working business, and with the proceeds purchased two newer houses near the pleasant little square at Third and Diamond Streets in a neater and more fashionable neighborhood that had many German families.[73]

Visiting Philadelphia in the 1860s, a European noted the

good quality of most of the housing and one of the reasons why better housing conditions prevailed in the city:

> Almost all the streets, where the working classes and even the small proprietors live, have been built by asssociations. Nothing could be simpler than the plan which they have adopted. Several house builders form themselves into a temporary association; they buy their ground, and pay for it in part by means of mortgage loan. Each one furnishes to the association his special work, masonry, carpentry, woodworking, glass, etc. As soon as the houses are built, they are sold, and the profits divided in proportion to the work of each man. Half of Philadelphia has been built in this way, and the workmen construct for themselves also houses, which make an extremely good appearance; they are healthy, airy, and provided with everything conducive to comfort and salubrity. . . . There is certainly not a city in the world where the working population lives with the comfort they enjoy in Philadelphia, and we must add that they owe this superiority solely to themselves and their intelligent activity.[74]

What was observed in this instance was that remarkable institution, the building and loan association. A sort of people's bank, it became a phenomenon of considerable renown and admiration. Since it was difficult for ordinary working people without collateral to obtain credit, groups of them began to develop their own credit systems. Each person deposited a small sum, usually weekly, until enough equity was established to warrant an extension of credit. If a man could pay the nominal ground rent on a lot, he could after a time borrow perhaps $1,400 from his local building and loan association, have a house built, and repay the loan over a period of years. This original mortgage system in the city grew spontaneously and extensively. The first such associations were begun in the late 1840's, and by 1875 there were 600 disbursing a half-million dollars a month. The depositors were the only stockholders. The overhead was low, since usually only the secretary of the association drew a salary. These associations were the fiscal mainspring behind the city's building in the 1850s and 1860s. They were a convenient and popular device, approbated because they encouraged the habits of "frugality, steadiness and the elements of finance." [75] This moral role was as acclaimed as were the actual business advantages. Between 1849 and 1876 an accounting for only 450 of these associations showed that they did $50 million worth of business.[76]

These building associations became one of the vehicles for improvement for Irish families intent upon achieving better housing and a modest respectability. With some of that dogged thrift that could often be found among the extraordinarily penurious Irish cottiers in the old country, the Philadelphia Irish took to the building and loan associations. As early as 1848, the Constitution of the Aramingo Building Association in Port Richmond listed Irishmen at the highest executive level: John O'Brien as its treasurer and Francis McManus and Hugh Malone among its eight directors. The Union Land and Homestead Association in 1854 listed as officers Hon. Charles Gilpin, president; Henry Smith, M.D., vice president; Edward Brady, treasurer; and as secretary, Ignatius Donnelly, that same activist and reformer who was to become a prophet of populism later in the century. With offices at 179 Spruce Street, the Board of Managers included Lewis Cassidy, the prominent Democratic political leader and noted trial lawyer; and also a dentist, an alderman, a carpenter, and two tavern keepers, all Irish. Such leadership would assure the association a strong Irish following. In 1855 the Flanagan Building Association had Hugh Cassidy as president, and 95 of its 150 stockholders bore clearly recognizable Irish names.[77]

These associations took on a distinctly Irish character in many instances. As adjuncts to Catholic churches, fraternal organizations, and Irish neighborhood and workingmen's groups, they flourished. One man alone started thirty-five such associations, eventually building their capital to $15 million. Usually serving as secretary, he avidly promoted these organizations of mite-saving depositors with formidable honesty and persistence, from 1847 until he died in 1880. This man, Bernard Rafferty, was something of an impresario for housing and building development for the Irish community. The names of some of the associations indicate the mixture of religious, patriotic, and ethnic appeal involved. There were associations named for Hibernia, Emerald, Erin, Shamrock, Saint Patrick, Mathew Carey, and Daniel O'Connell.[78]

The role of the Catholic parishes in this popular financial invigoration of the housing market was substantial. Though rarely involving them directly, the groups often operated in close conjunction with the parishes and sometimes were named after them, as was the Saint Patrick's Building and Loan Association. The connection with the parish implied honesty, and stability and provided a ready network of relationships together with a regularly attended locus for promotion and activity. And if the association encouraged thrift and family improvement, this was one of the aims of the church as well. The correspondence of their goals engendered in the two institutions a common interest in solid local development and neighborhood spirit.

In addition to this process of residential upgrading, there was the movement of well-to-do Irishmen into the select districts of the city. Stuart Blumin has shown that the center city in antebellum Philadelphia, despite its contiguity to mercantile activity, was a desirable residential area for the affluent. The area around Third and Spruce Streets was a fashionable quarter, while many of the old Quaker families lived on Arch Street.[79] Although by the early 1860s the street railways were making the outlying areas more accessible, the center city still retained the strong attributes of convenience, attractiveness, and fashion. In the outlying areas new housing was being built—the elegant houses of Germantown are an example—and the well-to-do Irish were already installed in middle-class and upper-class areas by 1860. Out of a sample of fifty such Irishmen, most Irish-born, nineteen resided in the center city between Vine and Cedar Streets, between the two rivers. While some of the political figures lived in Kensington and Moyamensing, others lived in more reputable areas. In the pleasant precincts of Germantown lived William McAleer, a city councilman; James Donnelly, a commission merchant; and Philip F. Kelly, a banker. Center-city residents included lawyers, physicians, editors, manufacturers, a railroad president, and various merchants and distillers. Among them was Congressman Charles O'Neill at 1408 South Penn Square, publisher Thomas Fitzgerald at 337 South Seventh Street, and Dr. William V. Keating at 283 South Fourth Street.

Norman Johnston has developed a pattern of zones based on the "class ecology" of Philadelphia. Five members of the above-mentioned sample of fifty affluent Irishmen lived in the mid-city area classed as "fashionable";[80] fourteen lived in the surrounding middle-class areas; and fifteen, among them Charles Kelly and Bernard McCredy, textile manufacturers who had large holdings in Delaware County, lived the lives of country gentlemen, in homes beyond the built-up areas of the city. It is clear from this sample that there was a selective residential dispersion of well-to-do Irish Philadelphians before the Civil War.[81]

The available evidence demonstrates that the infusion of Irish immigrants into the city resulted in concentrations of segregated slum living. But the immigration also coincided with a period of extensive residential building. This home building was of a special kind. It was diffused, often popularly sponsored through building and loan associations, and economical enough to permit an increasing number of working people to obtain homes. Thus, there was a prospect for liberation from the slums. Even the older areas of Moyamensing and Schuylkill, between one-fourth and one-half of the property owners were Irish. There was the possibility of housing improvement and social movement for Irish families. The attainment of a tidy row house on an orderly city street meant that the immigrant would have an actual stake in the urban community. It meant that the period of privation would be shortened, and that the hostility engendered by poverty and residential isolation would be tempered somewhat.

For the immigrant, the acquisition of a decent brick row house, however modest, was the fulfillment of one of the goals of migration. Where in Ireland could one of these men from the barren shores of Clare or the rugged wastes of Donegal hope to obtain such a dwelling? Where could the struggling tenant farmer amass the money to pay his rent in Ireland, let alone purchase a whole six-room house for his family? The answers are patent in view of what has been related about the Irish background. In Philadelphia there was opened to the Irishman an opportunity for domestic life and security that was only a dream in Ireland. Beyond the city's slums was a way of neighborhood life that was as beguiling as it was attainable. For people whose family ties and customs of sociability were strong, the residential pattern of Philadelphia held a deep attraction. Their entry into that pattern and their interaction with it would make a pervasive contribution to the stability of the city.

# FOUR

## WORKING
## TO LIVE

It is in the changes introduced into work life that the industrial revolution and its counterpart of urbanization had their most evident effects. Multitudes of men who had been conditioned to work centered on seed and its sowing, harvest, and hubandry were detached from agricultural pursuits and mobilized into the growing productive systems of industry founded on "the uses of inanimate sources of power and the use of tools to multiply the effect of effort." As T. S. Ashton states, "Labor became more mobile, and higher standards of comfort were offered to those able and willing to move to centres of opportunity." [1]

For Ireland the movement of workers came after a long period of economic reverses. During the eighteenth century the island had developed rather precociously in mercantile and manufacturing activities. Within the largely domestic technology of the eighteenth century, its developing economy expanded rapidly. In the 1830s, however, proximity to England, the leading nation in the industrial revolution with its dramatic reductions in transport costs, made Ireland's small-scale, domestic industries vulnerable in a fiercely competitive age. The result was a striking contraction that combined with agricultural decline to reduce both the vitality and the structure of Irish economic life.[2] Not only was the industry of the country subverted, but the trades and skills that were an adjunct to rural life were eroded. An account by a Gaelic speaker in Donegal portrays the effect on a townland of famine and economic depression: "There was no trade in the world but some man of Beltany could try it—the best weavers in the country were there; there were masons, carpenters, coopers, thatchers and every kind of tradesman you could name in this townland; and after the famine years neither tale nor tidings of them was to be found. They all went into strange and distant lands and never returned since.'' [3] Poverty in town and country fostered an alertness to opportunities elsewhere. News from those who had already gone to America excited wonderment at the benefits to be had there. As one Thomas Mooney wrote to his cousin Patrick, even an unskilled man could learn a trade in two or three years, then earn $1.25–$2.00 a day, with fine food in the mechanics' boarding houses and prospects for betterment at every hand. [4] The man who already had a trade could do well, but for the great majority of emigrants, those with no trades, the promise was different. Still, the news from America beckoned them. Newspapers told of the great railway boom and economic progress in the United States. [5] They told also of extensive labor agitation for a ten-hour day there. [6] To men struggling against poverty in Ireland, such intelligence was almost irresistably attractive.

An analysis of Irish immigrants arriving between 1850 and 1865 shows that 84.5 percent were farmers, farm laborers, servants, ploughmen, graziers, and herdsmen. Whatever the skills these men had, they were clearly emigrants from rural areas. [7] Among immigrants generally, laborers constituted slightly above 35 percent of the total. [8] Among the Irish the percentage was even higher; Handlin, for instance, found that in Boston 48 percent of the Irish were laborers. [9] Although the Census of 1850 listed 253 occupations in its tabulations, laborers constituted 21 percent of the total labor force. [10] The growing American economy used an enormous number of unskilled laborers, but the Irish from rural backgrounds were so disproportionately unskilled that they faced great hardship in obtaining a livelihood.

The economy of Philadelphia thrived in the decades after 1850. Except for the brief depression of 1857 and the adjustment problems at the beginning of the Civil War, the industrial and commercial growth of the city continued at an unprecedented pace. In 1852 R. A. Smith could write that "the enterprise of her citizens was never more displayed than at present." And even during the 1857 depression, Edwin T. Freedley, the man who had taken care to find out the most about the city's industrial structure, could laud its progressive vitality.[11] In iron, machinery, textiles, clothing, shoes, transportation, and construction, the city was alive with productive animation.

In 1850 the labor force, according to the census, was 59,903. By 1860 it had expanded to 107,931.[12] This force was distributed throughout several areas of industrial activity that were primary to the industrialization process; textiles, metals, and transportation led the way, spurred by the use of new sources of fuel and power.[13] It was in these areas that Philadelphia's labor force was concentrated by 1860. In textile production there were almost 10,000 workers; in carpet production, 2,500 in clothing and shirt manufacture, over 17,000; in iron, 2,300; in machinery fabrication, 2,000; in locomotive production, 1,200, in the city's two huge engine plants.[14] Philadelphia was widely reputed to be a workshop of marvels in machinery and technical innovation.[15]

The city was more than a series of manufacturing establishments, however. It was also a school, a vast educative network for the learning of behavior in the industrial urban environment. It represented a new human experience on a vast scale. The working population was developing a widening range of skills, there was increased occupational as well as geographical mobility, and higher levels of education led men to better positions in a highly structured work force. These factors promoted a new understanding and tolerance of diversity in society—a tolerance, however, that was balanced by an increase in rules, regulations and norms to which men had to conform if they were to function in the industrial order.[16] Into this learning process, the neophytes on the urban scene had to enter.

Although rules and regulations increased, the rate of change and the extent of the diversity in occupational life were confusing. Men who presided over new processes and enterprises might try to set forth detailed rules, but the bursting energy and inventiveness that characterized the industrial milieu generally tended to contradict their efforts. This was true with respect to occupations. The old apprenticeship and hierarchical patterns were constantly retreating in the face of innovation. Sam Bass Warner, speaking of occupational change in the developing city, states that "perhaps the only uniformities common to all these many different arrangements of urban manufacturers were that all were responses to the new opportunities of the city." [17]

It was not only the primary industries that were escalating. Much of the dynamic interaction and self-stimulation of the economy derived from other sources. "The increased size of the urban community promoted the development of auxiliary, supplementary and complementary industries and services." [18] In Philadelphia, for instance, by 1860 the making and installation of gas fixtures employed over 1,000 men; the making of cigars, 1,200. [19]

Into this great proliferation of change and construction the Irish were poured. "The availability of the immigrants in the labor force accelerated economic growth and assisted in the process of industrialization." [20] They were generally regarded as sturdy and diligent workers. In 1851 the *Evening Bulletin* reflected this opinion in commenting upon Henry Mayhew's *London's Labor and London's Poor,* in which he ranked the Irish poor above the unfortunate cockneys of the London slums. The paper ascribed Irelands' poverty, not to the character of her people, but to her land system. [21] In 1850 the Iron Masters of Philadelphia sent a memorial to Congress strongly urging the importation of immigrants: "We should employ hosts of laborers and attract them hither from all quarters of the world; and for every million people which this scene of industry would draw to our shores, we should be furnished with an additional home market." [22] This evident desire for more labor could never really be satisfied during this period of heady expansion. Scarce labor, then, and evidence of the greater production, efficiency, and economy to be gained from machines and new power sources led manufacturers to turn to mechanization.[23] The immigrants thus became part of a cycle of economic development that placed labor in competition with machines, a competition that was to lead to great suffering and stormy protest.[24]

The employment of throngs of Irish immigrants coincided with the development of a transportation network that was to set the stage for the tapping of resources and the distribution of products throughout the home market. As early as 1831 Irishmen were engaged in the great labor to build the first rail line across the Alleghenies between Holidaysburg and Johnstown. One of their number took the first canal boat across the mountains to the Ohio River, on that extraordinary construction of locks and rails the Portage Railroad, which ascended the heights west of Holidaysburg.[25] By the 1850s the Irish had become the standard workers of the railroad system.[26]

As a prelude of the transportation revolution, canals were built in the effort to provide access to the fabulous wealth of the hinterland. Although the Erie Canal was the most outstanding example of a waterway to the riches of the young nation, Pennsylvania had its own network of canals and canal ports. The primary links in this system were the Schuylkill Navigation Company's canal to Reading along the Schuylkill, and two canals connecting with the Delaware—the Delaware and Raritan Canal to Northern New Jersey, and the Lehigh Navigation Canal above Easton to Mauch Chunk.[27] It was on such works that the Philadelphia Irish often labored. Recruited in gangs, they would be transported to the work sites, where they would lodge in nearby boarding houses, makeshift workers' barracks, or shanties. The work was, by modern standards, arduous beyond belief. In the construction of a new canal, the process of clearing, grading, and banking the land along the route required intense effort. The felling of trees, movement of earth, and digging of the "cut" and the canal path in all kinds of weather was an operation leaving little room for sympathetic human relations. The construction gangs had to be driven, in the worst sense of the word. So grueling and dangerous was the work that Irishmen, considered less valuable than Negro slaves, were used at times in preference to an investment of black labor.[28]

There were a variety of nefarious practices related to the work. Pennsylvanian Simon Cameron, later a member of Lincoln's cabinet, recruited 136 Irish laborers in Philadelphia for work on the New Basin Canal outside New Orleans. After being transported to Louisiana, the Irishmen found conditions so bad they went on strike and denounced Cameron, claiming that he had practically sold them as redemptioners, that they had to buy food at double price, and that the only doctor available was a drunken quack.[29] Such experiences would not produce jolly laboring men. A poet might write,

> Work, work, my boy, be not afraid
> Look labor boldly in the face,
> Take up the hammer and the spade
> And blush not for your humble place.[30]

But the digger in the mire would not be so enthusiastic.

By the year 1850, the greater part of the canal boom had passed, and the labor used on canals was for maintenance and occasional extention. Subsidence had to be corrected, dredging was a constant operation, and portions of the canals had to be drained and rebuilt. In this work of mud, slime, and exertion, the Irish were regularly immersed. In the 1850 records of the Land Office of the Board of Canal Commissioners of Pennsylvania, for instance, at least half of the names of laborers on the canal between Easton and Bristol are readily recognizable as Irish. The pay vouchers show that they earned $87\frac{1}{2}$ cents a day for working in January weather. On one voucher, eighteen of the thirty-one names were Irish, and of these Irishmen twelve had to sign for their pay with an "X" mark.[31] Since the numbers of men listed on the vouchers from week to week vary, weather and other considerations probably caused uneven employment.

This kind of labor was a transient occupation, unenviable even under the best of conditions. How many laborers left families in Philadelphia to earn 87½ cents a day on the canals, living in loneliness in unsanitary, makeshift camps and working their twelve-hour day in the mud holes? The evidence does not provide a gross figure, but surely the number was very great, for brute labor was the only means of constructing those water roads across the countryside, and they were built despite the human cost.

As the canal boom subsided, the railroad boom began. This was an even greater conquest of wilderness and distance. If a man could dig a canal, he could dig a railroad right-of-way, and the Irish were recruited by the thousands to that task.[32] To excavate by hand a "cut" of 600 cubic yards a day required approximately one hundred men. The work of cutting, banking, tunneling, laying ties and rails, and building all the far-flung facilities required by railroads involved a mass of unskilled labor. Tunneling was the most dangerous operation, but practically all the work involved hazard. The use of "barrow runs," for example, was especially dangerous. A plank walk, often perilously steep, was built up the side of a bank, perhaps several hundred feet high. A rope line was run through a pulley at the top and attached to a horse. With the horse pulling at the top, the rope was attached to a barrow guided by a man at the bottom who walked the barrow up the plank path. Only the strongest men could do this work, and the mishaps were frequent.[33]

The shady practices of the canal days also plagued the railroad era. The Philadelphia Emigrant Society found in 1854 that "greenhorns" were victimized as soon as they left the incoming ship. Ten Irish newcomers were charged $3 each by a "forwarding agent" and were sent to Philadelphia for railroad jobs. Upon arriving, they found that the jobs were fictitious.[34]

As the construction work proceeded, the Irish gradually moved up from diggers to gang bosses, and then on into the actual operation of the roads.[35] Edward C. Kirkland notes that "not only did railroad employment involve a variety of skills. At the outset it required novel ones—for in the thirties and forties railroading was a new industry. . . . There was no uniformity in the placing of hand holds and grab irons, the position of ladders, in the position and dimension of running boards, in the height of cars and in the intervals between them. At best, these incalculable variations endangered the trainmen who, in response to the whistle, ran along the cars to their positions and braked the train to a stop with hand brakes.[36] Even if a man got out of the ditch, the dangers of this new industry surrounded him. Some men, like Waterford-born Richard O'Brien, who came to Philadelphia in 1851, could cultivate special skills. O'Brien became chief telegrapher for the Pennsylvania Railroad and was chief operator of all military lines for the Union in the Civil War.[37] But, for most of the immigrants displaced from Irish fields, the only way to earn a livelihood on the railroads was to dig, and dig hard.

How did the Irish immigrants find the jobs—in canal·work, on railroads, or in anything else? Many relied on relatives, friends, or acquaintances for information about employment. It was unusual for an immigrant to arrive in Philadelphia without some relative or other reference to whom he could appeal. Barring such contacts, the natural gravitation of the newcomer to persons of similar background readily established links. Persons from the same area or county in the old country grouped together for social reasons and at times even formed little residential clusters; and the parish churches, of course, were gathering places. Among a people noted for their "clannishness," the extension of information and aid was not long in forthcoming. There were more organized approaches available, also, such as the well-known "intelligence offices" that served as employment services. O'Conner's Emigrant and Intelligence Office advertised in the *Catholic Instructor,* one of the Philadelphia Catholic weeklies.[38] The railroads and other businesses relied on these offices to recruit part of their labor.[39] Organizations of mechanics and trade unions, too, served as grapevines for information about occupational conditions and opportunities. All these sources gave the immigrant a chance to locate and apply for jobs in which he could use what skills he had.

Aside from jobs in the transportation network, a system that was central to the growth of the new industrial economy, the immigrants could seek livelihoods in the textile industry, for which the city was already famous. Certainly one of the major features of the industrial revolution in the city was the expansion of textiles. Freedley lists over two hundred textile establishments in the city proper in 1856, with a total annual dry-goods production valued at over $21 million. There had long been a tradition of textile workers' emigrating to Philadelphia.[40] In the 1850s the production operations in the industry were still very diversified, with hand and domestic workshops, neighborhood shops, and big new mills all competing for a share of the growing market.[41]

Freedly gives a good view of this textile activity as of 1857. The city was the greatest seat of hand weaving in the country, and Freedley counted 4,760 hand looms in it. The work was done in the houses of the weavers or in small buildings or "sheds" containing 10 or 12 looms. Most were in the seventeenth and nineteenth wards, that is, in Kensington and Port Richmond. Entrepreneurs would deal with from 20 to 200 weavers, gathering the output for processing or sale. These hand weavers included numerous Irishmen, some of whom were jobbers of cloth as well; in a list of twenty-five large jobbing businesses given by Freedley, eight of the owners' names are Irish. However, the ancient skill of hand weaving was under increasing pressure, for it was competing with the new factories. The operatives in the factories in the 1850s were still heavily English or ''Anglo-American.'' Working a ten-hour day, these factory weavers, most of whom were women, earned $4–$5 a week tending power-driven machines, while spinners and spoolers earned $2–$3. Freedley's list of owners of textile factories includes few Irish names.[42]

Yet the entry of the Irish into the factory system in textiles was not long in coming. By 1850, the Irish had entered the mills in New England in great numbers, and Howard Gitelman has shown that they invaded many operations in the factories, including carding, spinning, weaving, and dressing. He also points out perhaps the preeminent reason for the adaptability of the Irish in the textile industry. In Ireland the hand production of cloth was a widespread trade, and one of the major elements of the rural economy even in times of poverty.[43] Although the machinery of the factories was new, the processes were the same. The movement of the Irish into the textile firms should have been even more extensive in Philadelphia, where mills were numerous and the numbers of hand weavers great, but, as in New England, the Catholic Irish would face discrimination from English, North of Ireland Protestant, and native American workers. In a highly competitive business in a competitive era, however, the need for labor would create openings in spite of such obstacles.

Various writers take note of the worsening plight of the hand weavers.[44] Their skill was one that had been cultivated over centuries, and most owned their own looms. Liam O'Flaherty, in his moving novel *Famine,* depicts one of these men. Proud of his skill, clinging to it tenaciously, he is driven to the roads by want and still refuses to part with his loom. But hand weaving was doomed in the factory world of the city, and the mass-production system gradually eliminated it. In this process, the hand weavers, though suffering terribly, hung on.[45]

An adjunct to the city's large textile industry was the

manufacture of ready-made clothes, and this work, long to be an occupation of immigrants, employed many Irish. A young girl in Philadelphia wrote to her brother in Dublin in 1851 that, "no female that can handle a needle need be idle." [46] In 1860 the city had 352 ready-made-clothing establishments, with 8,078 female and 6,309 male workers. Their products were valued at almost $10 million. The invention of the sewing machine and its perfection by Isaak Singer in 1851 began a new era in clothing manufacture. The factory system developed for sewing and tailoring. But if tailors or seamstresses could buy or rent sewing machines, it was common for them to do work in their homes, sometimes after a long day at the factory. In addition to the new factories, tenements, loft rooms and even old stables were used as shops to help fill the demand for ready-made garments.[47] Something of the same condition was prevalent in shoemaking, in which a reputed 7,000 workers were engaged by jobbers and retainers. Many of these worked under "garret bosses" in groups of 10.[48]

For the immigrants, practicing these trades of spinning and weaving, tailoring, and shoemaking in the city meant something different from practicing them in the villages of Ireland. It meant a new work setting, changes in materials and techniques, much more collaboration with others, and a new way in which the product of one's labor was sold. And more and more the machine and the factory system subsumed the old trades.

At the heart of the new industrial structure was the metal-working industry. Smelters, foundries, and metal-fabricating plants were numerous in the city. Freedley cites 10,000 workers employed in the industry in dozens of firms. The value of total production was above $12 million in 1856.[49] In the age of iron, Philadelphia was a leading producer of rails, bridge iron, boilers, and the thousands of other heavy items forged from this metal. For the Irish to be truly part of the industrial structure of the city, they had to be part of the strenuous cycle of transforming ore into the iron frames and products on which so much of the new technology of urbanism rested.

Thousands of laborers in ironworks stoked the furnaces, shoveled the ore, and carried the ingots. The Irish were a considerable portion of this unskilled labor force, working at such large plants at the Union Works at Nineteenth and Hamilton Streets and the Keystone Works at Front and Girard Avenue, which were part of the booming Stanley G. Flagg Company. Flagg, a gifted Yankee, was a technical leader in the industry; he used steam power, jigs, and dies to make malleable- and grey-iron pipes and fittings for the expanding gas, water, and steam systems that served a growing number of communities. His older craftsmen grumbled at his innovations, but the production rise was huge.[50] Firms like this, the Norris Locomotive Works, and the sprawling Baldwin Locomotive Works used great numbers of unskilled laborers.

Although the Irish were hired largely for menial tasks, some moved into the more technical and supervisory levels in the metals industry. More and Gallagher had an iron foundry on Ridge Avenue; T. P. McDonough built engines and printing machinery;[51] James Dougherty, partner in Bement and Dougherty, headed one of the outstanding machinery firms in the nation.[52] John Murphy, who started as an immigrant blacksmith with a smithy at Broad and Wood Streets in 1833, later joined a wheelwright named Allison to build railroad cars and streetcars, a business that was to prosper immensely as the transportation industry flourished. The Murphy and Allison Company became a major supplier to the great railroads that threaded through the city and beyond.[53]

Despite the generally animated condition of the economy, it still confronted the immigrant worker with many problems. The 1840s had brought a decline in the wages of laborers. Gradually they rose again through the 1850s, but the turnover for both skilled and unskilled labor was very high, especially during the Civil War years.[54] This turnover added to labor unrest and distress even while it provided the opportunity for men to find different jobs.

In 1848, Pennsylvania's legislature passed a law limiting the workday to ten hours, but mill owners simply cut wages to compensate for the work hours lost through the law, and by 1853 the hours had crept up again to twelve a day.[55] Child labor was accepted and was excused by one commentator on the grounds that "these half grown persons or children are at light work."[56] Religious and ethnic qualifications hedged employment opportunities. To obtain jobs the immigrants had to compete, and some of the competition, as in the building trades, was racial, with the Irish displacing Negro mechanics. This was one cause of the intense Irish-Negro hostility that produced intermittent violence.[57] Congressman Mike Walsh from New York said in 1854, "The only difference between the Negro slave in the South and the white wages slave of the North, is that the one has a master without asking for him, and the other has to beg for the privilege of becoming a slave. . . . The one is the slave of an individual; the other is the slave of an inexorable class."[58] Although there were few formal contract-labor importations in the 1850s and 1860s, labor recruitment for railroad and mining interests in cities like Philadelphia drew thousands of immigrants into bad working conditions.[59] Reverses in the economy, such as that of 1857, created severe unemployment in the coal, iron, and textile industries.[60] Even when times were good, inflation drove prices up and imposed a hardship on workers whose wages left little margin.[61]

The large proportion of the Irish who were laborers is an important factor in evaluating their position in the occupational complex of the industrializing city. Laborers in the 1850s and 1860s were in a marginal position with respect to the opportunities that the new industrialism afforded. They ιould not fully share the opportunities and benefits of the new urban culture from such a position. It was the laboring class that was the most subject to the disabilities of unemployment, poverty, and bad living conditions. An analysis of census schedules for 1850, 1860, and 1870 shows that the percentage of laborers among Irish-born males aged fifteen to sixty-five in one neighborhood in South Philadelphia, though gradually declining, remained large. In the 1850 census listings of occupations, 34.4 percent of a sample composed of Irish-born males were laborers, and 12 percent of a sample of a native-born Irish; in 1860, and in 1870 the laborers composed 22 and 25 percent of the Irish-born samples, respectively, and 8 percent of the native-born.[62]

Because of the limitations of the sources giving occupational data, these percentages may not be entirely accurate, but they do provide a general estimate of the proportion of the Irish whose level of skill did not afford them ready entry into the occupational matrix of technical industrialism. The census figures can be corroborated somewhat, however, by recourse to other sources. The Commonwealth of Pennsylvania conducted its own Septennial census for tax purposes. Of samples of males with recognizable Irish names taken from the population lists for four wards, between one-fourth and one-third were laborers (see table 1). The proportions varied from ward to ward.

Further confirmation that a large proportion of the Irish were laborers was provided by a sample of 750 names drawn from a list of 6,800 unemployed persons receiving meals, lodging, or other aid from the Philadelphia House of Industry from 1861 to 1870. Since these men, averaging thirty-five years of age and unemployed or traveling to some place of employment, gave their places of birth, the Irish-born are identifiable. In a sample of over 10 per cent of these names, the Irish-born constituted some 46 percent, or 345, of the total, and of these, 40 percent were laborers.[63] This very high per-

## TABLE 1

PERCENTAGE OF IRISH LABORERS, 1863

| WARD | % LABORERS | NO. IN SAMPLE |
|---|---|---|
| 1 (South Philadelphia) | 32 | 470 |
| 7 (South Philadelphia) | 24 | 537 |
| 8 (South Philadelphia) | 23 | 271 |
| 19 (Port Richmond) | 33 | 375 |
| Total | ... | 1,653 |

SOURCE: Record Group 7, Septennial Census Returns, boxes 6–12, Records of the General Assembly, House of Representatives, 1863, Archives of the Commonwealth of Pennsylvania, Harrisburg, Pa.

centage of laborers could be explained by the fact that it was the laborer whose services were the most easily dispensed with and who was the most vulnerable to unemployment, and hence the man most likely to be in need of a free meal and lodging.

This population of immigrant laborers was the problem group of the period. Although unskilled labor was an economic necessity in the industrial city for the tremendous tasks of moving raw materials and engaging in large-scale building operations, the laborer was a social liability. His minimal earning power, his marginal status, his cultural disabilities all constituted a problem. Living in the side streets, courts, and alleys where overcrowding, disease, and family breakdown were common, he was prey to all manner of ills and problems. In good times he was often given to heavy consumption of alcohol and boisterous, even riotous, behavior. In bad times he could be a formidable antagonist in strikes and disorders. The Irish immigrant laborer was a paradox. Though economically necessary, he was a burden. Though marginal in the increasingly elaborate urban occupational structure, he would remain a regular feature of the labor force for decades.

If laborers composed one-fourth to one-third of the Irish immigrant work force, the rest of the immigrant workers were distributed throughout a growing variety of occupations. The number of occupations represented among an Irish immigrant sample drawn from a heavily Irish neighborhood in Moyamensing (South Philadelphia) in 1850 was thirty-two. By 1860, a sample drawn from the same general area showed forty-nine occupations, and in 1870, sixty-two. Some of the occupations listed on the census schedules were unskilled, such as hostler, porter, or carter, but there were also highly skilled craftsmen such as machinists and carpenters, and even a few professional men.[64] Even the unemployed listed in the House of Industry's *Record of House Relief* represented thirty-five different occupations, with weavers composing the largest group besides laborers.[65]

The trend indicated by these listings is one of rapid occupational dispersion. In the period from 1850 to 1870 the work life of the inhabitants of Philadelphia was being transformed through the industrial revolution, which called for new trades and skills. Within the space of twenty years, the number of occupations engaged in by the Irish immigrants almost doubled. According to census figures, their leading occupations in 1850 were: laborer, tailor, and shoemaker; in 1860: laborer, weaver, and shoemaker; and in 1870: laborer, shoemaker, and tailor. These remained fairly static. But the occupations listed show a growing diversification. Merchants increased among the immigrants; urban occupations such as street-car conductor, gas fitter, and stereotyper appeared; occupations stemming from the high mercantile activity of the city, such as clerk, bookkeeper, printer, and salesman, appeared and increased. Contractors and even manufactuers appeared among the Irish-born.

In those two key areas of urban industrial expansion, metals and textiles, the Irish show some infiltration. In the sample drawn in 1850, there were no engineers, only two ironmoulders and one machinist. By 1870, the sample included two engineers, four ironmoulders, two machinists, and two typefounders. In textiles, although the designation "weaver" is less frequent, especially after 1860, the census samples show such occupations as loom boss, spooler, warper, and dyer in 1860, and 1870 a marked increase in factory hands. In addition, the number of women with occupational designations increases among the immigrants in 1860, and by 1870 seamstresses, foreladies, shirt-factory workers, and loom tenders are cited among the females in textile work.

This occupational diversification apparently proceeded in the face of a continued influx of unskilled immigrants who added to and replenished the ranks of the laborer class. To the old occupations of blacksmith, cordwainer, hatter, and stonemason, mentioned in the 1850 listings, were added plasterer, plumber, policeman, and others by 1870. If the proportion of laborers remained relatively static, the diversification for the greater portion of the immigrants grew apace. Although samples of native-born workers show greater occupational variety and a similar increasing rate of diversification, the absorption of the immigrants from rural backgrounds into the urban labor force at such a rapid rate is notable. Industrial production, by dictating the division of labor into new patterns of skill, provided the immigrants opportunities of assuming occupational roles they could hardly have conceived of in their homeland.

One of the significant features of the rapidly growing industrial pattern of Philadelphia in the mid-nineteenth century was the distribution of the mills and factories throughout the city.[66] Some localization of industry by type did exist, as in the textile areas of Kensington, but plant sites and factories were also located in most other sections of the city. This heightened their accessibility to immigrants seeking or holding employment. Thus, while the Irish populations of South-

wark, Port Richmond, Moyamensing, and Grays Ferry had
easy access to the docks, where much unskilled labor was employed, they were also within easy walking distance of a variety of mills and plants. There were ten major iron foundries and mills in the city at different locations, and with
major mills in Kensington (Kensington Iron Works) and
Spring Garden (Norris Works, Seventeenth and Hamilton
Streets; and Wood and Perot Company, 1136 Ridge Avenue).
The large Merrick and Sons plant was in Southwark, in South
Philadelphia. Although textile mills were concentrated in
Kensington, large mills were scattered in other locations as
well; the William Horstmann Company was at Fifth and
Cherry Streets, adjacent to center city and within ten blocks
of Southwark. Ready-made-clothing factories were scattered
in both North and South Philadelphia, and the city's fifty
brickyards, which employed many Irish, were almost equally
divided between North and South Philadelphia. An immigrant living in Grays Ferry could walk to work at the brickyard of George Sweeney and Company at 1310 Ridge Avenue.[67] The commercial and industrial development of the city
was such that the working people of the time, with their
strong walking habit, were not isolated from work sites in any
of the major areas of immigrant concentration.

The coming of the street railways made possible even greater
mobility for thousands of Philadelphians. While it is un-
likely that a girl making three dollars a week in a textile mill
would pay sixty cents of that wage for horse-car trips to and
from work in one week, for various tradesmen and skilled workers the fare of five cents a trip was not prohibitive.[68] By 1861
seventeen street-railway lines had been chartered in the city,
and most of these were in operation. Beginning in 1858 the
lines ran north and south through the center city from Kensington and North Philadelphia to Southwark and Moyamensing. Lines were soon in operation running east from the
Schuylkill–Grays Ferry area to center city, with two-cent

transfers to other lines available. By 1860 lines were operating to Port Richmond, and out Ridge Avenue to Fairmount, West Philadelphia, and Manayunk.[69] In 1858 these lines were carrying a combined average of 46,000 passengers a day, and by 1864 an average of 120,000.[70] Thus a large proportion of the city's population was patronizing the new street railways, and their existence increased the employment opportunities and general mobility of natives and immigrants alike.

Although skilled labor was generally unsympathetic toward the organization of the unskilled, and the unskilled Irish were in the least enviable labor position, the Irish were very much a part of labor agitation. Commons states that "by the mid-1850's the forty-one organized trades in Philadelphia specifically barred unskilled labor in general." [71] If the unskilled Irish could not organize, at least they could strike, and this they did. In 1851, coal heavers in Port Richmond struck to keep their wages at twelve and a half cents an hour. A marshal and five deputies confronted them and read the riot act, after which the workers rioted. Of the sixteen men arrested after a violent affray, fourteen had Irish names. A strike by a predominantly Irish group of brickyard workers in the Schuylkill area produced similar problems.[72] Although the major labor leaders in the 1850s were not Irish, the Irish were often the most vigorous spokesmen. In 1857, they took the leadership in conducting and speaking for a convention of the unemployed held in Kensington. As second-echelon men in the existing labor organizations they were gaining experience. By 1856, J. F. Finnegan was secretary of the Journeymen Lithographers Society, Frank Mallon was an officer of the Hatters Union, and C. C. Scanlon was an officer of the Journeymen House Carpenters Association.[73] By 1870, when the Iron Moulders International Cooperative and Protective Union debated its secrecy oath at its Philadelphia headquarters, leading spokesmen on the issue included William McHugh, P. M. Ryan, Thomas Walsh, Thomas Casey, and John Leahy.[74]

Two of the founding members of the Knights of Labor in 1869 were Philadelphia Irishmen Robert McCauley and Joseph S. Kennedy.[75] The entry of the unskilled into labor organizations was to be long delayed, but skilled Irish workers were sharing the organizational struggles of labor in Philadelphia by the late 1860s.

The laborers, mill hands, skilled workers, and a great number of the craftsmen such as shoemakers and carpenters worked for others, but there were hundreds of immigrants who preferred to work for themselves. In an age of rapid business growth and free enterprise, they conducted businesses, shops, stores, and service enterprises of many kinds. It should be recalled that one of the images of success for the Irish countryman was the well-established shopkeeper of the town. Among a spirited people like the Irish, business competition could be keen. Possibly for these reasons many entered small business with alacrity.

Some evidence of business activity among the Irish can be gleaned from a lugubrious account of the Philadelphia Irish by Jeremiah O'Donovan. This traveler, a seemingly irrepressible person—avidly sociable, inquisitive, and bombastic—toured the city in 1854. O'Donovan traveled through a number of cities in the United States. His major preoccupation seems to have been the collection of small sums from Irish people, in return for which he promised to include their names in a book. This he eventually accomplished, and the book, *A Brief Account of the Author's Interview with His Countrymen and of the Parts of the Emerald Isle whence They Emigrated together with a Direct Reference to Their Present Location in the Land of Their Adoption*, appeared in 1864.[76] It is an extraordinary compound of pompous effusions, stilted tributes, and homely details. The merit of the work is that it does list hundreds of Irish people in America, along with their occupations and a profusion of miscellany. In Philadelphia, the energetic O'Donovan visited several dozens of immigrants, who, far from home, probably welcomed the opportunity to be listed by O'Donovan in the hope that relatives and friends would read of their whereabouts.

In Philadelphia the effusive O'Donovan rambled from one contact to the next. He lists 137 persons, all but 2 of them Irish-born. They had come from twenty-one of Ireland's thirty-two counties, with Donegal and Cork the most frequently mentioned. Businessmen must have been especially favored by O'Donovan, for his listing is composed mostly of shopkeepers. He lists seventeen grocers, nine bootmakers, eight tavern- and hotelkeepers, four tailors, three hatters, and a variety of others. He includes three physicians and two lawyers. In all, he lists seventeen occupations among the 135 Irish immigrants he saw in Philadelphia.

The locations of the thirty-one businesses for which he gives addresses tell something of the distribution of Irish-operated enterprises. Twelve were in center city, seventeen in Moyamensing (South Philadelphia), two in Kensington, and a few in Port Richmond. This distribution, of course, may be simply the result of the author's indeterminate perambulations. There is a listing in another source of center-city businesses as of 1859, and among 168 owners, only 12 have names recognizable as Irish.[77]

The O'Donovan visitation demonstrates, at the least, the fact that in 1854 Philadelphia Irishmen were conducting a considerable number and variety of small businesses. Although concentrated in the Moyamensing area, the businesses are a varied testimony to petty capitalism. Judging from the florid encomiums with which O'Donovan attempted to flatter his contributors, they were already disposed toward bourgeois pretensions.

The extensive commercial and small-business activity of the city between 1850 and 1870 afforded many opportunities for immigrant ambition. Large-scale merchandising techniques had not yet displaced the simple, personal service of the constellations of neighborhood stores and institutions that catered to the wage-earning population. Retail and wholesale trade, commission merchandising, small banks, and building and loan associations attracted what was, in effect, an immigrant middle class.

One of the organizations in which such business-minded men gathered was the Friendly Sons of Saint Patrick. This group was venerable long before the 1850s. Founded in 1771, it counted many distinguished Irishmen among its members, and it was one of the few Irish groups that brought both Protestant and Catholic Irishmen together. An analysis of the biographies of forty-four Catholic Irish-born members of this organization who were active in the two decades from 1850 to 1870 showed that twenty-four occupations were represented among them. Eight of these were in skilled trades; twelve were in retail or wholesale businesses. There were also three manufacturers, three contractors, six lawyers, two teachers, one editor, and one physician. They included one member of the Board of the Chamber of Commerce, a member of the Board of Trade, a Gas Works trustee, and two bank directors. Such men were part of a successful elite within the Irish community. Their fraternal, ethnic, religious, and business ties interlocked. As entrepreneurs, most had come up the hard way. Owen Brady, who came to the city in 1852 from Kill, County Cavan, worked in a shipping warehouse, then for the U.S. Quartermaster's Department during the Civil War; he later founded his own shipping and commission business. Patrick Duffy from Culduff, County Donegal, arrived in 1850, worked as laborer, porter, salesman, and grocer, and finally became a lawyer and businessman. Hugh McCaffrey, who arrived in 1859 from Banbridge, County Down, was apprenticed as a file cutter and eventually owned a hardware-manufacturing firm. John P. McGrath, after coming to Philadelphia in 1850, was apprenticed as a machinist at the Norris Locomotive Works. He became a master mechanic, worked in Cuba, and later returned to the city and developed a factory for manufacturing textiles.[78]

These two samples of immigrant entrepreneurs suggest a

vital phenomenon of the period considered: by the 1850s, the
Irish population, though maintaining a heavy concentration
of unskilled workers, was already producing an active business
class. Of 612 grocers listed in 1857 in *McElroy's Philadelphia
City Directory*, 146, or 22 percent, had Irish names; of 257
dry-goods dealers, 32, or 12 percent; and of the real estate
dealers, 8 percent. By 1867 the same directory listed 225 of
866 grocers, or 28 percent, with Irish names; 44 of 343 dry-
goods dealers, or 12 percent; and 11 percent of the real estate
agents.[79] Certain of the immigrant entrepreneurs would eventually attain real wealth: Bernard McCredy, a cotton manufacturer and real-estate holder; the Kelly family of Kellyville, Delaware County, Pennsylvania, just outside Philadelphia, which built textile mills; Thomas Cahill, a coal shipper,
who endowed the city's first diocesan Catholic high school;
and Colonel Thomas Fitzgerald, son of an immigrant and a
journalist, playwright, and later publisher of the weekly paper
*Fitzgerald's Item*, who left $3 million on his death.[80] These
were exceptions, men who prospered greatly in a time of rapid
economic growth. For most of the immigrants a lifetime of
work produced only enough earnings for necessities or for a
modest improvement, but even this could be seen as success
for a generation that had emerged from famine conditions.

A distinctive feature of the immigrant effort for economic
adjustment reflected in these sources is its diversity. The
Irish washerwoman might toil away for a pittance at the
edge of a fashionable residential district, but a skilled crafts-
man could make a good living. The Irish could only very slowly
begin to make their way into the ranks of the police, and almost all the laborers could be Irish in a given area, but as
early as 1854 practically all the paving and construction contracting in Port Richmond was being handled by the firms
of Irishmen. Immigrants would work by the thousands as
domestic servants, but they would also conduct large brick-
making, glass-making and iron-manufacturing companies as
well as liquor and food businesses.[81] As one writer states,

"The entire period was characterized by labor mobility. . . . There are innumerable openings for private adventure, which require only an adventurous spirit and a very moderate amount of capital. The step between the situation of a journeyman and a master mechanic, a clerk and a small tradesman . . . is a short one and easily taken." [82] It was a time of steadily rising activity. The Civil War imposed shifts in the direction of development, and the consensus of scholars seems to be that it acted as a great stimulant. The number of manufacturing establishments rose from 6,467 in 1860 to 8,262 in 1870.[83]

It would be misleading to imply that the Irish were a major segment of the manufacturing, let alone the financial, leadership in the city. The exceptional man stood out. The Irish businesses were usually in smaller, more specialized activities or in retail trade. R. A. Smith included over three hundred businesses of all kinds as advertisers in his book in 1852, and only twenty-five owners or partners had Irish names. Freedley in 1857 listed over eight hundred manufacturers by name, and only twenty-six had recognizable Irish names.[84] By this index the Irish were hardly a major group in the manufacturing and commercial life of the city, but they had begun the process of penetrating its economic structure.

Handlin asserts that the course of economic adjustment in Boston created a fundamental difference between two categories of immigrants; one merged its skills and interests with those of the native American immigrants, and the other made its way only with the utmost difficulty. Thousands of uprooted Irish countrymen could not readily become merchants or clerks, shopkeepers or artisans, and according to Handlin, the majority of them were forced into an "unemployed, resourceless proletariat." In 1850 the single occupation of laborer accounted for 48 percent of the Irish labor force in Boston.[85] This kind of concentration of the unskilled, according to Maldwyn Jones, had no parallel among other immigrants. An unskilled class of diggers and servants unable to rise to decent levels of urban economic proficiency certainly represented an impasse in social development in an age of rapid urban industrial and commercial growth. ''Tossed in the swell of impersonal economic currents, the Irish remained but shabbily equipped to meet the multifarious problems imposed upon them by urban life.'' [86]

The basic disjunction between those who could compete and those forced into a proletariaan underclass applies to the Phildelphia Irish, but the severity of the disjunction must be called into question in the light of the occupational evidence set forth in this chapter. The samples of Irish in the Quaker City had only one-third of their number identified as laborers in 1850, and the proportion declined in succeeding census enumerations. The number of occupations represented among them increased from thirty-two in 1850 to sixty-two in 1870, which compares favorably with the increase in number among native Americans; the occupations did not attain the diversity represented among the natives, however. This increase occurred despite ethnic competition and the difficulties of transition from rural to urban standards of work life. It included entry into the metal and textile fields that were the mainspring of the city's economy.

Further affirmation of the occupational mobility of the Philadelphia Irish is their entry into businesses. Retail trades, small manufacturing, and contracting attracted them. Various sources agree that the economic conditions from 1850 to 1870 encouraged individual enterprise. The Irish in Philadelphia appear to have entered business more rapidly than those in Boston. Handlin found that in 1850 about 1 percent of Boston's grocers were Irish, whereas in Philadelphia in 1857 over one-fifth of the grocers listed in the city directory were Irish. The difference between the proportions is hardly attributable to the seven-year interval between the two calculations. Also in 1857, 12 percent of the Philadelphia dry-goods dealers listed were Irish. By 1867 the number of Irish businesses in Philadelphia had increased further, which contrasts markedly with Handlin's findings for the Boston Irish.[87]

Stephan Thernstrom, in examining records of the small town of Newburyport, Massachusetts, found that the outward mobility among Irish workers kept the town from developing a "degraded proletarian class with fixed membership in the 1850–1880 period." Further research led Thernstrom to state that "in no American city has there been a large lower class element with continuity of membership." [88] The proletariat may have persisted, but its membership constantly changed, with outward and upward movement and further immigration. The Philadelphia evidence in this chapter tends to confirm this view; indeed, in Philadelphia, job mobility and small businesses offered a route away from the laboring class for Irish immigrants in larger measure than appears to have been the case in Boston.

To what can the contrasting conditions of the Irish immigrants in Boston and Philadelphia be ascribed? In Philadelphia the textile industry may have been easier for them to enter because of their rural familiarity with cloth production. No such circumstance existed with respect to many other callings, however. The Philadelphia immigrants were fully as rural in background as those of Boston, for the samples drawn from Jeremiah O'Donovan book and John Campbell's *History of the Friendly Sons of St. Patrick* only rarely include men from Irish cities or large towns. The immigrant to Boston was just as likely as his compatriot in Philadelphia to find the city a strange environment. The factors of difference lay outside the immigrants themselves.

Philadelphia was much larger than Boston. In 1840 Boston's population was 85,000; Philadelphia's, over 220,000. In 1850 Boston's was 113,000; and Philadelphia's, 340,000, exclusive of the adjacent county population. The 1840–50 decade had brought the Irish influx. In 1850 Boston's population included 35,000 Irishmen; Philadelphia's 72,000—over twice as many.[89] In both cities the Irish represented slightly more than one-fifth of the population. On the basis of demographic proportions, the cities seem to have had problems of somewhat the same dimensions.

The differences between the difficulties of the immigrants in Boston and Philadelphia can be plausibly attributed to the economies of the two cities. Boston in 1840 was a tightly knit commercial town. Its industrial base was limited by its resources, transportation, and tradition.[90] As early as 1840, Philadelphia had well over 600 manufacturing establishments with 29,000 employed in them; [91] by 1860, 6,467, with a labor force of 107,000.[92] Boston's record of industrial growth was much less spectacular than the Quaker City's,[93] as the rates of population increases of the two cities reflect. In the decades 1840–50 and 1850–60 Boston grew by 19.6 percent and 29.9 percent respectively; Philadelphia, by 54.9 percent and 65.4 percent.[94]

The capacity of Philadelphia to absorb new workers and give opportunities to incoming residents was much greater than that of Boston. The huge and growing industries, the steady construction, the new mills and processes all demanded labor to an extent that was not paralleled in Boston. The occupational and business opportunity in Philadelphia was marginal, nevertheless, since the basic economic disadvantages were not fundamentally altered; in Philadelphia there was simply a better chance for Irishmen to compete.

# FIVE

## CHURCH AND
## SCHOOL

For the rural Irishman the American city was an educational experience of great complexity and sweeping cultural impact. Even if he was forced to reside in an urban slum, the compass of his life was expanded enormously. Compared with the Irish countryside or small town, the city, because of its density if for no other reason, provided a much greater field for human interraction, and thus for the exchange of human experience. Social organization and channels of information—the media for this exchange—were widely expanded by urban life; institutions unknown in rural areas offered opportunity for involvement and instruction.

If the city afforded more avenues and opportunities for learning, it also imposed new standards of thought and behavior. Daily life amid urban complexities demanded a knowledge of city geography and customs, as well as literacy, punctuality, and a breadth of information unparalleled in Irish rural situations.[1] The constant, driving change of the city required a capacity for adaptation and reorganization of experience far greater than that demanded by a rural environment. All these influences increased the need for and the value of education in both the formal and the informal sense.

Conversely, the infusion of masses of immigrants into the city would lead to many changes in urban institutions and media. Newspapers would be developed to cater to them. Employment of certain kinds would be assigned especially to them. A whole circuit of social activity and entertainment would be developed by them as a supplement to the general facilities offered by the city. Their effect upon the existing school system would be pronounced and long-lasting, as would the effect of the construction of their own religiously oriented schools.[2]

A comparison of the educational opportunities and facilities available in Ireland and in Philadelphia provides some evidence of the contrast between the rural and urban experiences in the Irish and American settings. Formal schooling is only one element in education, but available data on schools in Ireland and America permit some comparison of the learning situations in the two widely different environments.

The development of a school system in Ireland in the first half of the nineteenth century is one of the few positive social achievements brightening an otherwise somber period. The Catholic Emancipation in 1829 opened the way for the elaboration of an educational system for the Catholic population. The old Gaelic tradition of education had been reduced so that its facilities, modes, and teachers were hardly accessible. The "hedge schools," informal gatherings of youngsters for instruction under itinerant teachers, were a folk institution inadequate to the needs of the population.[3] The political compact arranged by Daniel O'Connell that permitted the development of the National Schools in Ireland came at a time when the need was great. Although the cultural effects of the imposition of an English-speaking school system upon a Gaelic-speaking population were bitterly criticized, the National Schools grew rapidly, with 432,000 pupils by 1845.[4] In 1849 Ireland had a larger proportion of its population enrolled in school than either the United States or France, and in 1851 it was estimated that 60 percent of the Irish aged twelve to forty years were literate.[5] The Irish schools, working against poverty and other great difficulties, had by the 1850s become a remarkable system. Nationalists would long suspect the schools as the chief agency of the English imperialists, but the influence of the schools could not be denied.[6] The system, functioning under a board of commissioners, taught English, geography, history, political economy, natural history, and mathematics. It included model schools, a teacher training department, and workhouse schools. The extension of the education system in Ireland was one of those anomalous advances that were fostered in the country because of the relative lack of resistance in a society weakened by depression and exhaustion.[7]

For the Irish child in a rural area, access to a school was a difficult problem, for, although the schools served many, attendance was still a privilege. The distance to school, the availability of adequate clothing, and the ability of the family to forego the children's earnings all influenced attendance. In addition, the Catholic authorities looked down on a system that did not provide formal religious instruction in Catholicism. Few children were as fortunate as those in Tipperary town, who had twelve schools, poor though the schools were, available to them.[8]

The villages in the poorer areas of the island, from which emigration was the heaviest, were the least likely to have schools. A boy like Thomas Tierney, who came to Philadelphia in 1866 from the little village of Shercock, County Cavan, would have had only a "Dame" school. Such schools, common enough in the 1840s and 1850s, were presided over by village matrons in barns or outbuildings. The pupils paid half-pence a week to learn reading, writing, and "sums" from the untrained teacher, and each pupil brought his own piece of turf for the fire. Though National Schools were authorized in Ireland in 1831, Shercock did not build one until 1879, and the nearest National School was six miles distant. Emigrant Thomas Tierney's situation was not unusual.[9]

Certain characteristics of the Irish background brought to the United States by the immigrants marked their educational development in this country. The collapse of the Irish Catholic middle class after O'Connell failed to obtain legitimized political power for them promoted the rise of the clergy to a preeminent position of leadership in Irish life. Lacking state support for religion, the Irish Catholics elevated their tradition of voluntary support for religion and its works into an ethic resistant to all intimidation.[10] Since they were subjected to steady proselytizing efforts, they became keenly sensitive to and wary of such influences.[11] As the survivors of a conquest that eradicated much of their indigenous culture, they were without elaborate cultural interests. This simplified cultural outlook prepared them to confront American conditions with a relatively plastic view, unencumbered by preferences and biases based on language, a learned class, or extensive cultural strictures. Finally, their church had been adapted by rude necessity to the tasks of survival and the service of basic human needs, and its tradition of direct service and works of mercy was to be one of its great assets in the process of promoting immigrant adjustment.[12] These social and religious considerations would have an influence upon the way in which the Irish confronted their educational problems in Philadelphia. Clerical leadership, voluntarism, religious separatism, social service, and cultural simplicity would be prominent in their American educational activity.

In Philadelphia, which was relatively fortunate in its early educational history, the Irish very early sought to organize for their educational needs; in 1781 for example a subscription for the support of a school was taken up among Irish families in Old Saint Joseph's parish. A wide variety of private and religiously sponsored schools marked the colonial history of the city.[13] Schools for pauper children were set up in the early nineteenth century, and although in 1837 the pauper qualification was dropped and the schools opened to any child, by 1844 the pauper stigma was still attached to these public schools.[14] The Pennsylvania Society for the Promotion of Public Schools tried in the 1830s to promote a general system of education for the state, and such a system was founded in 1834.[15] In its struggle to build and extend a new institution, the public school, the society found many allies in Philadelphia. "Urban interests, on which the impact of the Industrial Revolution had been felt most keenly, were largely in favor of public schools."[16] By 1843 the city had 214 public schools with

499 teachers and over 33,000 pupils. In 1850 Philadelphia
County's eleven separate school districts had 1 high school, 1
normal school, 29 secondary schools, 53 grammar schools, and
130 primary schools, plus several special schools for orphans
and the handicapped. The 1850 census figures credit Philadelphia with 150 schools and 45,382 pupils, Boston with 200
schools and 21,000 pupils, and New York with 100 schools and
35,000 pupils. In absolute numbers of pupils, Philadelphia
easily led its rivals in public school attendance, although
Boston enrolled 16 percent of its total population; Philadelphia, only 11 percent; and New York, about 5 percent. The
census figures do not include all the schools in Philadelphia
County, but only those within the old boundaries of the city.
In 1852 R. A. Smith listed a total, for all of Philadelphia
County, of 256 schools with 50,000 students.[17] It is apparent
that the Philadelphia area had a very large public school
enterprise.

It is notable, too, that Philadelphians were not content with
the system they had. Public education was a major social issue,
and the trend was toward development and improvement.[18] By
1850 a group known as the Friends of Education was leading
an educational movement, of which teachers associations and
an independent board of education at the state level were a
part, aimed at improving facilities and instruction. Profes-
sionalization of education and the extension of educational opportunities were two trends that gained momentum in the
1850s;[19] the 1860s saw a boom in school building.[20]

One of the primary goals of the education system was to im-
part social discipline: "The great end and aim of elementary
instruction in our schools is not so much to acquire any given
amount of knowledge as to discipline and give proper direction
to the impulses of the mind."[21] Merle Curti points out that
some of the strongest proponents of public schools stressed the
need for intelligent voters and morally reliable and intelligent
trainees for industrial work, and Maxine Greene notes that the
public schools represented, and were seen by contemporary

leaders as representing, a mass vehicle for the social training
of the urban population, both native and immigrant. Ignatius
Donnelly, the son of an immigrant, attended Philadelphia
public schools and credited them in retrospect with success in
precisely this function. "They have humanized the new generation," he wrote.[22]

The administration and curricula of the public schools were
suited to the task of inculcating discipline. Teaching methods
were highly formalized, with one teacher generally giving attention to a wide span of children within a strict classroom system.[23] Although there was no mandatory curriculum before
1860, the subjects taught were usually reading, writing, spelling, arithmetic, and geography. An analysis of textbooks used
in the Philadelphia schools of the period illustrates that the
subject matter was appropriate for the initiation of youth into
a world of accuracy, literacy, and regulated behavior. The
books reflect the accepted preoccupation with classical models
and elevated language. Although the exercises for reading
largely contain stories with rural settings, some concessions to
the urban environment are made in science and arithmetic
texts.[24] It can safely be assumed that children did not learn
much of their own social backgrounds or of the community
conditions in their city in the schools. For example, a geography text used by a girl named Rachel Dougherty in 1867
devotes only one line to Ireland, calling it a "fine fertile island." [25] They learned the skills of literacy and computation
and models for expected behavior. Even in academies, high
schools, and the more select grammar schools, the curricula
were designed to fit students into special social and economic
positions in society. It is not surprising, then, that the schools
often failed to arouse enthusiasm among immigrant children.
As Maxine Greene says, "The three R's, the McGuffey-style
preachments, the drills and punishments—all these removed
the schools from what they knew as 'reality'." [26]

The movement of Catholic children into Philadelphia's public schools was retarded, however, by the bitter religious con-

troversies that were to inflame the 1840s and cast a pall of prejudice and antagonism over the 1850s. As early as 1838 Catholic children who attended school were largely in public schools, and during the 1830s Catholics had served as directors or controllers for the public schools.[27] The efforts of Archbishop John Hughes to obtain some formula for the support of Catholic education that would not violate the constitutional principles barring state aid to religion in New York failed in the 1840s.[28] The Catholic prelate in Philadelphia, Dublin-born Bishop Francis Kenrick, had at first taken a pragmatic attitude toward the problems created by public school attendance among his flock. He originally argued for a nonreligious education but gradually changed his attitude. In the early 1840s the entry of Catholic children into the public schools in growing numbers, and the bishop's concern over the Protestant orientation of those schools, led him to take the leadership in precipitating a controversy over the propriety of regular reading of the King James Version of the Bible in schools attended by Catholics. The preference of the Catholics, who used the Douay Version, was denied. The controversy was one source of rancor that helped to promote the disastrous riots of 1844.[29]

The development of an alternative school system by the Roman Catholics was a major social and financial undertaking for a part of the city's population that contained many of the poorest and most disadvantaged citizens. This school system represented a phase of the Catholic expansion that was among the most dynamic features of the city's life in the 1850s and 1860s. The Catholic church was a source of precedent, guidance, talent, and cooperation for institutional development. Its fund of precept and ritual naturally fostered educational goals and programs; its organizational and administrative structure provided a framework based in tradition for the immigrants' attempts to organize to meet their needs; and its extensive network of communications fostered cooperative activities such as the bringing of leaders and teachers from abroad for work in Philadelphia. It would be difficult to overestimate the church's role, especially among the Irish, whose denial of religious liberty in Ireland was central to their consciousness as a people. For the immigrants, their church was the foremost instrument at hand for promoting educational growth and social adjustment, and they used their American freedom to advance the church with great energy.

The Catholic schools were usually adjuncts to parishes, although a number of academies and secondary schools were conducted by various orders of priests and nuns. In 1850 there were twelve parish churches in the City of Philadelphia proper and five others in other areas of the County of Philadelphia. By 1860 the number of parishes had grown to twenty-eight, and in 1870 to thirty-six. These parishes were the base for the voluntary financial support of parochial schools. It is worth noting that the rate of expansion in parish churches that Philadelphia experienced was not maintained in Boston, which had nine churches in 1850; eleven in 1860; and twenty, plus five mission chapels, in 1870. Philadelphia parishes grew by 100 percent in each decade, but Boston's Catholic growth in institutional terms was slower, requiring twenty years to increase by 100 percent.[30]

The Philadelphia Archdiocese progressed in the face of great suspicion and hostility.[31] Carleton Beale asserts that anti-Catholic publishing became a "regular industry." Aside from the great riots in the 1840s, intermittent clashes were not uncommon. In 1855, one immigrant wrote a letter advising Irishmen to stay in Ireland because of the intensity of Know-Nothing feeling against them. Philadelphia was a city with a great deal of Protestant vitality, and the revivalism among Protestant congregations in the 1850s led to campaigns to seek out Catholic children for proselytizing through charitable "ragged schools," and to attempts to "reform" Catholic adults through prohibition activities.[32]

The arduous task of building and maintaining churches was hampered by a shortage of priests to lead the effort.[33] Saint Michael's Church at Second and Jefferson Streets, burned in the riots of 1844, had to be rebuilt, as did the Holy Trinity Church at Sixth and Spruce Streets, which accidentally burned in 1859. The poverty of the parishioners was a consistent problem. In 1856 the parish collections for Saint Stephen's Church in outlying Nicetown totaled only $16.58 for the first three months of the year. Despite their poverty, the Irish carried the financial and administrative burdens of the parish work. In 1838, when Saint Augustine's parish was organized, Irish-born parishioners constituted one-half of the congregation, and from 1844 to 1870 fifteen of its twenty-two priests were Irish. When pews were finally installed in Saint Patrick's Church at Nineteenth and Spruce Streets, twelve years after its foundation in a former vinegar factory, only 8 of the 111 pew holders were non-Irish, and of the parish's twenty-six priests over the period 1839–70, only six were non-Irish.[34] Although by 1870 five of the thirty-six local parishes were predominantly German in leadership and congregation,[35] the others were largely Irish.

The Irish response to the religious agitation and discrimination they faced was less than temperate on many occasions, for, although the church as an institution was conservative, its parish spokesmen were easily provoked. Such figures as the Reverend Patrick Moriarty of Saint Augustine's Church were defiant protagonists of Irish Catholic grievances and interests. Even after the Civil War had diminished hostility toward the immigrants because of their wartime contributions, polemics were still common. The style of the interreligious controversy is evident in Saint Patrick's Day sermon by the rector of Saint Patrick's Church, Rev. James O'Connor, in 1867: "The essential tendency of Protestantism is to distract and divide, in politics as well as in religion, the people who profess it." He saw Protestantism producing "perpetual anarchy." Protestantism "seems to have devoted all of its proselytizing energies to the kidnapping, the stealing of the children of the Catholic poor." He cited examples of Catholic children in Protestant orphanages whose faith was destroyed under the pretext of philanthropy and charity. This, he asserted, was a "burning shame on Irish Catholics." He also said that "the newly arrived immigrant has strong claims on the attention and care of his brethren" and urged Catholic organizations to meet immigrant ships and give counsel to newcomers. He saw Protestantism as unequal to the task of providing America with solidarity and greatness; no power but Catholicism was equal to such a task.[36] Such fulminations give some idea of the agitated response of the immigrant Irish Catholics to the harrassment they suffered.

It was in this atmosphere of distress and polemics that the parishes pressed forward with their educational work. Saint Francis Xavier had a school in 1839, and other parishes began schools soon after: Saint Philip Neri (1840), Saint Augustine's (1842), Saint Paul's Select Classical Academy (1842), Assumption Parish School (1849), and Saint Patrick's (1849). In 1850, the city had five parish schools; in 1860, fourteen; and in 1870, twenty-six, in addition to twenty-one Catholic academies and boarding schools of various kinds.[37] In 1858 the *Catholic Herald* proudly called attention to the fact that a dozen schools had been erected in only a few years, at a cost of over ten thousand dollars each. This educational network reached to the higher levels as well. The Seminary of Saint Charles Borromeo for the education of future priests had been established in 1832 and by 1850 had ordained twenty-one priests.[38] Villanova College was founded in 1842 by the Augustinian fathers, the Jesuits set up Saint Joseph's College in 1851, and La Salle College was incorporated in 1863.[39] These schools provided both a higher level of education to which Catholics could advance and a training system for leadership and teaching personnel.

Again, a comparison with Boston serves to highlight the Philadelphia achievement. In 1850, Boston, with a Catholic population roughly half the size of Philadelphia's, had only one Catholic parish school; in 1860, three, plus two academies; in 1870, fourteen. The Catholic system in Philadelphia developed more rapidly in the 1850s than that of Boston, and it was also more diversified.[40]

In addition to the founding of parish schools and academies, some special efforts were made to reach the immigrant poor. In 1856 the Sisters of the Holy Cross established the Industrial School for Girls at Seventeenth and Filbert Streets to teach girls of secondary school age housekeeping, sewing, English, and other subjects.[41] In 1861 a night school for immigrants was set up through Saint Joseph's parish by the Sisters of Saint Joseph in quarters at Juniper and Filbert Streets.[42]

The parish schools were at first unstable and difficult to maintain.[43] Most began with lay teachers. Saint Patrick's parish school, for instance, which began in 1849, had six female teachers who received $150.00 a year. Saint Malachy's, which opened in 1860, was able to obtain Sisters of Mercy for the school from the outset.[44] The academies were beyond the means of most of the immigrants; yet Saint Joseph's College had sixty-five students in 1852 despite its tuition of $12.50 a quarter.[45] Mount Saint Joseph's Academy, a girls' school opened in 1858 to teach German, French, art, and other suitable subjects, charged $135.00 in tuition a year.[46]

The curricula of the parish schools generally included English, grammar, spelling, geography, arithmetic, history, and religion. The religious study consisted of Bible history and catechism, with a pervasive citation of and allusion to Catholic models, customs, and principles of moral formation. The academies, such as that advertised in the *Catholic Herald* in 1851 conducted by the Visitation Sisters, taught foreign languages, painting, drawing, and music for girls.[47] Saint Joseph's College, really a secondary school at the time, was teaching the Jesuit *ratio studiorum* with Greek, Latin, rhetoric, mathematics, poetry, and religion in 1852.[48] By 1858 local Catholics were asking for a Catholic high school that would be operated by the Archdiocese and would be more reasonable in tuition.[49]

This Catholic school network, functioning within and in coordination with the archdiocesan and parochial framework, became a powerful social medium for Catholic life in the city. For the Irish immigrants it provided a means of maintaining a coherent pattern of social separation from the indigenous Philadelphians, whose reception of the immigrants had proved to be less than enthusiastic. The immigrants' children, or first-generation Philadelphians, were from their earliest years part of a parish community in which their identities and childhood psychological experiences were informed by Catholic consciousness and influence, moral as well as visual and intellectual.

The parish and school network became sufficiently comprehensive that the individual could proceed from cradle to career without substantial non-Catholic contact. It represented a great social and financial investment in group solidarity and tradition. It was a strong influence upon local neighborhood life, reinforcing residential ties and amenities. As part of the Catholic subculture, the schools provided a medium for the fostering of Catholic marriages and vocations to the priesthood, as well as a tutoring system for Catholic orientation and practice. The parishes and schools were a response to Catholic needs and non-Catholic pressures, and as such they formed a responsive institutional fabric in which the immigrant could find the self-assurance, familiarity, and practical aid he needed.

Parishes and schools facilitated collaboration for many purposes. As early as 1851 the Catholics had established Saint Joseph's Hospital, and by 1856, Saint Joseph's Orphanage and Saint Anne's Widow's Home.[50] Saint Joseph's Hospital was only one good work of the Daughters of Charity, which had long been active in caring for the ill at the Blockley Almshouse and for victims of epidemics.[51] The parishes were the vehicles for charitable groups such as the Society of Saint Vincent de Paul. The first group began caring for the poor in St. Joseph's parish in 1851, and by 1858 seven groups were at work in other parishes. There were Sunday schools for children who attended public schools; literary clubs like the Philopatrian Literary

Institute and Saint James Literary Institute for young adults; social clubs like the Carroll Club; and regular lecture series featuring such notables as Thomas D'Arcy McGee, Thomas Francis Meagher, and Orestes Brownson. All these associations, with their rounds of meetings, outings, drives, and campaigns, formed a thriving interaction of Catholic effort and support. Thus, the drive that collected $3,317 for the support of Saint Charles Seminary in 1856 could rely on a cadre of diligent collectors, the overwhelming number of them Irish, in each parish.[52] Nor did the attention to local needs subvert the memory of persistent needs in Ireland. Bishop James Wood, in 1863 alone, was able to send to Ireland for relief work over $4,000 collected in Philadelphia, and smaller remittances—such as $660 sent in 1853 by Saint Anne's church in Port Richmond to aid the Catholic University in Ireland— were common.[53]

Because of such variables as distance, family choice, and available space in schools, not all Irish children attended parish schools. Young Ignatius Donnelly went to public school, then to Central High School, where he was made to feel somewhat ill-at-ease in the school's "aristocratic" atmosphere.[54] Thomas Twibill, born in Philadelphia of Armagh parents in 1858, attended public elementary school, La Salle College, and the University of Pennsylvania Law School.[55] Between 1850 and 1870 only three Irish Catholics attended the University of Pennsylvania College.[56] Attendance at public schools did not prevent Irishmen from becoming leaders of their community, but the common Catholic pattern was for Catholics to be educated in their own institutions. As the Catholic institutions grew, their absorption of Catholic youth became a matter of course. This pattern was to become more characteristic of Philadelphia than of perhaps any other major American city where Catholics were a large minority.

The educational work of the church was not limited to schools. As a means of promoting communication, instruction, and the defense of Catholic interests, the newspaper conducted on behalf of the archdiocese was an important influence, and it provided a major source and outlet for Irish news and opinion. But Philadelphia's lack of a continuous Irish paper independent of clerical control is significant. The nationalist Irish press of New York, including such well-edited papers as the *Irish American*, provided a secular view of Irish affairs, with due deference shown to the religious disposition of its readers. That the Philadelphia Irish relied heavily on their Catholic paper for news of Irish affairs— although other papers serving Irish readers appeared intermittently—suggests that they were somewhat more closely attuned to clerical opinion than their more diverse and politically active compatriots in New York.[57] New York, rather than Philadelphia, was the overseas mecca of Irish nationalism largely because of differences such as this in the conditions affecting immigrant life in the two cities.

The coverage of Irish affairs in the *Catholic Herald*, the weekly archdiocesan paper, was extensive. Whole pages were given over to news from Ireland, carried under the headings of the thirty-two counties. Religious, political, social, and personal items were reported. Pastorals of Irish bishops, British parliamentary affairs dealing with Ireland, editorials commenting on Irish events, and notes on emigration were steady fare. Dispatches direct from Ireland by correspondents occasionally appeared; a letter from an Irishman exiled to Van Diemen's land would be reprinted; an appeal from County Donegal for "800 families subsisting on seaweed, crabs and cockles" after evictions reminded the Philadelphia Irish of the grim privation that had a claim upon their charity; advertisements asking information about immigrants in behalf of their families, or listing offices in Irish towns through which remittances could be sent back to the old country, were carried.[58]

The regular and extensive Catholic press coverage of local affairs reflected the vigor of the Irish Catholic population of Philadelphia. The heavily Irish orientation continued after the *Catholic Herald* was supplanted as the archdiocesan newspaper by the *Catholic Standard and Times* in 1866. Illustrations of the kinds of coverage given Irish concerns are: the report of a meeting in 1851, chaired by Governor William F. Johnson and called for the purpose of requesting the United States government to petition for the release of John Mitchel, William Smith-O'Brien, and Thomas Francis Meagher, leaders who had been imprisoned in the futile Irish risings of 1848; [59] regular notices of meetings of parish groups and Catholic clubs, and of lectures by Irish leaders on Ireland's grievances; [60] and editorials on such matters as the prospects for colonization of western land by Irish immigrants.[61] In addition, coverage of local religious controversies was continuous; for example, the recurrence, in the mid-1850s, of the Know-Nothing controversy inspired editorial militancy in the short-lived *Catholic Instructor* (1854–55), which vigorously opposed the movement.[62] Clearly, the church's communications service illustrates the fusion of its broad concerns with the ethnic concerns of the Irish immigrants in their new urban environment.

The services of the church, however, extended beyond those of providing schools and communication. The social problems that came to the attention of priests, nuns, and charitable societies were formidable. Family disorganization and discord, unemployment, and the more calculated vices of the city took a heavy toll among the Irish. Houses of prostitution, for instance, were a peril to both health and morals. One concentration of such houses was in heavily Irish Southwark.[63] In 1851 the *North American* editorialized against the ruffian life with which such areas abounded.[64] Catholic clergy and laymen could work to rescue girls engaged in prostitution, but they were often contending against organized vice rings that were cynical and powerful. Catholic authorities in 1851 collected funds to build the House of the Good Shepherd for Penitent Females.[65] A prostitute's register kept at the Blockley Hospital in 1868 reveals that 80 of the 205 women who sought commitment to the hospital gave Ireland as their place of birth.[66] Although exact figures on the extent of prostitution are lacking, the fact that over 200 women sought admission to one hospital in one year indicates that the size of the traffic and the toll due to venereal disease were by no means negligible.

Certainly one of the most prominent problems with which the church had to deal was alcoholism, the target of campaigns and crusades from the 1840s onward. Father Theobald Matthew, the Irish "apostle of temperance," visited Philadelphia during his tour of the United States in 1849, his fame and crusade preceding him.[67] The *Catholic Herald* recorded temperance activities in 1840, and in 1841 Pennsylvania led all other states in temperance pledges, but the problem of alcohol was not to be surmounted by pledges alone. It was common practice for contractors to provide workers with liquor as part of their remuneration.[68] The temptation to forget daily troubles in heavy drinking was hard for the immigrants, who had a surfeit of troubles, to resist. Whiskey was a traditional drink for the Irish, and its use sanctioned by strong cultural supports, and its illicit distillation—in Ireland never fully controlled by British authorities—continued to be practiced among some of the immigrants.[69] For many of the Catholic clergy, as Archbishop John Ireland was to say later, "the saloon keeper is America's danger and disgrace." [70]

Catholic temperance activity in Philadelphia, after a surge of organization and propaganda in the 1840s, ebbed until it was revived after the Civil War.[71] The establishment of the Catholic Total Abstinence Union as a national organization in 1866 stimulated the movement. The persistent need for such work was widely recogized, for "drunken" as modifier for "Irish" became a stereotype. The newspapers and social agency records of the city contain many references to Irish inebriates.[72] As late as 1879 the case books of the Philadelphia Society to Protect Children contain entries showing that 58 percent of the cases of child neglect and abuse among the heavily Irish case load involved problems of alcohol.[73]

The temperance movement, however, was large and enthusiastic. Its growth had a notable effect on the Philadelphia Irish community. The national headquarters of the Total Abstinence Union was located in the city, and Philadelphia had the highest number of local societies affiliated with the national group. These societies sponsored a number of services including an immigration bureau, libraries and reading rooms in parishes, and eventually, they built halls in every parish for recreation and "dry" celebrations.[74] These parish halls provided the setting for a whole range of activities that were alternatives to the lusty delights of saloons and whorehouses. They added to the neighborhood fabric of the city's life and the self-segregation of its Catholics. Philadelphia had more such halls than any other city.[75]

The emergence of the Catholic temperance movement not only associated recreation and social life more closely with the parishes, but it helped to displace the old pattern of firehouse rowdyism and nationalist agitation. The temperance societies countered the nationalist secret societies and gave the Irish a respectable outlet for social activities.[76] In the Saint Patrick's Day parade of 1875, which included 10,000 Irishmen, thirtynine of the marching units were temperance societies.[77] That fire-eating nationalist organizations like the Fenians were outnumbered by representatives of Victorian sobriety indicates that the Philadelphia Irish were becoming increasingly subject to the conservative influence of a well-organized local Catholic system. If Philadelphia was less a center for Irish nationalist activities than New York and Boston after 1870, one reason was the ascendency of the temperance cult.

The influence of school and church on immigrant adjustment to the new culture of the city was decisive. In addition to providing means for dealing with the disruption and pathology induced by the city, the educational systems, both formal and informal, permitted the maintenance of ethnic tradition and the alignment of immigrant aspirations. This was more true of the parochial- than of the public-school network. The extensive elaboration of church-related schools, organizations, and institutions bore the imprint of the cultural experience of the Irish people, whose traditionally defensive religious outlook was exacerbated by the general civic hostility toward Irish Catholics. This network reflected the tradition of generous voluntary support of the church by the people themselves, confirmed the pattern of strong clergy leadership, and maintained an ethic of direct social-service activity by the church. It should not be overlooked, of course, that the dynamic pace of urban development in Philadelphia encouraged more rapid and substantial institutional growth than was possible in Ireland, where a deeper poverty and a more effective hostility surrounded Catholic efforts.

The examples of educational and religious experience cited in this chapter illustrate only one phase of the cultural adjustment made by the Irish to city life. Their work in constructing a school and organizational system parallel to the general community's facilities would have profound long-range effects on the city, among which were the creation of the city's first full-fledged ghetto complex and the ratification of a growing urban pluralism.[78] The conscious separation of so large a group from many aspects of the city's general life contravened basic ideals of democratic social growth such as full civic participation and untrammeled secular intercourse. But the Irish Catholic institutions also affirmed democratic values such as the freedom of religious conscience and the freedom of association. As a response to the complex new learning needs imposed on the immigrants by city life, these institutions represented an impressive achievement.

# SIX

## CLANS AND
## CAUSES

Although the immigrant from rural Ireland to urban Philadelphia may have been estranged in various ways from full participation in the life of the city because of poverty and cultural difference, he did contrive his own elaborate network for social activity. A part of this network was connected with the church. Much of it was not. In character and complexity, it was quite different from the structure available to the ordinary resident of an Irish rural village or small town, where, in the nineteenth century, a folk quality pervaded social relations. Traditionally, the institutions that provided the structure for socialization were the face-to-face local agricultural community, the parish church, and the local fair for the exchange of produce and livestock. There was also the "big house," the landlord's estate, remote because of its English character and higher status but intimately related to the community because of its economic significance.[1] Within this rustic framework thrived that sociability for which the Irish were noted.

Sunday mass at the parish church commanded all but the English establishment to a weekly concourse for gossip, speculation, and friendly interchange. The periodic fairs were even larger occasions for sociability, with their bargaining, matchmaking, impromptu auctions and sales, drinking, barter, and political activity. Political rallies and elections, often coinciding with the fairs, provided additional rural excitement; and on a rare occasion, some religious pilgrimage or larger political event, such as one of Daniel O'Connell's mass rallies, would take the farmer or village man out of his locality. For the most part, local life was just that, enlivened by visiting

106

among families for the exchange of gossip and homely information; evening gatherings around the turf fire for converse,
story telling, and singing; weddings, wakes, and christenings;
or some local scandal.[2] The life of the Irish countryman was
indeed confined, with limited opportunities for making new
acquaintances or discussing more than crops, weather, and
immediate local affairs.

If there was a distinctive vitality to Irish rural social life, it
was an achievement of the people themselves rather than of a
formal organizational structure. Their love of language and
discourse, a rich folklore, traditions of generosity and hospitality, and an alert disposition toward political development
helped to counter the rude simplicity, loneliness, and confining
poverty of the rural environment. The emigration of these
country people to the urban conditions of Philadelphia would
require more complicated responses for social organization,
with the familiarity and presumptive intimacy of the village
community replaced by a substitute system of primary relationships. Parishes would have to be organized, since there
were none to inherit; new gatherings would have to replace the
fairs and crossroads dances; and the immigrants would have
to set up a new pattern of social groups without the landlord
or the fair. In the city, the consciousness of their own ethnic
identity, their need for mutual aid and recreation, and the performance of religious obligations would form the major themes
around which the Irish would organize themselves.

In addition to organizations formally related to the Catholic
church, the immigrants established an extensive framework of
groups and societies for ethnic association. The oldest of these,
the Friendly Sons of Saint Patrick, later combined with the
Hibernian Society for the Relief of Emigrants from Ireland.
Dating from 1771 and continuing to this day, it counted
among its founders luminaries of the Revolutionary period
such as General Stephen Moylan, Commodore John Barry,
and Thomas Fitzsimons and had as honorary members George
Washington, Andrew Jackson, and Ulysses S. Grant. It was

always a fairly select group of the more prominent Philadelphia Irish, numbering among its leaders successful businessmen, political figures, military men, and scholars. It was one
of the few Irish organizations in which the Irish Catholic and
the Irish Protestant could meet in fraternal association. Many
of its presidents were Protestants, for its tradition of ethnic
pride dated from that eighteenth-century period of Irish nationalism when Protestants such as Theobald Wolfe Tone led
the movement.

In the mid–nineteenth century the Friendly Sons of Saint
Patrick was a vehicle for the spirited expression of Irish
loyalty to the United States and for charitable concern for
immigrant welfare. Among its members were many self-made
owners and operators of large businesses whose backgrounds
were humble in the extreme. A review of fifty biographical
notes on Irish-born Catholic members in the 1850–70 period
reveals that the memberships ranged from relatively unknown
small businessmen to wealthy entrepreneurs. There were men
like William McAleer, director of the Chamber of Commerce
and city councilman; Bernard McCredy, graduate of Dublin
University and textile manufacturer; Richard and Thomas
Cahill, members of a family grown wealthy in coal shipping
and brick making; John and William Keating, sons of Baron
John Keating, a veteran of the Irish Brigade in France and
fellow bank trustee with Clement Biddle; John B. Colahan,
engineer and lawyer, was married to a Quaker and was an
intimate of the Drexel family; and Dennis Kelly, born in
poverty in Donegal, who owned cotton mills in Kellyville,
Delaware County, and raised thoroughbred horses and prize
cattle.[3] These men were leaders of the Irish community. They
were bank directors; heads of church building drives; trustees
of schools, hospitals and orphanages. And they were largely
conservative, which was reflected in the Friendly Sons of
Saint Patrick. Although some of its members were tireless
Irish nationalists, the organization contented itself with me-

morializing its own members, attesting patriotism, and dispensing modest charity.[4]

The organizational life of the Irish community interlaced fraternal, beneficial, and political groups. Some organizations arose in response to a need or series of events in Ireland—for example, an organization supporting Daniel O'Connell's drive to repeal the Act of Union binding Ireland to England, which collected $2,000 in one week in Philadelphia and sent it to Ireland.[5] If personal experience did not suffice to remind the Philadelphia Irish of the chronic destitution of their native place, newspaper accounts giving details of the misery there prompted intermittent appeals for funds.[6] Other groups were military, such as the "Irish Brigade" that paraded on Saint Patrick's Day in 1857.[7] Still others were devoted to meeting needs in Philadelphia. There were mutual beneficial societies providing sickness and death benefits and savings plans—a typical such group, the Emerald Beneficial Association, formed in 1869, met in following years at five locations in the city [8]— and also the numerous fire brigades, some, like the Hibernia Hose Company, completely Irish.[9]

The annual high point for these groups was Saint Patrick's Day, which had been observed in the city by Irishmen since colonial times.[10] The celebrations increased in magnitude after the great wave of immigration in the 1840s and perhaps reached their apogee after the Civil War when parading veterans groups provided a colorful military panoply. On Saint Patrick's Day, Catholics would attend mass, enjoy festive meals with family and friends at home, and attend some of the many events sponsored by the Irish organizations. There were lectures such as the redoubtable Father Patrick Moriarty's "Ireland: A Sovereign State in the American Union"; [11] recitals of Irish music; [12] oratory in the elaborate rhetorical style of the day; [13] and banquets and balls, which were occasions for pleasant association, toasts, and the renewal of ethnic pride. Even non-Irish institutions at times adverted to the celebration. In 1870, for instance, the Academy of Fine Arts scheduled a showing of the popular painting ''Sheridan's Ride,'' by T. B. Read, to honor the day.[14]

The Irish newspapers of the city had a troubled history. The first one of them *Erin,* emerged in 1823 as a result of religious disputes; a number ceased publication in the 1870s; and those of the 1890s were pompous fraternal or political sheets. With the exception of *Erin,* they were poorly edited, bombastic, and highly selective in their coverage. Ritual anti-English editorials alternated with over-heated declamations. These papers, however, were important personal platforms for ambitious men, and also important vehicles of ethnic news and symbolic ties.

Coverage of Irish affairs by newspapers outside the Irish and Catholic presses was only occasional. A lecture in 1856 entitled ''The Irish Emigrant: His Memories, His Duties, His Hopes'' was described in the *Evening Bulletin* in slightly satirical terms. The lecturer's plea for the ''re-establishment of Celtic nationality'' was treated lightly, and the presence of pickpockets in the audience humorously noted. The *North American* editorialized against ''gabble about Anglo-Saxon blood'' in 1853, asserting that Celts and Saxons had been mingled inextricably for centuries. The *Press* used Saint Patrick's Day as an opportunity to encourage interreligious fraternity among the Irish. In 1867 it saluted the day in a three-column editorial and, in wry juxtaposition, ran another, entitled ''The Evils of Intemperence,'' on the same page.[15]

Thus, Irish organizations provided a medium for association, celebration, and nationalist activity. They were based partly upon nostalgia for the old country and a concern for its welfare and partly on the need for ethnic solidarity and interaction. At their affairs the music, lore, and reminiscences of Ireland could be enjoyed, and projects for Irish independence and exile agitation formulated and promoted. They were also channels for business or political advancement, and an arena for the exercise of personal influence or the assertion of social status. In many ways they represented an interim step between the relative isolation of the newly arrived immigrant and his full social acceptance in the urban milieu. As an expression of the values and interests of a subculture within the city, they fitted into the nineteenth-century configuration of fraternal and ethnic organizations. If they were filio-pietistic, they were also practical as devices for fund raising and publicity in behalf of Irish causes. Their observances and appeals were the outlets through which Irish identity was conserved and expressed. If that identity, so beleaguered in Ireland and so skeptically regarded in America, was at times expressed in terms of implacable hostility or antic rhetoric, the aberrations are understandable. For most of the immigrants, the organizations yielded an emotional gratification that was at least as valuable as their practical benefits.

It is important to consider, also, those Irish organizations that did not conform to the canons of respectability and propriety. Among the most notable was the Fenian Brotherhood, which was a secret society formed in 1858 to work toward making Ireland an independent democratic republic. The society had an ambiguous character from the outset that was to contribute to its eventual isolation and demise. On the one hand it appealed to those whose spirits rebelled against the oppression that characterized Ireland's political and social life.[16] On the other hand, secret societies were outlawed by the Catholic church, and the Fenian espousal of violent methods to achieve political ends frightened and alienated many people. But the growth of the Fenian Brotherhood in the years following the potato famine was one of the few symbolic expressions of Irish nationality in a time when the political fortunes and spirit of the Irish people had been depressed almost to the point of expiration. The Irish in America afforded a fertile field for the propagation of Fenianism, and the organization's secrecy added to its romantic appeal.

In 1859 the Fenian Brotherhood, headed by James Stephens, a relentless organizer, began a drive to gather American members.[17] The waning of Know-Nothingism at that time had somewhat diminished the ascendency of the clergy in the Irish community.[18] One of the first Philadelphians to join the brotherhood was James Gibbons, owner of a printing business. In 1859 he became a member of the Central Council, the American directorate of the organization; for a time was acting president of the society nationally; and remained one of the chief conspirators in the brotherhood for the next decade. He was a respected businessman in the city, and his connection with the Fenians was an open secret.[19] He was to join other Philadelphian Irishmen, such as Colonel James O'Reilly, Hugh McCaffrey, Michael Kerwin, and Dr. William Carroll, one of the most talented and realistic of the Irish-American revolutionary conspirators, in a decade of intrigue in behalf of Irish freedom.[20]

In 1861 the Fenians were organized well enough to hold a large rally addressed by Colonel Michael Doheny, one of the survivors of the imprisonments growing out of the Irish rising in 1848.[21] Strains between the Irish and American wings of the brotherhood soon created a factional split, and Thomas Clarke Luby, another former prisoner, visited Philadelphia in 1863 to help heal the schism.[22] In addition to factionalism, the increasing antagonism of Catholic bishops toward the organization—exemplified by Philadelphia Archbishop James Wood's condemnatory circular letter in 1864—created further problems. In response to episcopal condemnation, the Fenians asserted that they were a military organization, and bound, like any such group, by orders from and obedience to superiors.[23]

The venerable nationalistic cleric, Rev. Patrick Moriarty of Saint Augustine's parish, was close to the Fenians. In 1864 he gave a speech entitled "An Oration: What Right Has England to Rule Ireland?" The speech was something of a cause célèbre, since Archbishop Wood had forbidden Moriarty to give it. The priest later publicly apologized to the archbishop, but James Gibbons reprinted his indictment of Britain as "tyrant, robber, murderer . . . infidel England."[24]

An invasion of Canada was planned by the Fenians in 1866, and in preparation Philadelphia Fenians were actively arming their echelons. C. Carrol Tevis—a Philadelphian whose father was Irish-born—and Major William O'Reilly, both veterans of the Union Army, arranged for purchases of Pennsylvania militia muskets stored at the Bridesburg Arsenal, but although 4,220 guns were purchased, negotiations for artillery fell through.[25] After the failure of the Canadian venture, Fenian leaders throughout the country met in Philadelphia in 1867, and James Gibbons and five others issued a report on the hapless affair.[26]

Philadelphia newspapers gave the Fenians fairly generous coverage. The group's intrigues, daring schemes, and violent methods were exciting to the city's large Irish population, and to urban newspaper readers beginning to taste the delights of sensational news coverage. The *Press*, a Democratic paper, at first found the Fenians "imperfect and premature," then adopted a tone of mild reproof. The *Evening Bulletin* gave the group extensive coverage all through the summer of 1866. The *Catholic Standard and Times*, while pointing out that British repression had fostered Fenianism, editorialized against it as "anarchy and bloodshed" bringing nothing but "trouble and misery" both in Ireland and in America. On the occasion of the ill-starred Fenian rising in 1867, the *Press* maintained a moderate tone, affirming England's guilt for prompting misguided Fenian violence. The *Inquirer* held to nonpartisan position but noted that the underlying causes promoting Irish risings would persist.[27]

The Philadelphia Fenians were worthy participants in the conspiratorial web organized by the Irish in a dozen countries. If, as William D'Arcy, the American who has studied the movement the most intensively, states, the Fenians were too few to be able to win the support of the more influential Irish

Americans, they were still honest and dedicated.[28] They were
brave as well; many were veterans of the fiercest fighting of
the Civil War. Among these was Michael Kerwin, who was
born in Wexford and raised in Philadelphia. After cavalry
service with General Philip Sheridan, he was sent to Ireland
in 1865 by John O'Mahony, head center of the Fenians, as
one of 300 Americans sworn to prepare an uprising. Seized by
British authorities, he was imprisoned but later freed.[29] Dr.
William Carroll, another Civil War veteran and a Presbyterian born in Donegal, settled in Philadelphia in 1867. After
his Union Army service, he joined the Fenians. His career as
a selfless organizer in the Irish revolutionary movement was to
last until his death in 1926 at the age of ninety. A friend of
archrebels John Devoy and "Pagan" John O'Leary, he was
also friend and physician to Charles Stewart Parnell.[30] Such
men were irreconcilable foes of British power, exponents of a
revolutionary creed that placed them outside the religious institutions of their time. Having witnessed the sufferings of
their people, they were prepared to sacrifice all security, even
life itself, to relieve those sufferings.

If revolutionary activity placed some Irishmen under a
cloud of suspicion or subjected them to religious censure, there
were others whose activities were conclusively outrageous to
decent Philadelphians. Poverty, as the Philadelphia Emigrant
Society stated in 1854, was a fruitful source of crime.[31] The
slum areas of the city seethed with gangs of rowdies, some of
whom were hardened criminals, and the most prominent of
them were Irish.[32] Distinguished by locality and colorful
names such as the "Bouncers," "Tormentors," "Killers,"
"Spitfires," "Smashers," and "Flayers," they vied for noto-
riety. Gangs like the Kensington "Black Hawks" competed
with the "Schuylkill Rangers" in burglary, riot, and intimidation.[33]

The *North American* in 1851 attributed the gang problem to
a long neglect of youth in the city. Burglary was the least of
the evils the gangs perpetrated; the Schuylkill Rangers were

linked to arson, murder, intimidation, and control of vice. The
*Evening Bulletin* in 1856 ascribed the genesis of the group to
the anti-Irish disorders of 1844 when the Irish in the Grays
Ferry and Schuylkill areas on the western edge of South
Philadelphia banded together for mutual protection. Whether
this explanation of their origin is correct or not, the Rangers
soon became the terror of the district. As they grew from a
tough base amid the Schuylkill River barge wharves and coal
yards, they began to extort tribute on the rich river and canal
traffic, eventually reaching as far up the river as Pottsville.[34]
They also engaged in counterfeiting, robbery, and intermittent
war with the police.[35] The Rangers were unusual only in the
spectacular success of their activities. It was a Lieutenant
Flaherty who broke the Schuylkill Rangers, driving their
leader, Jim Haggerty, from the city during the administration
of Mayor Richard Vaux. Although the Irish policeman became one of the stereotypes of American urban folklore, the
entry of the Irish into the police ranks in Philadelphia was
rather slow. Colonel John K. Murphy was marshall of the City
of Philadelphia before the Consolidation Act in 1854, which
provided the base for a much stronger and larger police force;
but an examination of the police personnel listed in Oscar
Sprogle's *Philadelphia Police: Past and Present* indicates that
Irish-born policemen were the exception from 1850 to 1870.
More Irishmen appear on the list in the late 1870s, but these
tend to be American-born.[36]

At the neighborhood level, the Irish used to good advantage
two institutions that were to serve as the base for grass-roots
political organization. The first of these was the saloon. Public
premises for the dispensation of alcoholic beverages were an
accepted and flourishing institution among the Irish in the
old country. There was hardly a village so remote, mean, or
impoverished but that it had its little *shebeen,* or public house.
Indeed, the exclusion of Catholics from the professions and
from businesses preempted by town-dwelling Protestants increased the recourse to the liquor business among them. The

saloon transported to the American urban setting was an oasis of camaraderie for the worker, the unemployed, the troubled, and the calculating. Since saloons were spread throughout the residential areas and drew a largely male clientele from all classes, it was natural that they should become the arenas for political discussion and confederation. The saloon keeper was a figure of some status. Well known, independent, and often well-to-do compared with his working-class patrons, he was commonly called on to aid or represent his neighbors and customers. E. L. Godkin wrote in the *Nation* in 1875, "Liquor dealers are the medium and the only medium through which political preaching or control can reach a very large body of voters. . . . The liquor dealer is their guide, philosopher, creditor. He sees them more frequently and familiarly than anybody else, and is the person through whom the news and the meaning of what passes in the upper regions of city politics reach them. . . . They are the natural administrators of Boss government." [37] When combined, the power of the saloon keepers was a formidable aggregation of political contacts and influences. Young Ignatius Donnelly, an otherwise gifted and promising political aspirant, took leave of Philadelphia politics in 1855 when, after being nominated to run for the state legislature, he failed to get the endorsement of the Liquor League.[38]

The second neighborhood institution that served as a political mechanism for the Irish was the fire company. Chartered fire companies were first formed in the city in colonial days, and by the 1840s there were a score of them in Philadelphia.[39] Their colorful uniforms, exciting dashes to fires, and competition for community recognition made them attractive to young men in the city. Some of the groups took on a paramilitary character. Various fire companies were involved in the riotous fighting that terrorized the city in 1844, and clashes among them were common. In 1852 there were thirty-five fire companies competing for subscribers in the city.[40]

Typical of the fire companies that became bases for strong

political fiefs was the Moyamensing Hose Company, which was taken over by William McMullen, a native-born Philadelphian, when he returned from the Mexican War. In 1854 McMullen opened a saloon, and for the next twenty years he was regularly returned as alderman from the Moyamensing area.[41] The Hibernia Hose Company, the Wecacco Company, and the Franklin Company were all part of a political infrastructure that launched the careers of such veteran city politicians as Lewis C. Cassidy, William V. McGrath, and Congressman Charles O'Neill.

Ethnic concentration, saloon and fire-company associations, and a turbulent energy thrust the Irish into the political life of the city. Long before 1850 commentators on the American scene had noted the zeal with which they took to electoral contest.[42] The Irish political proclivity was stimulated by the demands of native Americans that newcomers make steady professions of devotion to the republic, but because the Irish were living under the strains of poverty, social disability, and the necessity of making an adjustment to a difficult new environment, they developed strong feelings of grievance and hostility. Politics was a safety valve for these feelings, a channel for the expression of distress and aspiration.[43] Politics mirrored the conflicts created by the process of urbanization.

By 1850 the Democratic party in Philadelphia had a devoted Irish Catholic following.[44] Especially in South Philadelphia, the Democratic party benefited from the heavily Irish population. Moyamensing and Southwark were Democratic strongholds in Jacksonian days, and Thomas B. Florence built the area into a district machine in the years before 1850. The same Irish attachment to the Democratic party revealed by Lee Benson for New York seems to have prevailed in Philadelphia. This Democratic following was founded on attention to the interests of the workingman. Patronage, favors, and campaigns against Whig privilege kept the "Democracy" in good form. Perhaps the explanation of Democratic appeal to the Irish is to be found in their conditioning in the political

tradition of Daniel O'Connell. At any rate, the saloons and
firehouses were the redoubts of the local political wars.[45]

The vitality of the political contests of the period was as-
sured by more than simple competition for electoral preferment. Religious and ethnic antagonisms were a virulent ac-
companiment of political combat. Thus, James Campbell, a
judge of the Common Pleas Court and a favorite among the
Irish Catholics, was defeated for office in 1851 by a strong
sectarian vote. In an attempt to assuage hurt feelings, Governor William Bigler appointed Campbell state attorney general, but instead of smoothing the religious feelings, the move
only provoked more bitter nativist hostility.[46]

The impact of the immigrants upon the city, their cultural
and religious difference, and the memory of the violence involving the Irish in 1844 promoted a broad political crisis in
municipal affairs. The immigrants were steadily gaining political influence. Under professional politicians such as lawyer Lewis C. Cassidy, they were in virtually undisputed control of Southwark and Moyamensing, and their significance in
Port Richmond and Kensington was growing. The prospect
of the old and eminent City of Philadelphia perhaps dominated by raucous Irish political blocs was frightening to the
city's older leaders, and even terrifying to those Protestant
clergymen and laymen who saw Irish Catholicism as a massive
threat to the moral and civic welfare of their city. Philadelphia County had more than sixty local councils of the Order
of the United American Mechanics, a Know-Nothing organization only too ready to campaign against the Irish Catholics.[47]

The confrontation with the immigrant political phalanx
came in 1854, when under the Act of Consolidation passed by
the state legislature, the city's boundaries were extended so
that the City and the County of Philadelphia were cotermin-
ous. Sam Bass Warner attributes this governmental transformation to the public's insistence that better police and administrative measures be taken to control burgeoning violence

and corruption.[48] Since the Irish were closely identified with both conditions, the Act of Consolidation did have ethnic implications. To many of the Irish, the act must have seemed an effort to reorganize the city to include outlying non-Irish districts so that a permanent native-born Protestant ascendency could be maintained.

Richard Vaux, a gentleman Democrat in the Jacksonian tradition, ran for mayor in 1854 with the backing of Lewis C. Cassidy's Irish cohorts. His opponent was Robert T. Conrad, a nativist former Whig and a man who saw immigrants as the chief source of disorder in the city. The Democrats lost the election, but they fought on, and in 1856 Vaux won the mayoralty. He was aided by a Democratic demonstration of anticorruption zeal; for the duration of the electoral campaign "Boss" Bill McMullen was held up by fellow Democrats as the symbol of machine dishonesty.[49] After the election it was widely asserted that aliens in large numbers had been illegally naturalized in order to vote Democratic. As a result Charles Penrose introduced a bill into the state legislature to tighten naturalization procedures and increase penalties for fraudulent naturalization.[50]

The movement of the Irish into public office was limited. They were a minority in the City Council even when the council was controlled by Democrats. In 1850 the only Irishman on the 30-member Common Council was Joseph Flanigan. As a result of the enlargement of the city's boundaries in 1854, the bicameral municipal legislative branch, with its Common Council and smaller Select Council, swelled to 149 members, but although by 1857 three-fourths of these members were Democrats, only a small number were Irish. In 1858 only 8 of the 85-member Common Council were Irish, and no Irishmen were on the Select Council. By 1864 the City Council had again revised its size, and Patrick O'Rourk and Peter McElney were the only Irishmen on the 27-member Select Council, while four Irishmen were on the 52-member Common

Council. This small number of Irish council members indicates that the Irish were far from constituting a dominant political group in the city.[51]

As the slavery controversy grew in intensity in the nation, Pennsylvania became a key state in the effort to marshal political sentiment behind Free-Soil and Abolitionist slogans. The emergence of an energetic new Republican party sorely pressed the Democrats. The "Democracy" was split, with the more conservative, Protestant wing led by Charles Ingersoll, and the Irish Catholics by Lewis Cassidy, a Stephen A. Douglas, popular-sovereignty Democrat. So hard pressed were the Democrats that in the congressional elections of 1858 one Democratic leader financed candidates of the Native American party to split the strength of the Republican opposition.[52] The local affairs of the city were eclipsed by the mounting discord over secession and slavery.

The Irish Catholics had little sympathy for the Abolitionist cause. Although the *Catholic Herald* took a position against the extension of slavery to Kansas, the religious, political, and economic gulf between the average Irishman and the Yankee Abolitionist leaders was too great to bridge.[53] The fervent Protestant evangelism and the Republican party identification of the antislavery leaders rankled the Catholic Democrats, and the link of the Abolitionists to British antislavery circles alienated Irishmen who could see such British moral reformers only as hypocrites blind to the near serfdom in Ireland. It was not unusual for the Irish to regard themselves as in a social and economic position that made them as vulnerable and as worthy of sympathy as the black slaves.[54] To the Irish laborers of the city, the Abolitionists were "disunionists." Even though the Democrats were able to win statewide elections in 1862, they lost ground in Philadelphia.[55]

The disruption of the Democratic party by the Civil War and the split along class lines between Whiggish "old family" Democrats and the Irish political bosses doomed its political hopes in the city.[56] The threat of Negro economic competition confirmed antagonism between blacks and Irishmen in the city and added fuel to a tradition of racial discord that was to mar the ethnic history of the Irish for generations.[57] In the postwar years, the egalitarian appeal of the Republican party and efforts by its Philadelphia leaders to win Irish adherents produced two effects. One was to draw off some of the Irish Catholics into the powerful Republican machine, and the other was to cloister die-hard Democrats into a compact, isolated bloc in Sam J. Randall's First Congressional District in South Philadelphia.[58] By the 1870s the Irish were producing bosses for the Republican machine that was to become a hoary monument in Philadelphia for generations. James McNichol was the first Irish Catholic to head that machine, but this was not until the turn of the century. The Irish Catholics remained subordinate in the city's Republican circles until that time.[59]

When the Civil War broke, there were widespread misgivings about the reliability of the Irish as loyal Unionists. Their attachment to the Democratic party and their feelings about Negroes gave them a doubtful image. General Winfield Scott felt it appropriate to issue a letter defending the Irish troops who had served under him in the war with Mexico against charges of cowardice and desertion.[60] Professions of Irish loyalty to the Union were quick in coming in Philadelphia, however. Commodore Charles Stewart, a grand old man of the U.S. Navy with strong ties to Ireland, wrote a widely circulated letter condemning the Southern Secession.[61]

Daniel Dougherty, a lawyer and fiery orator who was to be one of the founders of the Union League Club, began a series of speeches in behalf of the Union that stirred the Irish and Philadelphia at large.[62] Recruiting for an all-Irish regiment was active by the end of 1861.[63] Colonel James I. Galligher's Irish Dragoons became the Thirteenth Cavalry of the One Hundred Seventeenth Regiment of the Pennsylvania Volunteers, and former City Marshall Colonel John K. Murphy recruited for the Twenty-ninth Regiment, Pennsylvania Volunteers. The Hibernian Target Company united with the Pennsylvania Volunteers as numerous fraternal groups and local organizations sponsored recruiting drives. The men who led these forces included some professional soldiers, such as Colonel Henry O'Neill of the Corn Exchange Regiment, who had served with the British in India, and Colonel Dennis Heenan of "Meaghers Guards," who saw British service, but most were new to military life: Colonel Dennis O'Kane and Captain James O'Reilly of the Sixty-ninth Pennsylvania Regiment; Captain John O'Farrell and Timothy Hennessey, a well-to-do lawyer, of the One Hundred Sixteenth Pennsylvania Regiment. The latter regiment was to vie with New York's Fighting Sixty-ninth as the inheritor of the military legendry of the Irish brigades that had served with colorful daring on dozens of European battlefields.[64] Irishmen in great numbers were attracted by enlistment bounties or were drafted. There were no draft riots in Philadelphia to trouble President Lincoln, possibly because no inflammatory incident occurred to set off disturbances, as in the famous anti-draft riots in New York in July 1863, or because the large number of Union military encampments in the city discouraged such outbreaks. The Irishmen joining the ranks, though far from being spit-and-polish martial figures, would prove to be ferocious antagonists as early as the first Battle of Bull Run. One Philadelphia Irishman, Patrick Dunny, writing to his family in Ireland in 1861, described in shocked awe the contest between Northern and Southern Irish contingents in that battle as they struggled for a green flag, the sentimental symbol of the country of their origin.[65] The hardships of war would fall heavily on men such as those who fought with the One Hundred Sixteenth Pennsylvania Regiment through the holocausts of Fredericksburg and Gettysburg. The strain was reflected in an editorial that commented soberly on the inconsistency of those who pointed the "glorious Irishman" to the wars and yet discriminated against his brothers on the home front.[66]

Service in the Union army benefited the Irish in terms of public opinion. Men like General St. Clair Mulholland were welcomed back from the war with honor and moved into careers in public service; in 1869 St. Clair Mulholland became the city's first Irish Catholic chief of police. Opposition to immigration almost ceased because of general respect for the military role of the foreign-born.[67] The wartime economy also provided many opportunities for the immigrants to enlarge their businesses or advance their careers. Philadelphia as the industrial heart of the Union, the largest staging area for troops and supplies north of the Mason-Dixon line, and the financial center of the North was the scene of great enterprise during the war. Alexander K. McClure wrote, in recalling those years, ''Wealth came suddenly and in large measure to a class of our industrial people who had never dreamed of gaining more than a modest competence in their business.'' [68] Irish entrepreneurs were part of this acquisitive activity.[69] Existing businesses expanded and new ones prospered. These developments set the stage for a greater tolerance toward, and a greater degree of acceptance of, the Irish in the general life of the community.

The problems of crime and slum disorders continued to stigmatize the group, of course. Such organizations as the Fenians and the Schuylkill Rangers perpetuated the stereotype of the Irish as alien, sinister, erratic, and incorrigible malefactors. This stereotype was to attach to the Irish for generations, shadowing their achievements and compromising their relationship with the broader community.[70]

An Irish ''underclass'' persisted, with its problems of poverty and adjustment, and this category was maintained by steady immigration, but the Irish middle class and its political and civic leadership were growing. The Irish community had built a strong network of churches, schools, and self-help and civic groups by the end of the Civil War. This fabric of social and ethnic organization constituted a broad and inventive response to the challenge of urban life, and, in addition, it provided for the perpetuation of Irish ethnic identity within the framework of the city's civic life, sustained the ties to Ireland, established a tradition of association available to the successive influxes of Irish immigrants, and made possible the maintenance of that cult of exile nationalism that was eventually to prove so important to the attainment of Ireland's independence.[71]

The development of Irish organizations and models of economic and civic success also set up a channel for social mobility that stimulated individual and group advancement. The invigoration of self-esteem, morale, and social competition within the Irish community through this medium abetted the process of adjustment to the individualistic and competitive urban environment. It fostered mutual aid and provided a system of status devices and social amenities for an ethnic community that had been transplanted from its previous rural social system.

In politics the alacrity with which the Irish took to organized vote getting spurred the growth of that anomalous institution, the city political machine.[72] The machine, part welfare establishment and part political and governmental adjunct, was a distinctively American response to the problems presented by urban growth and the commitment to a broad franchise. The rural domination of the state legislatures and the narrow definition of government's role prompted city politicians to develop a pattern of local affiliation and service that begot the machine.[73]

The Irish contributions to this process involved the transmission of certain factors from the old country, a pragmatic sense of immediate needs, and their arrival in large numbers at a time when expanding urban areas required some integrating political influence. From Ireland the Irish brought a precocious experience in mass politics generated by the campaigns of Daniel O'Connell, and also a certain language facility and gregarious habits that made them adepts at political promotion, compromises, and alliances.[74] These traits and their immigrants' grievances in cities like Philadelphia enabled them to capitalize upon an urban situation demanding political hegemony and a flexible pattern of services to the poor, the unemployed, and the bewildered immigrant. As William Forbes Adams says, they added a picturesque and dramatic quality to city politics equivalent to that of the hard-cider and log-cabin campaigns of the West.[75]

Some among the Irish recognized the perils of large-scale corruption and political jobbery. Long before Lord James Bryce inveighed against the immigrant influence in American urban politics, Philadelphian Daniel Dougherty in 1859 stirred wide interest with his address questioning whether self-government was a failure in large cities. Dougherty's solution was probity in politics and high moral standards.[76] But the exigencies of politics overrode such counsel. The Irish bosses continued to cope with the electoral and social needs of their followers with cynical effectiveness, allowing themselves a margin of personal gain in the process. This does not, however, diminish the strategic significance for urban life of their shaping of the city political machine and of the tactical virtuosity with which they ran it.

It is clear, then, that the Irish created a subsystem within Philadelphia's urban structure that suited their needs. To their religious and educational enterprises, they added a varied complement of social and ethnic organizations, some of which extended into the political arena. This accomplishment not only served them, but it became a model for imitation by other ethnic groups as the population of the city grew.

# SEVEN

## HIBERNIA
## PHILADELPHIA

In the last third of the nineteenth century, the Philadelphia Irish concluded a compact with the rest of the urban society surrounding them. It was a Victorian compromise. Under it the Irish would largely remain within the institutional framework they had been constructing for themselves. They would avoid any attempt to overthrow or supplant the native Philadelphia institutions that dominated the city. The aristocratic clubs, schools, and elite family business connections that structured the leadership levels of the city's life went on unhindered. The Irish were content to deal with more pragmatic and immediate concerns. There was sufficient latitude within the expanding industrial society to accommodate their enlarging Irish social achievement without disrupting the traditional monuments of Protestant upper-class sway. However severe the continued sufferings of the Irish working class, they could not basically threaten the ascendent capitalist group. Whatever the religious and educational goals of the Irish community, they no longer imperiled public order. The intermittent rampant nationalism focused on the old country and was peripheral to the life of the city even though it was central as a concern to the Irish community. The economic and political roles of the Irish in the city were utilitarian in that they provided a medium for manipulation more than a challenge to the status quo.

As the Victorian period moved toward its ponderous consolidation in the 1870s, the Irish began settling themselves into the city's life in an extensive way that previous conditions had not permitted. They helped build the 1876 Centennial celebration site in Fairmount Park to fete the nation's inde-

pendence. The exuberance and festivity of the occasion typified the brighter side of the 1870s; the Civil War had be-
queathed a passion for parading and military drill to the
public at large. In 1872 the annual expression of Irish vitality
brought forth a Saint Patrick's Day parade of 6,000 march-
ers—1,100 from beneficial societies and over 300 from "literary" societies—and the mayor reviewed the parade at Fifth
and Chestnut Streets.[1] In 1875 one newspaper devoted three
columns to the Saint Patrick's Day event, describing the rich
regalia, banners, and decorations.[2]

Parades as civic institutions reflect the acceptance and popular participation of groups in a community. The famous Mummers parade that became the fixture of Philadelphia's New
Year's Day celebration had a long history. Earliest records of
it date to the eighteenth century. By the 1870s the custom of
gaily dressed New Year's Day parading was general throughout the city, but South Second Street in Southwark, the lower
reaches of South Philadelphia, and Kensington, heavily Irish
areas, were especially notable for the rites.[3] Pistol firing,
dancing, strutting "cake walks," and generally uninhibited
frolic were part of the parade. Such displays were compatible
with the Irish propensity for enjoyment. The folksy panto-
mime, the jingling music, and the ardent defiance of freezing
winter weather made the Mummers famous, and the Irish were
an eager part of the tradition.

By 1883 the tireless statistician Lorin Blodgett could show
one-half of the workers in the city owning their own homes
and working a ten-hour day.[4] The Philadelphia achievement of
working-class betterment was being enacted, and beyond it a
bourgeois entrenchment in the comfort of the city's more
pleasant areas was under way. All the way across North Philadelphia, from Kensington on the east to Strawberry Mansion
near the Schuylkill River, the big three-story houses were
flying the lace-curtain flags of domestic satisfaction. Parlors
full of bric-a-brac, huge Sunday dinners, and a short walk to
the friendly saloon were part of the cult of residential content-

ment. The image of the Irish underwent some rehabilitation as these improvements took place.

In 1875 an editorial both touted the Irish and provided some insight into the social condition of the Irish women in the city:

> And everywhere we find them the same, Irishmen always, but still adapting themselves to every condition and improving it. Brave, enthusiastic and loyal, making the best citizens of the Republic and the finest soldiers of the kingdom. . . . But what shall we say of the daughters, compelled to be the drudges of our households and the victims of a social aristocracy and of outrages utterly at variance with democratic notions and often cruelly unjust? . . . they too have their compensations. . . . They are secure from competition and can afford to laugh at their detractors. . . . And they have fewer faults, too, than are charged to them. Tidiness seems their natural state, and no people are more obedient, affectionate and faithful when kindly used.[5]

The Irishman might bear the soldier-hero image, but the Irish girl was still the upstairs maid to the public.

For those who were talented or lucky enough, fortunes were being made in the city in these times.[6] Among this ambitious group were the Irish striving upward toward rewarding careers and prominence. Their rise could be traced in the swiftly running gossip at wakes, political meetings, and saloon exchanges: "Tom Fahy's on the Board of Education." "Did you hear that Alex McClure made Frank McLaughlin editor of the *Times?*" "Tom Ryan is the only Democrat on the Council now." "Christy Gallagher's on the Fairmount Park Commission, you know." If Thomas Powers was coroner, he would let Stephen Farrelly of the Central News Company know of a death so the obituary writers could get busy; Farrelly, in turn, might call lawyer William O'Brien, who specialized in handling bequests both in Ireland and in Philadelphia.[7] The

Irish in the city constituted a highly sensitive communications system that registered individual ascents and descents with equal relish and alacrity.

There was an echelon of the Irish community that transcended petty gossip, however, for its affairs were topics for grave consideration. This group comprised the very important men—the wealthy, the venerable, and the powerful—such as James Campbell, who was born in Southwark in 1812 and was the "best known leader of the Catholic Democrats in Philadelphia";[8] James F. Sullivan, who was born in Cork and became vice president of the huge Midvale Steel Company and president of the Market Street National Bank; Thomas Dolan, who was noted for the large library in his home on Rittenhouse Square after becoming wealthy in street-railway transactions and utilities; Thomas E. Cahill, a coal merchant who left $1 million in 1876 to establish the first archdiocesan Catholic high school in the city; Colonel Thomas Fitzgerald, who grew rich publishing the *Philadelphia Item;* and John B. Colahan, who was married to a Quaker and was a trustee of the Drexel estate.[9] These men were at the upper level of the flourishing economy of the city and reaped its rewards.

Still, there was a gulf between the Irish and the "proper Philadelphians." In 1882 Alexander McClure felt impelled to admonish the Irish to profess their devotion to America more readily, and to place less emphasis upon their devotion to Ireland; Goldwin Smith depicted them as an inferior race with a mad propensity for "assassination, dynamite, bloodthirsty bluster and delirious lying"; and a book by Edward O'Meagher Condon was entitled *The Irish Race in America.*[10] The Irish were regarded, and regarded themselves, as a separate race of people, "Celts," and the classification could be variously interpreted. This attribution, in a country that took race very seriously, was potentially dangerous.

The affinity of the Irish was increasingly reinforced by their huge religious establishment. Between 1869 and 1882 seven more Catholic churches were built in the city, bringing the

total to forty-three.[11] In 1889 the Reverend J. P. Loughlin
stated that America desperately needed to be converted to
Catholicism, for it lacked "that better food which fills the
soul." Similar exhortations were common in the Catholic ser-
mons of the time. The reaction of Protestant Philadelphians to
Irish Catholic religious expansion and missionary purpose can
readily be imagined. The widely known historian Henry C. Lea
saw a clear threat in the Catholic presence, a threat of foreign
Italianate intrigue against American institutions. As minions
of the Papacy, he saw the Irish as inherently disloyal.[12] Such
sentiment continued to promote strong religious dissension in
the city. As late as 1897 the American Protestant Association's
anti-Catholic drives found strong support in Pennsylvania.[13]

In addition to "racial" and religious factors, the half-world
and the underworld of Irish misery in the slums continued to
be a scandal and a testimony of failure to those who traced
these conditions to something inherent in the Irish themselves.
Many of the Irish workers suffered through the severe economic depression of 1873 and took part in the disorders of the
violent railroad strike in 1877. For the poor there was continuous distress even in rich America. In 1875 a writer noted the
"Celtic" character of those patronizing the soup kitchen of
the Bedford Street Settlement House and said, "John Bull
grumbles at the money he spends on his poor. . . . We give
without grumbling." [14]

Between 1876 and 1895 the movement of the Irish onto the
police force was very slow. In this period, the number of Irish
on the force was less than 7 percent of the total and increased
only 1 percent in a decade. By 1876 the only notable concentration of Irish officers was in the Fourteenth District in the
Schuylkill area in South Philadelphia.[15]

Poverty and drunkenness were familar elements in the cycle
of degradation besetting the immigrant Irish. There were
worse failings in the Victorian period, none more dreadful than
the "life of shame" of the fallen woman. A reformer estimated that in the 1890s there were 1,500 houses of prostitu-

tion, employing over 7,000 girls, in the city. "Children of Irish or German or English parents many of them are. Girls of generous temperament or too trustful dispositions have been betrayed by employer or friend, and have found no door open to them but that of the house of shame.[16] He stated that most of the girls came from the lower class and worked as domestics, among whom Irish girls were legion at the time. Thus, the "proper Philadelphians" could find much that was scandalizing about the Irish, and the religious and social ideas of the time did not afford redeeming explanations for the multiple afflictions borne by the Irish.

If the misfortunes of the Irish gave ample cause for derogatory concepts of them as a group to arise, their actual deeds as lawbreakers and criminals added to the picture of the Irish as a fallen race. In one month in 1872, the *Evening Bulletin* would report that Denis Shea, who had testified against tavern-keepers' making illegal Sunday sales, was beaten; that James McMahon and Philip Monegan had attacked police, Monegan with a knife; that Donald Cullen and John McMenamy had been arrested for burglary and drunken assaults; that Sarah Kelly had been arrested in a raid on a disorderly house; that James Scullion had tried to cut a woman's throat; that James Connolly had been seized as a wife beater, and Maggie Casey for larceny; and that, in a magistrate-court scandal, Mr. Florence McCarthy had been taken in on conspiracy charges after making false arrests. Such stories did not inspire confidence in the Irish as peaceful citizens. In 1885 the foreign-born Irish alone accounted for 35 percent of the arrests in the city, while representing only a tenth of the population. Occasionally there were sensational stories about great outrages perpetrated under Irish auspices, such as the Phoenix Park murders in Dublin in 1882, in which the viceroy for Ireland was assassinated; and the murder of Dr. Patrick Cronin in Chicago in 1889, as part of a Fenian plot.[17] Such items rounded out the local tales of crime and mayhem to depict the Irish as a race of desperadoes.

Bishop John Lancaster Spalding, one of the most gifted of
the country's Catholic prelates, was all too familiar with the
toll exacted by the urban slums. In his "Religious Mission of
the Irish and Colonization," he tried to promote once again the
solution of rural settlement for immigrants.[18] But the accessibility and attraction of the city were simply too great, and the
cycle of misfortune and exploitation continued to trap more
and more victims.

Against this background of preoccupation with earning a
living, getting ahead, and dealing with social problems, the
Irish community maintained its distinctive activites in promoting the liberation of the old country. The incessant rounds of
rallies and drives, the organizing and reorganizing for "the
cause" were regarded by many as mere "bloodthirsty bluster," the feckless indulgence of a crowd of bombasts, charla-
tans, and malcontents. Such a view was mistaken, for behind
the orotund declamations and rambling recitations of Ireland's
wrongs was an intense conviction among the exiles that, somehow, something must be done for the stricken country of their
nativity. There was also the steady purpose of a cadre of
shrewd men, diehard leaders of factions and complicated
schemes, who would spare no effort and stop at nothing to
achieve the Irish liberty they dreamed about.

Such a man was Dr. William Carroll of 617 South Sixteenth
Street. Born a Presbyterian in Donegal, Carroll performed the
unusual feat of identifying with his landless and reviled Catholic countrymen. After coming to the United States he served
as a major in the Union army during the Civil War and later
joined the Fenian Brotherhood. In 1875 he was on the Clan-na-
Gael Executive Committee and helped to plan the dramatic
rescue of six Fenians, including the poet John Boyle O'Reilly,
from a penal colony in Australia. In 1877 he was in touch with
Charles Stewart Parnell and became his friend and personal
physician, but he later broke with Parnell when that leader
gave greater emphasis to land reform than to revolutionary
activity. Carroll was fully dedicated to Irish nationalist ideals,

however, and was more knowledgeable and far-sighted than most of the other revolutionaries. In 1880 he collected more than eleven thousand dollars in Philadelphia for those suffering from crop failures and eviction in Ireland. He was deeply interested in the Gaelic language and its literature and tried to foster bonds between the Irish and the Scots Highlanders. He died in his ninety-first year in 1926, a man thoroughly respected by those who knew him in his unselfish struggle for Irish emancipation.[19]

As the 1880s unfolded, the Irish mounted a momentous drive to wrest the land on which their existence depended from the tenacious grasp of the hereditary English landlords. Not since the days of Daniel O'Connell had these people been so moved by a cause. Crucial to the effort was the participation of thousands upon thousands of emigrated Irishmen, whose money and commitment swelled the mounting pressure of their landless brethren. Michael Davitt, son of Gaelic-speaking tenants who had been evicted from their pathetic patch of land in Mayo, returned to Ireland from a boyhood of toil in English mills, full of burning purpose and ideology. Davitt founded the Land League in 1879, setting in motion a political and economic movement that was to at last shake free a portion of the land of his country from English control. The goal of the Land League as he stated it was "to link the land or social question to that of Home Rule, by making the ownership of the soil the basis of the fight for self-government. Tactically it would mean an attack upon the weakest point in the English hold on Ireland, in the form of a national crusade against landlordism, while such a move would possess the additional advantage of being calculated to win a maximum of auxiliary help from those whom the system had driven out of the country." [20]

Davitt toured the United States in 1878. In mining camps and in the basements of slum churches, on public platforms and in rented halls, he forged a following. He visited Philadelphia, where he had relatives living in Manayunk among the railroad workers and laborers in Saint Brigid's parish. A speaking tour of the whole country was planned at meetings at the home of Dr. William Carroll, and Davitt, despite his ill-health resulting from his servitude in English prisons, set off. His enthusiasm spread. By 1881 there were thirty local branches of the far-flung American Land League in the city.

When the British government proscribed the Land League in Ireland in 1883, a tumultuous convention met in Philadelphia to form a new structure for American support. This organization, the Irish National League, collected funds to advance the movement and to sustain the brilliant parliamentary agitation of Charles Stewart Parnell, the relentless strategist of its political program. "Fair rent, Free Sale and Fixity of Tenure" became the war cry of the land-hungry country people; "Agitate, Educate, Organize, Win!" became the slogan of their American allies.

As agrarian outrages, boycotts, and parliamentary struggle grew, the Philadelphia newspapers championed Parnell's cause. To Americans of many backgrounds, the movement of the Irish to purchase the land they tilled offered a sane alternative to famine, violence, and misery. When the British passed new coercion acts to suppress the movement, the *Philadelphia Record* called for "emphatic utterances condemnatory of the cruelties toward the people of Ireland." The *Philadelphia Press* saw such acts as "a return to despotism and barbarism." The leadership of Parnell was threatened in 1889, when the lofty *Times* of London used forged documents to try to link the Irish leader to violence. The forgeries were later exposed, and the *Philadelphia Press* lauded Parnell's vindication and hailed the "utter ruin of this great plot." [21] In the midst of the controversy, Parnell visited Philadelphia, addressed a wildly cheering mass meeting in the Academy of Music, was feted by the city's leaders, and given a check for $1,000 by G. W. Childs, editor of the *Evening Bulletin.* [22]

The achievements of Parnell and Davitt stirred the hearts of Irishmen in American cities. In behalf of the land movement they conducted a steady campaign of propaganda and financing.[23] The "bloodthirsty bluster" was transformed into a hard-hitting, practical endeavor that for the first time in centuries helped to open a path for social and economic advancement to the mass of the Irish people. Through churches and clubs, in saloons and in thousands of meetings, the Irish Philadelphians shared in the effort to purchase the fields their families had forsaken under the duress of famine and eviction. The Land League was more than a sentimental enthusiasm for the American Irish. It was an exercise in trans-Atlantic fidelity that was to presage an even more potent coalition in the twentieth century.

During this period, the tension between the "constitutional," or moderate, Irish nationalist groups and the more radical advocates of violent revolutionary methods formed a bizarre undercurrent in Irish affairs. This split was partly along class lines, with the bourgeois Irish maintaining a relatively temperate stance, and some less restrained Irish in the working class advocating terrorist methods. There were, however, educated and even prosperous men who backed violent tactics, as the career of Dr. William Carroll illustrates. In 1880 there was a split in the Clan-na-Gael, the secret extremist organization that succeeded the Fenians. "Red" Jim McDermott, then a resident of South Philadelphia, tried to organize a more radical splinter group around the slogan:

> Not one cent for blatherskite,
> Every dollar for dynamite!

McDermott was later exposed as a British agent provocateur. The position of the dynamiters was simple: blow up every English institution, connection, and appurtenance in sight, whether it was the London Bridge, an army post in Ireland, or a British ship in an American harbor. With such men at large, the Pennsylvania Assembly saw fit to pass a law against "infernal machines," that is, explosive devices. Archbishop Frederick Wood refused to permit the Ancient Order of Hibernians to meet in Catholic halls in 1880, for this group, too, was suspected of advocating violence at the time. In 1883, at the Land League Convention in Philadelphia, the dynamite faction barely missed taking over the organization that was promoting the land movement. As late as 1900 one of the Philadelphia dynamiters, Luke Dillon, was arrested by Canadian officials for attempting to blow up the Welland Canal near Buffalo, New York, as a protest against the British war on the Boers in South Africa.[24] Dillon served a fourteen-year sentence in Canadian prisons for his trouble.

Most of the Irish followed more circumspect leaders. One of these was Michael J. Ryan, a lawyer, an orator, a long-time president of the Irish National League, and a prominent political and fraternal figure. His organizational forte was not radicalism, but the formal addresses and resolutions proper to the Irish who had become part of the Philadelphia middle class. Ryan, a large man, was once physically thrown out the window of a meeting hall on Spruce Street by more radical Clan-na-Gael partisans. He adhered to his belief in parliamentary redress, however, and worked to maintain American support for John Redmond's Irish Parliamentary party. At one time the leadership of the three most powerful Irish organizations in America was concentrated in Philadelphia, in Ryan; in Maurice Wilhere, leader of the Ancient Order of Hibernians; and in Timothy M. Daily, the head of the Irish Catholic Benevolent Union. As the nineteenth century closed, the Irish of the city still formed a persistent network of nationalist activities and sympathies, and in doing so they preserved their ethnic identity and solidarity.[25]

Vying with the Irish "patriot" for the admiration of the Irish community was that symbol of American success, the businessman. During the Victorian years there emerged the archetypal urban figure, the contractor-boss—the builder-developer with strong political ties and influence. For the Irish he was the image of free-enterprise prowess. There is a considerable literature delineating the political boss, the machine politician whose influence is interpreted as nefarious or socially beneficial depending upon which historian or political scientist one reads. The ethnic identification of this figure has begun to be reconsidered without the prejudice of filiopietism that previously attached to views of it.[26] Although the political significance of the boss has been weighed, the boss as an agent of urban expansion and development has not been closely examined against the background of ethnic and political affliliations.

An examination of the occupational statistics concerning immigrants compiled by Edward P. Hutchinson shows a notable concentration of Irishmen in the occupation of builder and contractor. According to the 1870 and 1880 United States census figures summarized by Hutchinson, the Irish led all other immigrants in this occupational category. By 1890 the Irish had twice the proportion of builders and contractors as had other immigrant groups.[27] This concentration was not accidental. Rather, it was a function of the social position of the Irish in nineteenth-century America. The vast influx of refugees from the Great Famine in the 1840s coincided with a period of rapid industrialization and urban expansion in the eastern cities. Because the Irish, coming from a society that was singularly rural, initially entered the United States without skills appropriate to the new industrial technology, they entered the work force as unskilled labor, and such labor was in great demand for the construction of canals, railroads, and urban structures.[28]

For many men anxious to improve themselves, an opportune route out of the unskilled labor pool was to become a small building contractor. It was not far from the truth to say that any man with his own shovel and wheelbarrow styled himself a "contractor." Such an occupation required little capital, but aggressiveness and strong backs were important, and these the Irish had. They also had easy access to fellow countrymen who, after the initial adjustment to city life, had developed skills in bricklaying, ironwork, and most of the trades associated with building. Because of ethnic and religious discrimination in public schools, the overwhelmingly Catholic Irish felt impelled to construct an entire parallel network of churches, schools, and welfare institutions in the major cities, and the necessary building work provided a continuing source of construction operations for the Irish contractors. Also, the political proclivities of the Irish increasingly identified them with the municipal machines that would be fruitful sources of contracts for public works.

An illustration of this evolution of the Irish construction magnate can be found in Philadelphia after 1850. In 1854 the consolidation of the City and County of Philadelphia expanded the city greatly, and the development of street railways opened up the newly annexed hinterlands to working and middle classes alike. As early as 1852 Irish contractors were monopolizing most of the public construction work in the Port Richmond district. In 1853 builder Thomas Dugan was selling three-story houses in the Kensington area for $1,200 each, and in 1856 James Tagert, born in County Tyrone and president of the Farmers and Mechanics Bank, was promoting various building activities.[29]

In the 1870s David Martin, a Republican protégé of state boss Mathew Quay, opened the way for the recruitment of Irish Catholics into the Republican party and attracted many ambitious men to the huge machine. John C. Grady served the machine for thirty years in the Pennsylvania Assembly, and E. Tracy Tobin and Michael O'Callaghan labored for it in the city wards. Through connections such as these, the Irish contractors could obtain access to public works. Nor were Irish Democrats lacking during the administration of President Grover Cleveland: William F. Harrity, wealthy board member of a dozen local corporations, was a member of the Democratic National Committee; William McAleer, a hardy Democratic perennial, was a member of the party's National Executive Committee.[30] If there were political strings to be pulled to obtain public work, the chance was that somebody in the Irish community knew somebody who could pull them. Railroad and public-works construction was the meat and potatoes of the contracting business, and a prime area for lucrative operations. Tipperary-born Thomas Costigan did much railroad work, as did William J. Nead and Francis McManus.[31] The large pool of Irish pick-and-shovel laborers in the city provided practically the only resource needed for a smart contractor to organize an excavation crew to perform the enormously arduous work of digging cuts, grades, and tunnels for the railroads.

The business of Patrick McManus indicates the kinds of jobs the contractor could become involved in. McManus was born in Pottsville, Pennsylvania, of Irish parents in 1847. His first major project was the building of stockyards in Philadelphia. He laid special tracks to serve the grounds of the Centennial Exposition in 1876 in Fairmount Park. Later he and his partner, James B. Reilly, built stone bridges over the Schuylkill River and constructed track lines and stations for the railroads, including the Reading Company's line that took Philadelphians to vacations in Atlantic City.[32]

In a period when business and politics were closely allied, the contractors were engaged frequently in public-works construction. Martin Maloney, who started as a simple mechanic, invented a gas burner for street lamps, went into the business of laying gas utility lines, and helped organize the United Gas Improvement Company in the city.[33] The continuing expansion, renovation, and improvement of the urban landscape afforded such men repeated opportunities for public work. Unfortunately, it was not uncommon for them to engage in fraudulent practices in obtaining the work. Seymour Mendelbaum has written that the only way the burgeoning cities could be controlled politically and ordered physically was by resorting to massive payoff schemes.[34] Philadelphia's Republican politics became a national byword for corruption. Although the dollar costs of public gouging can be calculated in some cases, the social costs of not expanding and building the city can only be conjectured. Whatever the malpractice involved, many of the contractors did produce. The city is still full of their works, aging but usable, a century after their erection.

By 1900, 63 percent of the building firms in the nation were located in 200 cities, and urban construction was 90 percent of the national total.[35] After the 1840s there was an unprecedented development of urban areas, and the Irish contractors had ridden the wave of this growth. Asa Briggs has pointed out the primary role played by the provision of sanitation, utility, and public-works facilities in such growth.[36] It was in these areas of construction that the Irish contractors made a heavy contribution. They were one of the new categories of "talent and connection" called forth by the city expansion.[37] Starting in the ditches as excavators, they had gained command of a flexible medium for meeting the fast-breaking construction needs of the cities. Construction activity has historically been a speculative and economically eccentric field, more sensitive to cycles of boom and bust than most other areas of the economy. This has led to an old saying in the field that a construction man must perforce be a gambler. A sudden contraction of credit, a hard-rock stratum struck in excavation, a laborers' strike could jeopardize not only a single project but a whole business. Competition in a field where heavy capitalization was not required for entry was always keen, and although contractors could attempt to stabilize their work by obtaining jobs through political preferment, the high-risk element remained.

The contracting business interacted with politics in a system of mutual reinforcement. The system suited the Irish admirably. In Philadelphia the Irish political fortunes were divided, however. Their early strength in the Democratic party identified them with pro-Southern sentiment during the Civil War, and the ensuing ascendency of an unbeatable city Republican machine in a staunchly Republican state cast the Irish under a cloud from which they emerged only gradually.[38] But emerge they did, and as the new immigration from southern and eastern Europe commenced, they took up the role of political intermediary that has been such a notable feature of their political history as an ethnic group.[39] In contracting, also, they were intermediaries as well as principals. In hiring labor, in presiding over subcontractors, in reconciling architects, engineers, union bosses, and clients, they demonstrated the same facility for maneuvering and mobilization that they displayed in politics.

An example of the interaction of the contractor and the political boss can be seen in the career of James P. "Sunny Jim" McNichol, the first Irish Catholic to become top Republican potentate in Philadelphia. McNichol, born in 1864 in the tough Tenth Ward, formed a building firm with his brother, Daniel, as a young man. Between 1893 and 1895 his business forged ahead, doing $6 million worth of work in those years.[40] From 1898 to 1902 McNichol served on the Select Council of the city, and later in the Pennsylvania Senate. The factional disputes within the Republican party, and the shifting alliances of the Democrats who were intermittent handmaidens of one Republican cohort after another, made McNichol's political life a stormy one. In 1908, when he was at the height of his power, "Sunny Jim" faced challenges and patronage fights involving the commissioner of wharves, docks and ferries; the police; the city solicitor; and the antisaloon forces of the city. He was able to show that one of his challengers, D. Clarence Gibboney, secretary of the Law and Order Society and a mayoral candidate of the "reform" City party, was a stooge as well as a hypocrite in the pay of contractor rivals of McNichol.[41] Through it all "Sunny Jim" maintained the geniality suggested by his sobriquet. About one-fourth of the Republican City Committee, over which McNichol presided, was composed of Irish Catholics, and McNichol's reputation as a dispenser of jobs through his government contracts and his huge contracting business stood him in good stead.

In 1907 McNichol was reported to have said, after a controversy involving municipal contract work, "Never again under any circumstances will I go after municipal contracts." [42] But business sense overcame political irritation. In 1908 McNichol was completing the subway excavation from City Hall to South Philadelphia, building the million-dollar Torresdale water-filtration plant, laying pipe for sewers and other public utility projects, handling asphalt and granite-block paving contracts, and conducting a half-million-dollar garbage-disposal business through the Penn Reduction Company. A total of more than $2.5 million in contracts was thus handled by McNichol. During his career McNichol also built the subway tunnel for the Market Street transit line; the imposing Benjamin Franklin Parkway, which is still one of the most appealing features of the city; and the eight-mile Roosevelt Boulevard, which opened up the broad fields of the northeast section of the city to automobile traffic and residential development.[43] In terms of urban construction, few men in the last century changed Philadelphia's physical orientation more extensively than "Sunny Jim" McNichol.

The "New Immigration" of the period from 1880 onward brought to the city an array of immigrants different from that of previous arrivals. The foreign-born population of the city in 1880 was 204,335 and by 1890 would increase by 65,000, mostly because of immigration from southern and eastern Europe. The new immigrants crowded into the same slums, often into the same buildings, where the Irish had been crammed in the 1840s, and the same outrageous privation greeted them. In many ways the Irish assumed the role of "managers" of the new immigrants. As politicians, contractors, priests, and policemen, they dealt with the newcomers at firsthand, using their knowledge of the city well.[44] Often their ministrations were far from benign. "Sunny Jim" McNichol was not remembered happily by many of the Italian laborers who worked for him, nor were the Irish policemen known for their tenderness in their newly won status as keepers of the peace.

For the heavily Catholic immigrants from southern and

eastern Europe, the impressive institutional Catholicism built by the Irish and Germans in Philadelphia was to have great significance. The Irish clearly dominated that church structure. The kind of religious and cultural formulation represented by the Irish-built church was peculiarly Victorian in its characteristics. In Ireland the people had been weaned on a folk religion that was communal, rural, richly traditional, and often superstitious. Persecution had stripped it of many of the cultural attributes normally associated with Catholicism. From the simplified base of belief and worship brought to America, the Irish elaborated a Victorian religious style strongly influenced by contemporary and class factors. Victorian religion was generally both strenuous and stoic, in a tight middle-class image. The Irish developed a militant and vigorous catechistic religious style that matched anything stiff-necked Protestantism could produce. In an age that idolized competition, the Irish Catholics competed furiously with other denominations. If Protestantism viewed them as somewhat rowdy, they set up for themselves stifling standards of propriety for church behavior. They elevated the rationalist canons of the period into a creed and labored mightily to assure the perfectibility of their souls and institutions.[45]

As a religious body long denied state tolerance in Ireland, the Irish Catholic church was quite familiar with the realities of the separation of church and state. In the American system this proved to be a considerable asset, since it stimulated independent development and sanctioned ghetto separatism. If the resulting ecclesiology was pompous and inward-looking, it was also broadly conservative and committed to its constituency in the lower orders of society. Such a church could be relied upon to minister to the newer Catholic immigrants with fidelity and firmness. Of the newer immigrants, the Italians suffered the most from the hard-handed Irish church figures. But, if the Irish version of Catholicism was not congenial to the new immigrants culturally, at least the base was established upon which they could mold their own versions. The

Victorian character of the Irish brand of Catholicism would persist in the city right through the first half of the twentieth century.[46]

The social changes between 1870 and 1900 thus strongly shaped the urban deportment of the Philadelphia Irish. The social problems that plagued them were moderated but still continued as steady immigration from Ireland persisted. Economically and politically, the contractor bosses drew great numbers of them into the trades and commerce of urban building activities and the sharp dealing of city machine politics. Religiously they shaped a Catholic bureaucracy in a Victorian image that eventually attracted and held masses of other immigrants through its schools and influence. And they continued to agitate for and contribute to Irish nationalist causes. In these responses the Irish experienced the social and business currents of the Victorian period, while retaining their ideals of religion and romantic nationalism.

# EIGHT

## THE TRADITION
## PERSISTS

The twentieth century would charge the city with powers even greater than those which had earlier spawned its industrial might. New forms of energy and new inventions added vastly to its technical capacity. Ascending downtown towers looked out over intensive development that flowed beyond the old city boundaries in a sweeping pattern of metropolitan construction and settlement. The people of this city seemed driven by a new energy as well, but their course, like the people themselves, was highly varied. Changing residences, jobs, and goals, they moved ever outward, searching the urban landscape restlessly for the warmth and stability that became increasingly difficult to find in industrial society. In their restless search they left behind in the inner city the decay and wreckage of the first American urban age. Caught in that debris were the latest immigrants and those working-class Irish still experiencing gruelling exploitation in the lower levels of the industrial city.

The free-enterprise economy of the nineteenth century had left the city a legacy of bitter problems that festered during the years prior to World War I. As early as 1892 Joseph D. Murphy, editor of the *Catholic Standard and Times*, anticipated the reformers of the Progressive movement by excoriating the "sweater" in industry. He complained that any plans for housing improvement were quickly branded as "desperate Anarchistic schemes for driving the wealthy people out of Philadelphia." [1] Twenty years later the same problems existed, and another social critic of the same surname, John J. Murphy, rose to prominence as a labor leader whose efforts for the redress of working-class grievances went well beyond excoriation. John J. Murphy was head of the Central Labor Union in the city. In 1910 the Irish were the dominant element in jobs in the transportation system, which had been concentrated into a monopoly called the Rapid Transit Company. In a fight for better wages and working conditions, the unionized conductors and motormen went on strike in 1910 and stopped the trolley lines, vital in the preautomobile days, from operating. Violence errupted when the company tried to break the union by running trolleys with strikebreakers. John J. Murphy called a general strike of every unionized worker in the city, economic paralysis resulted, and Murphy was jailed for defying a court injunction as the hungry workers rioted. The hated state police, the "coal and iron police" who had broken many a mine strike for the Pennsylvania coal barons, were called in to restore order. The strike was lost, and the transit workers returned to work beaten.[2]

Events like these turned many of the Irish toward radical organizations like the International Workers of the World. Men who were avid readers, fiery speakers, and fearless organizers sought the "one big union" that would free workers from wage slavery. One such a radical was Irish-born Eddie McLean, a sternly anticlerical agitator who scathingly blasted priests as obstacles to proletarian progress, "workless broadcloth bums, bourgeois stooges, hypocrite leeches." "Bomb the Bosses!" was Eddie's shouted greeting on all occasions. Others, like John Keogh, were just as tough but pursued reform through the church. Ordained a priest, young Keogh was assigned to a dockside parish near the Delaware. Drunkenness, wife beating, and unemployment led the list of misfortunes that plagued the families there. A fierce proponent of total abstinence from alcohol, Father Keogh would tour the slum saloons on payday, hauling one huge stevedore after another out of the bars and ordering them home. Father Keogh's service to the poor, a career similar to those of dozens of other priests in the city, continued for sixty years.[3]

It is not surprising that such leaders' daily firsthand struggle with social problems was much more impressive to the Irish community than the lofty reformism of the progressive civic groups in the city. The downtown civic worthies who met at the City Club tended to see social evils in terms of hapless immigrants rather than in terms of an irresponsible or predatory upper class. Within the space of a few months the City Club listened to addresses entitled "The Immigrant Problem as It Affects Philadelphia," "The Education of the Foreign Population of Our Cities," and "The Civic Education of New Americans." Congressman (later Mayor) J. Hampton Moore made political capital by stressing his role in tightening provisions that would exclude immigrants from the country.[4]

For those who managed to, or aspired to, escape from economic insecurity, education was the magic medium. The Catholic school system worked steadily, and increasing numbers of Irish Catholics went on to high school and college. Saint Joseph's College, La Salle College, Villanova College, and a constellation of girls' convent schools served the middle-class families. For those who were sufficiently well-to-do, the family life-style could approximate that of the "Proper Philadelphians." Some Catholic families even became "proper" by proximity to them. One such family was that of Constance O'Hara, which lived on fashionable Pine Street. The daughter of a prominent physician, Constance O'Hara grew up in an atmosphere of pride, culture, religiosity, and talent and in adulthood was a journalist and a playwright. She recalled, "We were an Irish Catholic family living in the midst of the charmed circle of the Philadelphia gentry."[5] This was unusual. For most of the Irish the awkward distances between themselves and the city's socialites were more like those described in Christopher Morley's popular novel *Kitty Foyle*, a quandary of misjudgments and social disparity.

The chord of Irish identity sounded differently for different people as education and economics diversified the population. The romantic currents of the literature of the Celtic twilight stirred some. As the literary revival that was to mani-

fest Irish brilliance in the twentieth century began to flower,
the interest in Gaelic studies attracted devotees. A thin tradition of Gaelic scholarship had existed in the city since the
days of Matthias O'Conway in the 1830s. The enthusiasm of
the Gaelic League in Ireland was imitated in Philadelphia as
groups gathered to study the old language and its poetry.[6]
Some of the first products of the literary revival, however,
found a harsh welcome among those whose nationalism led
them to be overprotective of the Irish image. When John Mil-
lington Synge's classic, "The Playboy of the Western World,"
opened in Philadelphia with the touring Abbey Theater company in 1911, some local nationalists created an uproar and
had the manager hailed into court for producing an immoral
show.[7] Long sensitive to the stage image of the buffoon Irishman, these protesters mistook literary license for satire, be-
traying the cultural limitations that were such a long-standing
feature of the Irish community.

As Europe moved toward the First World War, which was
to involve England in the slaughter of Flanders and the Somme,
events in Ireland were building toward an eruption of national idealism that would almost completely cast off the yoke
of British rule. The long struggle for Home Rule within an
imperial framework first projected by William Ewart Glad-
stone culminated in the passage of a Home Rule measure by
the British Parliament. Its implementation, however, was sus-
pended with the onset of the war. As England turned to the
trembling Continent, determined revolutionaries in Ireland
laid the plans that were eventually to uproot the centuries-
old English domination of the island.

In Philadelphia there now emerged a man whose efforts in
the cause of Irish freedom were to have tremendous importance in the final battles for liberation. His name was Joseph
McGarrity. Born in Carrickmore, County Tyrone, in 1874,
he would reside in Philadelphia until 1940. Energetic, talented, and endowed with a far-sighted sense of Irish patriotism, Joseph McGarrity became the greatest single driving force

in the city's Irish nationalist circles. As he grew wealthy in distilling and real estate, McGarrity poured his money and energy into Irish revolutionary work. As a member of the three-man Directory of the secret Clan-na-Gael, he was close to John Devoy, the doyen of the rebel conspirators, whose career reached back to the Fenian days of the early 1870s. With Devoy and the other stubborn nationalists, he aspired to more than Home Rule for Ireland. Their goal was a democratic republic, free of imperial ties and free of English parliamentary politics.[8]

In March of 1914 McGarrity tested his strength and organized a large meeting in Philadelphia whose purpose was to protest English contentions about the use of the Panama Canal; and when the *Public Ledger* reported in May 1914 that the city's Irish population was overjoyed at the prospect of Home Rule for Ireland, McGarrity was conducting a drive to undermine such sentiment.[9] The nationalists in Ireland had begun to organize into military units called the Irish Volunteers, a name rich with memories of the ill-fated rising of 1798. The control of the Volunteers gradually slipped into the hands of the secret revolutionary wing. The old precept, "England's extremity is Ireland's opportunity," came to the fore as England moved toward war.

In July 1914 McGarrity received a letter from Eoin Mac-Neill, head of the Irish Volunteers in Dublin, which thanked him for a remittance of £1,000 but asked for arms, not merely money, from America. Loyalist Orangemen in Ulster were arming to fight against Irish Home Rule, and the Volunteers proposed to arm as well.

In the summer of 1914 McGarrity was host to Sir Roger Casement, a man whose exposure of the ravages of imperial rulers against the natives of the Congo had earned him the enmity of half the crowned heads of Europe. Casement was deeply involved in the Irish revolutionary movement. He was at McGarrity's house in West Philadelphia when they learned on 7 July that the Volunteers had successfully landed guns at

Howth in Ireland, the first major arming of Irish nationalists
since the Fenian days. The Clan-na-Gael arranged a mass
meeting at the Forrest Theater on 2 August at which Casement appealed for American support for Irish liberation.
McGarrity and the Clan later arranged for Casement to
journey to Germany to seek German arms for Ireland. This
led to Casement's eventual capture in a thwarted landing in
Ireland, and to his trial for treason by the British in 1916.
McGarrity sent Michael Francis Doyle, a gifted Philadelphia
lawyer, to London to proffer what aid he could during Casement's trial, but the verdict was "guilty," and despite pleas
for clemency from all over the world, Casement was hanged.[10]

The stakes were high in the struggle. England was at war
and would spare little mercy for her Irish enemies. McGarrity
knew he was involved in a bitter conflict. In December of 1914
he arranged another mass meeting, at which the main speaker
was the great Irish labor leader James Larkin, whose strikes
had brought Dublin to the verge of chaos. Larkin's speech was
entitled "Why Should Ireland Fight for Britain in This
War?" In his roaring voice he challenged those Irishmen who
would aid England: "What has Britain ever done for our
people? Whatever we got from her we wrested with struggle
and sacrifice. No, men and women of the Irish race, we shall
not fight for England. We shall fight for the destruction of the
British Empire and the construction of an Irish Republic.
. . . We will fight to free Ireland from the grasp of that vile
carcass called England."[11] At this point Larkin finished his
plea, the curtains of the stage swept back, and the audience
leaped to its feet to cheer the spectacle of a company of Irish
Volunteers with guns at present arms facing a company of
German Uhlans in a fraternal tableau.

McGarrity busied himself with Clan-na-Gael plans to fo-
ment an Irish rising. In collaboration with the Clan-na-Gael
Directory in the U.S., the secret group within the Volunteer
structure in Ireland planned the rising for Easter, 1916.[12] The
plans miscarried, but an abortive rising took place in Dublin

on Easter Monday, sending a shock around the world. England, mired in the carnage of trench warfare in France, was enraged. American opinion was incredulous. The British response was one of tough repression. Thus, the glory of the "Agony at Easter" was born. The leaders of the rebellion were executed in a protracted vengeance that turned Irish and American opinion in favor of the rebel martyrs.

In Philadelphia, the old dynamiter Luke Dillon, free again after his years in prison for his Canadian adventure, phrased the reaction of Irish-Americans, stating that 100,000 Irishmen in the United States would fight to avenge the men of Easter Week.[13] Indeed, Volunteer units had been drilling in the city for months. McGarrity promoted more meetings. "O God Free Ireland and Punish Her Enemies," read the announcements. The "blood was up." The Friends of Irish Freedom was formed, and an intense drive for money and public support was launched. As the situation in Ireland moved from rebellion to revolution over the next two years, the local effort swelled.[14]

Now the great contest in the ancient duel of the two peoples began. By 1918 practically the entire population of Ireland was involved in one way or another in the guerilla half-war that pervaded the country. At the end of 1918 Sinn Fein (Ourselves Alone), the political organization of the independence movement, won overwhelmingly in a national election. British propaganda was poured forth to discredit Sinn Fein and to brand the Irish patriots as "traitors," "murder gangs," and "miscreants" who had "stabbed England in the back" as she grappled with the Germans. In Philadelphia McGarrity and his friends worked to counteract such allegations. The *Catholic Standard and Times,* which had earlier characterized the 1916 rising and the declaration of an Irish Republic as folly, by 1918 had swung behind the rebels. The United States Post Office, yielding to British diplomatic pressure, banned from the mails the *Irish World* and the *Gaelic American,* the two leading Irish papers in the country, because of their criticism of England. McGarrity began his own paper, the *Irish Press*, which flayed English policy and published news of repression in Ireland that could not be found in the general press. This paper, vital in keeping the Irish in the country informed, was published at a reputed loss of $3,000 an issue, a loss largely compensated for by McGarrity's personal contributions.[15]

During 1919 and 1920 Britain, faced with losing its control of Ireland because of the daring guerrilla warfare of the forces of the new republic, resorted to terrorism and intimidation of the most savage kind. The Irish pressed the fighting in every county against the "Black and Tans," auxiliary terror units that defiled British military honor in their indiscriminate retaliations against Irish civilians and nonmilitary targets. An Irish Victory Fund target of $1 million was announced at the Irish Race Convention in Philadelphia in February 1919, and Joseph McGarrity personally purchased the first $10,000 in bonds issued by the Irish Republic. By 1920 $1 million had been raised in Philadelphia alone for the various phases of the independence movement.[16]

As the struggle mounted with ever greater ferocity, the strains began to tell in the Irish-American community. It is remembered with bitterness even today that many of the wealthy Philadelphia Irish, so prominently patriotic toward the old country on St. Patrick's Day, were found wanting when it came to contributing in its hour of great need.[17] It was the little people who carried most of the burden. Dozens of Irish organizations ran fund drives, their workers begging before churches after mass and setting up booths on the downtown street corners. Scrubwomen, housemaids, ditch diggers, and dock wallopers gave unselfishly.[18]

Michael J. Ryan, who had built his career on rallying Irish-Americans to support for parliamentary reform that would aid Ireland, was displaced and displeased by the whole Sinn Fein fervor. "I've spent a lifetime trying to free

Ireland," he told the young enthusiasts for Sinn Fein, "and now the work is in ruins." But Ryan served on a special mission sent to Paris during the peace conference of 1919 to present Ireland's case for recognition as a separate nation to to President Woodrow Wilson. Wilson, intent on fathering the League of Nations, and bitter toward the Irish, rebuffed the mission and it ended in frustration.

A crisis developed at the 1919 Irish Race Convention in the city. Old John Devoy and Judge Daniel Cohalan of New York wanted to use the Irish Victory Fund to fight Woodrow Wilson and his League of Nations. Cohalan's motives were not unmixed, for the Irish Democrats of New York were formidable, and they sought to wrest control of the Democratic party from the president. McGarrity opposed them, insisting that the Victory Fund be used in Ireland. Eamon De Valera, lone surviving leader of the 1916 rebellion, toured the United States speaking in opposition to the Cohalan forces. The American support for the independence movement hung in the balance as the factions maneuvered. It was Joseph McGarrity who dominated the situation. Siding with De Valera, he relentlessly wheeled American support behind him and away from Devoy and Cohalan. By so doing, he performed  the highest possible service to the young Irish republic. Without concerted support, it could never have obtained recognition and the money it needed. McGarrity insured that support and masterfully reinforced the establishment of Irish independence.[19]

When a treaty was signed between England and the Irish government representing twenty-six of the island's thirty-two counties, a deep split was created that led to a fierce civil war in the new "Irish Free State." The foes of the treaty, espousing a full republic, accused the Free State government of compromise. The divisions of the Irish civil war were reflected in Philadelphia, with the Clan-na-Gael and the Irish American Club on North Broad Street supporting the oulawed Irish Republican army. Others supported the Free State regime that

worked deviously in the years following the civil war toward
a de facto republican status, alternately placating and perse-
cuting the Irish Republican army diehards.

For most of the Philadelphia Irish, however, the troubles in
Ireland were only a dim background compared with the domestic excitements of the 1920s. The zestful spirit of the
decade added to the drive for success of Irish-Americans who
returned from World War I determined on careers in business
and the professions. These same men joined with enthusiasm
in the sports craze of the twenties, glorying in the Jack Dempsey–Gene Tunney fight in Philadelphia in 1926. The city's
own pugilistic pride, Tommy Loughran, battled with the prize
ring's best from knockout to knockout. Cornelius McGilli-
cuddy, "Mr. Baseball," piloted his Philadelphia Athletics to
thrilling triumphs. The sports craze accorded with the continuing effort of most Irishmen to attune their combative
working-class feelings to the disciplines of American life.
Those who sought cultural elevation, whether through the
drama of Eugene O'Neill or the packed concerts of John Mc-
Cormack, were part of the more successful current of families
aiming for the suburbs. The suburbs of the twenties, though,
were still largely alien territory, where the propaganda for
immigration restriction and a sympathy for the Ku Klux Klan
diatribes decrying Catholicism were far from negligible. More
than one Irish Catholic family was startled to find a flaming
cross planted on the lawn of its new suburban abode.

The Prohibition era in American life had a particularly
strong impact on the Irish community. In one puritanical
swoop it knocked out the saloon network that had been for
generations a key communications medium for the Irish. The
saloon was a major social institution in the city. Indeed, under
genial Irish administration it had done much to vivify the
life of a city long derided for its staid deportment. Tavern
owners, one day prosperous and respected, the next were
stripped of livelihood and status by Prohibition. Their bitterness against the largely Protestant "drys" was extreme.

With the demise of the legitimate liquor business came a proliferation of bootlegging and gangsterism that spawned a host of Irish "beer barons." Families without a secure adjustment to American life saw their sons drawn into the deadly underworld of hijacking, intimidation, and corruption; psychopaths and gun-crazy youths vied in beer wars; and fortunes were made by cynics with respectable fronts, who were undisturbed by the traffic in poisonous drink.

The gangsterism of the 1920s was to be the savage finale in the long story of Irish entanglement with the underworld. When New York mobster Ownie Madden seemed to encroach on the territory of the Philadelphia beer barons, gunman Reds Murphy killed a visiting New York hood simply as a warning to Madden. Happy-go-lucky Joe Curry kissed his moll, Aggie O'Connor, goodbye and went to the electric chair for murder after the sensational Olney bank robbery. Eddie Regan, crime lord of North Philadelphia, had a machine gun mounted in his $20,000 Dusenberg car and protected his interests with murderous zeal. The apogee of criminality was recorded in 1928, when a gangland hanger-on, hunchback Hughie McLoon, was shot down; two days later, Daniel O'Leary, his probable assassin, was gunned to death; and before the killing was over fourteen others had been slain in an underworld bloodbath.[20]

Through the 1920s and 1930s the Irish perpetuated their clubs and organizations. The MacSwiney Club in nearby Jenkintown was ferociously devoted to the ideal of an Irish republic completely divorced from English influence. The American Association for the Recognition of the Irish Republic supported the existing Irish government and played a vigorous role in its behalf. One of the key figures in this association was John J. Reilly, an American-born businessman, who for thirty years served in various positions in the AARIR, performing the roles of advocate, adviser, and organizer for American activity in behalf of the Irish nation. Along with such Irishmen as Judge Clare Gerald Fenerty, Owen B. Hunt, and Patrick McNelis, he conducted efforts to publicize and criticize the partition, imposed on Ireland by the peace treaty of 1921, that had excluded six of the thirty-two counties of the island from Irish rule and had retained them under English sovereignty.[21] These men gained little from their dedication to Irish affairs, but their attachment was second nature to them.[22]

Beyond this circle of Irish organizations and leaders were Irish-Americans who were becoming powerful figures in the Philadelphia community. Perhaps the most popular of these was John B. Kelly, a robust, handsome man whose family was unusually talented. John B. Kelly's rise from bricklayer's apprentice to owner of the largest brickwork company in America added a somewhat glamorous touch to the contractor-politico image. One of ten children of an immigrant from County Mayo, Kelly was raised in the Falls of the Schuylkill district of the city. After service in World War I, he made a spectacular record as an oarsman, winning 125 races and endearing himself to Irishmen everywhere by beating the British sculling champion in the Olympic Games of 1920.[23]

His brother George became a noted playright, and his brother Walter became a widely known entertainer. It was in the steps of brother Patrick, however, that John charted his career. Patrick had a contracting firm and built a number of public buildings. John worked successively as a bricklayer, foreman, and superintendent for his brother, then set up his own company. His business grew until "Kelly for Brickwork" became a slogan in Philadelphia. Detecting the slide of more and more Irish as well as others into the Democratic party as a result of the fiercely fought 1928 campaign to elect Alfred E. Smith to the Presidency against strong anti-Catholic prejudice, Kelly moved into politics. In 1933 he supported the New Deal of Franklin D. Roosevelt. "Until I saw a bread line for the first time, I stayed out of politics," Kelly said. "If I hadn't gone into politics, I would have made $100,000 this year . . . and never once did politics enter into my

getting a contract," he stated in 1934. But in the same interview he also noted, "I made money under the Republican
regime and I suppose most people would have stuck to a
system like that. It has cost me a lot of money to become a
Democrat." [24]

This statement indicates the ambiguous position of the contractor and the Irish as a group in Philadelphia. The New
Deal was beginning to split many of them from the powerful
Republican machine, luring them back into the Democratic
party to which other Irish families had adhered doggedly
through three generations of defeats. John B. Kelly ran for
mayor in 1935, losing an election that his cohorts and many
others believed to have been stolen by fraudulent vote tallies
by the embattled Republicans. The family image was further
embellished when John B.'s daughter, Grace, became a movie
star and wed Prince Rainier of Monaco. The rise of the Kellys
symbolized a change in the life of the city. James Reichley,
analyst of reform politics in the city, credits Kelly with
bringing about the rise of the city's first true opposition party
since the Civil War.[25] Yet, until the 1960s no Irish Catholic
was ever elected a mayor of Philadelphia. They might serve
the machine, but the weight of the non-Catholic sentiment in
Republican circles in the city and the state long denied them
the positions of ultimate political leadership. John B. Kelly
might be attractive, wealthy, and popular, but the old crust of
class and caste barriers did not yield.[26]

A keen competitor of Kelly's for contracting work was
Matthew McCloskey, whose activities took the contractor-
politico evolution one step further onto the national stage.
McCloskey was one of eight children. His forebearers were
from Dungiven, County Derry. Young Matthew went into
business for himself when he was only eighteen. His first big
job was the construction of a building at the Philadelphia
Navy Yard in 1917. It was a project that typified the hard-
driving McCloskey, whose men built 160,000 square feet of construction in sixty days. Reverses hit the young builder in 1923,

however, and he barely escaped bankruptcy after losing money trying to complete a barracks at the U.S. Military Academy at West Point. Recovering, McCloskey built more schools in the city than any other single contractor, an accomplishment not without significance politically. He built the Philadelphia Convention Hall, and government buildings in the state capitol. For six decades Matthew McCloskey pursued his business, with a reputation as an intense competitor and a shrewd calculator of contract costs.[27] One of his most notable successes was a $25 million project with the Pennsylvania Railroad for the Penn Center transportation facilities, part of the downtown renovation that transformed the center-city business district in the 1960s.

In 1932 McCloskey went into politics after discussions with James Farley, Franklin D. Roosevelt's able party chieftain. In 1934 McCloskey helped to elect one of the rare Democratic governors of Pennsylvania. His Democratic party work placed him on a first-name basis with four presidents. From 1955 to 1962 he was the national finance chairman of the Democratic party, a position he handled with mastery, producing contributions from across the nation to sustain the party's work. McCloskey's association with President John F. Kennedy was especially warm. In June 1962 he was appointed U.S. ambassador to Ireland, a post that was symbolic of the man's background and affections.[28]

Perhaps the largest contractor of all in this tradition of urban builders is John McShain. The son of a County Derry carpenter, McShain built an immense construction business. His ability to figure huge contracts tightly became legendary. Beginning in Philadelphia, he built the Board of Education Building in 1930, then the Municipal Court, as well as schools and churches. It is noteworthy that he served on the city's Zoning Board of Adjustment from 1936 until 1952. In Philadelphia he constructed the Veterans Hospital and the Naval Hospital and worked on the Philadelphia International Airport and various college and university buildings. He also became director of several banks and a transit company. The scope of McShain's work, however, spread far beyond the city. His contracts included work on the $40 million Clinical Research Building of the National Institutes of Health, the General Accounting Office, the National Airport, the Jefferson Memorial, and the State Department Building, and restoration of the White House in Washington, D.C. It is calculated that he has completed over $1 billion in government contract work. The largest of all his projects was the Pentagon in Washington, an $80 million construction.[29]

McShain's political allegiances are not as clear as those of John B. Kelly or Matthew McCloskey. He has worked with the administrations of both parties and has seemingly avoided close identification with either party. The scale of McShain's work on government contracts, however, is manifest testimony to unusual political acumen. His Irish ties have remained— a keen horse fancier, he has acquired an 8,500-acre estate in Killarney, where his racing thoroughbreds are stabled; he has entertained the Irish ambassador in the United States—but his status has placed him beyond contacts with the ordinary Irish organizations in Philadelphia.[30]

There are numerous other examples of the contractor-boss in Philadelphia, including Austin Meehan, long-time Republican power in the city, who fought the reform movement that finally broke the Republican party's ascendency over the city in 1951.[31] Such careers of the children of immigrants represent a latter-day enactment of the Horatio Alger cycle.

The period of general prosperity, political reform, and migration to the suburbs following the excitement and distress of World War II found the Irish en masse sharing the good life on a citywide basis. Conscious of their power, they were woven tightly into the urban fabric. For fifty years they had installed their own as chairmen of the Philadelphia Democratic party, which was finally basking in political success. John O'Donnell, Jack Kelly, Michael Bradley, James Finnegan, William Green II, Francis Smith, William Green III, and Joseph Scanlan ruled the City Committee in turn. It was William Green II who underpinned the reforms of "Proper Philadelphians" Joseph S. Clark and Richardson Dilworth with political know-how. While "Billy" Green put together a prodigious organization known as the "Green Men," the socialite reformers transformed the tired old city in a renascence of government and downtown improvement. And it was Green whose efforts gave critical support to John Fitzgerald Kennedy in his closely won bid to become the first Irish Catholic elected to the presidency in 1960.

The tragedy of the Kennedy assassinations signaled the decline of the Irish as controlling political arbiters in Philadelphia, as in numerous other areas.[32] The radiant image and long-delayed fulfillment of the Kennedy years faded swiftly as the tumults of the 1960s rocked the nation's cities. The entire structure of urban life had enlarged, become more complex, and escaped the grasp of ethnic networks and old-time political machines. New power elites with national and international ties, new communications media, and a radically changed population distribution outpaced the politics of Irish dominance. The Irish were part of the new urban dimensions, of course. In 1960 they were represented in the top executive levels of the fifty largest businesses of the city by men who either headed corporations or were in key positions. Some members of this elite group, like Ralph Dungan, former Kennedy aide and ambassador to Chile, were driving intellectuals; others were suburbanites—practical men who headed charity campaigns, sent their daughters abroad to study, and walked in the circumspect paths of business success.[33]

Such men were not exempt from the conservatism that is the concomitant of success. In his novel *Farragan's Retreat*, Tom McHale mercilessly satirized some members of the newly rich Philadelphia Irish Catholic class, with their limited sensibility and maudlin religiosity. McHale's novels provide an acid insight into the tensions that social change inflicted upon the Irish of the city who had huge incomes and stunted social

consciences. The contumely and bitter discourse between Irish
conservatives and liberals ruined many a family gathering,
organization meeting, and political love feast over the years.
Kennedy men like Ralph Dungan and Joseph Brady had to
contend with troglodite reactionaries in both religion and
politics.[34]

William Green's political achievement was inherited by
Mayor James H. J. Tate, who in 1962 became the city's first
Irish Catholic mayor.[35] Tate's accession coincided with a
period of intense urban crisis. The Irish community ebbed as
an organized group in the 1960s as two major forces greatly
changed it. The first was the vast increase of the Black population. In 1940 there were 250,000 nonwhites, or 13.1 percent
of the city's population; in 1970, there were 653,000, or
33.6 percent. Following World War II the Black popula-
lation expanded and displaced the Irish from many inner-
city parishes. There was grim resentment as the Irish left the
old neighborhoods and the parishes they had built. The attempt to temper antagonism by such organizations as the
Catholic Interracial Council was largely unavailing. Such
local leaders as Judge Gerald Flood, Robert V. Callaghan,
Mrs. Anna McGarry, and John A. McDermott strove mightily,
in the best tradition of liberal social action, to assuage the
anti-Black feeling, but church leaders were generally too
short-sighted or prejudiced to comprehend the requirements
of the new urban situation. As the Irish neighborhoods dispersed, the old ethnic ties became difficult to maintain.[36]

The second powerful force changing the Philadelphia Irish
was the Second Vatican Council of the Catholic Church.
Since first coming to the city, the Irish had bound themselves
closely to the church. Vatican II was to transform the cere-
monies and the outlook of religious life and education ad-
ministered by the church. The changes in orientation and expression of belief, and the liberalization of customs long
believed sacrosanct struck a blow at the simple pieties and
in-group morale of many Catholics. The folk quality was be-

ing taken out of the Catholicism most Philadelphians knew. The expunging of that folk quality, the hardy camaraderie of "our own kind," was divesting Catholics of one of the most familiar and amenable features of their religion. This religious transition with its social implications diminshed a principal factor in the ethnic cult of local Irishry. It was one more factor in the sequence of neighborhood change, class mobility, decreased immigration, and assimilation influences that were curtailing the animation of the city's Irish community.

In the 1960s the crisis in urban affairs brought on by social distress, rising municipal costs, and the exodus of the affluent from the city hit Philadelphia hard. Racial unrest and the difficulty of maintaining the vast complexity of an aging residential and economic base eroded confidence in the city and its future among many people. For many of the Irish, especially those in politics, however, there was no retreat. Building alliances with Blacks, Italians, and Puerto Ricans, they stuck to the tasks of civic and political activity. Often these were "new breed" types—educated, able, but quite capable of laughing at themselves. Congressman William Green III, son of the man who constructed the Democratic machine of the 1950s, provided a handsome and affable leadership to the Democratic machine in the 1960s. His combat with Mayor Tate was a classic Irish feud, but he survived and beat down a malignant attempt to oust him from his congressional seat. Gerald Gleeson, Gordon Cavanaugh, Miles Mahoney, Michael Stack, and Judge James Cavanaugh worked to attain justice and urban improvement amid the strains and alarms of urban riots, budget crises, political purges, and teachers' strikes. In the Republican party, temporarily out of power but far from dead in the 1960s, William Meehan and William Devlin worked to restore vitality and confidence. These men were conscious of the tradition they represented, but they were sufficiently perceptive and flexible not to permit it to monopolize them amid the pluralism of urban affairs. As exponents of political accountability and social development, they attempted to chart a future for the city in the face of manifold uncertainties.

The trenchant social criticism sparked by the Black rebellions of the 1960s and the Viet Nam war laid bare the massive cynicism and exploitation inherent in American urban life. From the perspective of minority social demands and a renewed populism, the sores of poverty and public neglect shook confidence in the free-enterprise ethic and the truisms of democracy. The Irish achievement of social advancement based upon political and electoral persistence and personal diligence could be seen as only a partial antidote to the disabilities imposed by the prevailing urban institutional system. As Black politicians asserted, upon succeeding to the leadership of the political machines constructed by the Irish, there was no human-service dimension to the municipal structures commanded by the elected officials. The Irish had satisfied their social needs through their families, their associations, and their church, but in their public structures they had stopped short of setting up the human services so vital to survival amid continuing urban crisis. The ward boss might give out coal and food, but the public welfare system was an inadequate hodgepodge. Far from the most successful of the minority groups in American urban society, as they were sometimes enviously considered by other minorities, the Irish could be viewed as the most long-suffering, or perhaps the most traduced.

Compared with their condition in the days of their immigrant prominence, the condition of the Philadelphia Irish at the close of the 1960s was diffuse and contradictory in several respects. While still very much in politics, they had lost the group basis of their previous participation.[37] While they were heirs to a huge school and college system, they were decidedly short of being able to claim intellectual eminence. While as leaders of urban construction they were prodigious, they were largely uncertain about the new influences for urban social reconstruction and environmental reform. While they now moved with freedom and assurance in the general society, the traditional minority tie to Ireland was sustained, subtly at times, demonstratively at other times. Affluence and jet travel permitted a steady traffic of tourists and students to gain first-hand experience of Irish life, and courses in colleges and universities in the works of the giants of modern Irish literature drew hundreds of students to a deepened interest in the old country and its links with America. Family traditions and the continuing currency of ethnicity as a factor in American life contributed to sustaining the Irish connection. The length of the connection was, itself, a strengthening element.

Thus, while some were predicting the ultimate assimilation of the Irish in the city, the crisis in the North of Ireland, beginning in 1969, brought forth a highly energetic local effort in behalf of the nationalist Irish behind the barricades in bomb-torn Belfast and Derry. When Bernadette Devlin appeared in the city in 1969 to plead the cause of the Ulster minority, the funds raised to support the civil rights drive of the North of Ireland Catholics were scanty. As the violence in Ulster increased in the next three years, however, a Philadelphia Irish network sponsored dozens of benefit dances, rallies, and demonstrations. The James Larkin Irish Republican Club, Marxist oriented and in close liaison with the Irish Republican Army, gathered audiences for touring speakers from Ireland. Tavern owners collected relief and "gun money" steadily. British entertainment groups were picketed, and a chapter of the American Committee for Ulster Justice worked to inspire local support at colleges for the final expulsion of England from her last foothold in Ireland. At meetings and rallies, hard-bitten veterans of the Irish struggle of the 1920s sat next to hirsute young radicals and cheered for the final extinction of colonialism in Ireland.[38] Once more the generation gap was bridged. Once more the bond between Irishmen defied time and distance to affirm a common interest, an interest that had been sustained in Philadelphia for three hundred years.

# NINE

## THE URBAN
## IRISHMAN

When Alexis de Tocqueville visited an impoverished Ireland in 1835, he speculated about what would happen if it became possible to provide the Irish people with commercial and economic opportunities that would "ever give the poor a thousand hopes."[1] Although the modern economic development of Ireland had to await the twentieth century, some part of Tocqueville's speculation was fulfilled when the great trans-Atlantic emigration of the nineteenth century placed Irishmen in the commercial and industrial centers of the New World. Because of the biases of our historical writing, the results of this transition have not been deeply explored, for, as Constance McLaughlin Green has noted, there has been a striking "gap in our knowledge of the statistically numerous, nondominant groups" in our society.[2]

If Philadelphia is taken as a case analysis, the adaptation of the Irish to the city in the eighteenth century can be seen to have been fairly successful. They contributed to the circles that led the patriotic and commercial movements of the time, as well as to the working classes. They were not so numerous, however, as to form a force for the disruption of the power relationships in the city. The Irish, by stepping carefully, could walk among the dominant Anglo-Saxon institutions without undue jeopardy. With the coming of heavier immigration and industrialization, a demographic and social challenge to the dominant institutions emerged. The Irish of the 1840s developed an intense minority-group morale that led them to build their own institutional system within the expanding city. In doing so they contrived to endow it with a pluralistic social dimension that it had lacked despite its growing size.

The evidence dealing with the adaptation of the Irish to urban life in the preceding chapters reveals that an important portion of the Irish population of Philadelphia began the process of social advancement prior to 1870. In terms of property acquisition, occupational diversification, and institutional development, a significant element of the Irish population had begun to take advantage of opportunities in the city and to expand an ethnic subcultural complex that would flourish for generations. Although the data presented do not permit generalizations about the proportion of the city's Irish population engaged in the process of active social development, they clearly testify to the evolution and vitality of that process.[3]

With respect to the residential adjustment of the immigrants, the Irish experienced all the misfortunes of slum conditions as an introduction to urban living. As undesirable newcomers, they were consigned by economics and custom to the least desirable areas at the edge of the city proper. Their concentration in these districts, especially in Moyamensing, Southwark, and Grays Ferry, created the city's first pattern of large-scale ethnic ghetto living, with overcrowding, poverty, and disease exacting a grim toll.

But even in the 1850s property holding by the Irish was substantial in these districts. The relative economy of the city's pattern of row-house construction permitted extensive residential building, and the steady expansion of the city made residential improvement a practical possibility for workers' families. This is especially notable in view of the fact that the immigrants actively joined in organizing and patronizing building and loan associations that made financing a home feasible, as well as provided a means for the residential upgrading and mobility of thousands of Irish families. Hundreds of such associations existed in the city by 1870.

The dispersion of the Irish throughout the city's neighborhoods in the Civil War period is indicated by the tabulations of Sam Bass Warner showing that in 1860 no ward in the city had a population including more than 28 percent Irish-born, and that seventeen of the city's twenty-four wards had Irish-born populations of between 10 percent and 28 percent.[4] This dispersion continued while the ghetto concentrations were maintained by new immigration. By 1864 the numerous street railways of the city enabled many of the Irish as well as other citizens to journey relatively long distances between home and job. That nine of the twenty-four Catholic churches built between 1840 and 1870 were outside the areas of heaviest Irish population concentration existing in 1850 also testifies to the residential dispersion of the Irish urbanites. And it is worthy of note that some of the affluent Irishmen had homes in the most fashionable residential district, the center of the city, and that others lived in adjacent middle-class areas or in outlying upper-class neighborhoods.

This residential dispersion provided the immigrants with a very important vehicle for social advancement, and a device for maintaining an equilibrium in urban life. The ghetto districts persisted, populated by a steady stream of newly arriving immigrants and those unable to become mobile. But for many of the Irish home ownership in a decent neighborhood was a practical goal, a goal that encouraged thrift, propriety, and family cooperation. Better housing brought the benefits of improved health and family life. A decent home, whether rented or owned, gave the immigrant or his son an increased stake in the community and a degree of social stability hardly attainable in the turbulent slum districts. Philadelphia's housing opportunities constituted a ladder for advancement that led to a residential situation in which home, school, and church were linked in institutional support of relatively attractive neighborhood life.

Philadelphia, because of the scale and variety of its economic activity, had a great capacity to absorb and advance the immigrant worker. During the mid–nineteenth century, the city was in the midst of its most active period of economic development. As a transportation nexus for canals and railroads and as a major port, it attracted an immense traffic. As a center for the manufacture of metals, textiles, and all the goods produced by the new industrialized system, the city was dotted with mills, factories, and warehouses. The subsidiary financial and commercial services related to the industrial establishment stimulated and abetted its activity. All these enterprises required unskilled labor, and Irish immigrant labor was readily available.

While approximately one-third of the Irish males in the city were laborers and unskilled workers in 1850, the occupational samples drawn from the South Philadelphia Irish population for this study show that there was increasing diversification in employment over the next twenty years. The Irish began to obtain jobs in factories, fabricating plants, and in some of the technical trades associated with metal production and textiles. The industrial geography of the city was such that the immigrants' living areas were not isolated but were near a large variety of plants and businesses. The rapid extension of street-railway lines between 1858 and 1870 permitted at least some of the better-paid Irish workers to reach employment that was relatively distant from home. The economy of the city was characterized by a high rate of labor mobility at the time, and this occasioned a diversified choice of job opportunities. In a time of economic growth and industrial expansion, new kinds of jobs were being invented rapidly as technology and production systems became more specialized. Thus, even though the city used great numbers of unskilled workers, its economy created opportunities for immigrants at a variety of levels.

The beginning of occupational diversification among the Irish wage earners coincided with a notable degree of Irish small-business activity, and some Irish ownership of large, substantial businesses. Grocers, dry-goods dealers, real-estate brokers, and commission merchants, as well as manufacturers and members of the professions, were not uncommon among the Irish in the 1850s and 1860s. There were some wealthy Irishmen, but it is more significant that large numbers of the

Irish were attracted to business in an age when individual enterprise was a potent and prevalent national ideal.

The occupational and economic diversity reflected in the city's Irish population was part of the upgrading cycle that was in progress. The unskilled and uneducated Irish in the slums, suffering from exploitation, unemployment, and privation, could look forward to entering semiskilled or skilled work. By becoming part of the skilled labor force of the industrial age, they and their Irish fellow citizens in business could begin to share in the residential, educational, and social benefits of urban life. The breadth and pace of this development, and the proportion of the Irish population involved in it, is a subject that requires further research. The conclusion stressed in this study is that the process of occupational dispersion by which the immigrants achieved economic mobility was begun in a substantial way before the Civil War. From backgrounds almost exclusively rural, the immigrants were becoming part of industrialized society.

Part of the earnings gained by the Irish was contributed to the network of parish churches they built throughout the city. To this parish network was appended a school system completely supported by the Catholic population, and a number of hospitals, asylums, charitable organizations, and social groups partially supported by it. The extent and organizational complexity of this Catholic structure is, in itself, surprising. That the structure was erected by the segment of the city's population that was the least affluent, the most beset by social problems, and the least able to have recourse to power and influence is remarkable. In furthering this Catholic religious and educational work, the Irish were the primary agents and chief contributors. Their religious and educational institutions perpetuated traditions of voluntarism, clerical leadership, and social service that had their roots in the history of the Catholic church in Ireland.

That a group of immigrants from a rural society could build such an institutional system in an urban setting testifies to its adaptability and inventiveness. While the Catholic schools served to provide the literacy, training, and skills needed for further urban adjustment, the parishes and religious organizations bound the immigrants together in a subculture that linked education, the home, the neighborhood, and a circuit of institutional facilities and associations that functioned on a citywide basis.

This religious network was a comprehensive medium aiding the immigrants in the attainment of careers and social stability in the urban environment. If Catholic institutions existed as a separate, partially segregated system in the city, they were not much different in this respect from the facilities of other denominations. If Catholic morality and opinion tended to be conservative and rigidly dedicated to its version of religious certitude, this was not untypical of other Victorian religious denominations. Its strict attitude toward sex, the total-abstinence movement against alcohol, and a preoccupation with propriety gave to Irish Catholicism features that were compatible with the social emphasis of much of the city's Victorian Protestantism. These aspects of Irish Catholicism, encouraged by the strong and concerted leadership of the clergy, left an impress not only upon the new Catholic middle class, but also upon the working-class Catholics for whom that middle class served as a model for imitation and aspiration.

In addition to the extension of Catholic institutional and educational structures, the immigrants also promoted a congeries of fire companies, beneficial associations, Irish ethnic groups, and nationalist societies. These organizations were another sphere for mutual aid and social advancement. They preserved the ethnic traditions and identity of the Irish and provided organizational ties for them at a variety of social levels for a variety of purposes. There were, in addition, groups that were unacceptable to the general public and to most of the immigrants as well, such as the conspiratorial Fenians and the criminal gangs of the slum areas. These would help to sustain the stereotype of the Irishman as an

antic and erratic figure. The coming of the Civil War, however, was the occasion for immigrant military service that im-
pressed public opinion and gave the Irish a somewhat more
favorable image.

The political participation of the Irish in the city involved
the development, at the neighborhood and ward levels, of a
grass-roots system of electoral activity based upon the saloon
and the fire company. These two local community fixtures
became the vehicles for an intense political effort that initially was chiefly of benefit to the Democratic party. This
effort was carried out under local bosses who, the prototypes
of a long line of political machine leaders, became masters of
urban party manipulation. The advent of the Irish immigrant
political organization coincided with the reshaping of urban
political life. The expansion of the city and its services and
the necessity of initiating a diverse urban population into the
processes of party campaigning and the exercise of the franchise required the creation of a broad and flexible mechanism
for political participation. In the fashioning of this mechanism, which was to accommodate the political aspirations of
ethnic groups and the new masses of industrial workers in the
city, the Irish played a leading role.

The fact that the Irish adhered initially to the Democratic
party was to have a significant effect on the political history
of Philadelphia. The Democrats were unable to consolidate the
Irish immigrant faction with the older party elements that
continued the tradition of Jacksonian Democracy in the city.
The Civil War and the identification of the Democrats with
Southern Secession struck a grave blow at the party. The
Republican party, identified with the victory of the Union
and the ascending forces of the industrial revolution, cap-
tured the political allegiance of the majority of Philadelphians
after the Civil War. The Irish Democrats remained a political
minority, and their influence dwindled as the Republican
hegemony became more complete. By the late 1870s Irish
Catholics were rising to prominence in the local Republican

machine, thus splitting the Irish as an ethnic political group. The Republicans drew more and more of them into their ranks, but, because the Irish did not represent a sufficiently large minority to dominate the city's politics, they did not rise to ultimate positions of power as Republicans. The broad base of Republican support in Pennsylvania extended beyond the city, and the Irish never constituted a major numerical element in the spectrum of Republican strength. Hence, even though the Irish Catholics did become intermittent leaders of local Republican factions, the preponderant Republican power base among native Americans, Protestants, and middle- and upper-class groups prevented Irish domination.

This denial of commanding political power, lasting till the mid–twentieth century, deeply affected the Irish and the city. It consigned the Irish Catholics either to political futility in the ranks of an ineffectual Democratic party or to the status of permanent minority stepchildren within the ranks of a Republican organization dominated locally by Anglo-Saxon businessmen and statewide by Scotch-Irish political bosses. This long-lasting minority political status induced among the Irish an ambiguity of purpose. On the one hand, they could not hope to control the city's political life; on the other, they had access to patronage and offices through the Republican party. The resulting ambivalence frustrated that combative morale and single-minded pursuit of power that Edward Levine finds a characteristic of Irish politicians.[5] The Irish in Philadelphia remained handmaidens of a machine they did not control—a group blunted in its political ambitions and fragmented in its political impact until the mid–twentieth century. In Boston and New York, however, the Irish dominated the urban machine.[6]

The picture that emerges from the evidence gathered about the Irish in Philadelphia in the critical period of the mid–nineteenth century, then, is one of modest but promising progress in the residential and economic life of the city. Through a cultural and religious network, the immigrants had developed their own institutional dimension of urban life. Despite the continuing disability of a large unskilled minority among them, the Irish were creating a viable and accepted subculture within a major American industrial city. If they could not break through to achieve political control of the city, they could function satisfactorily within the existing political framework, while enjoying an acceptable degree of latitude for social and economic advancement.

How can this picture of urban adjustment be reconciled with the initial resistance that greeted the mass Irish emigration in the 1840s? Although antipathy toward Irish Catholics was widespread in the city, the deep bitterness and aggressive hostility harbored by the Protestant Irish textile workers and tradesmen of Philadelphia, who, after all, were those most directly confronted by Irish Catholic immigrants, was not typical of the rest of the city. It is noteworthy, also, that the riots occurred in 1844, while the great wave of postfamine immigrants did not arrive until 1846. The growth of the Irish-born population to 72,000 by 1850, a figure representing 18 percent of the population of the County of Philadelphia, created so large a minority that violent repression as a response could only appear as folly to reasonable men. The institutional growth of Catholicism probably convinced many that the Catholic church, no matter how repugnant to them theologically and historically, was the chief agency for the maintenance of order and moral standards among the Irish. Protestant Philadelphia put the riots behind it, for such disruption was incompatible with the city's labor needs, progress, and stability.

If Protestant Philadelphia, with the city's new police force installed in the 1850s, could afford to regret and forget the riots, Catholics could hardly do so as easily. As the victims of the riots, they remained more sensitive to the implications of their minority position. The antagonism manifested in the riots, along with the stigma attached to them, worked to motivate the Irish Catholics toward positive achievements—ethnic

solidarity and self-reliance. Hence, the initial challenge to the
Irish immigrant community became a stimulant to its educational and social development. The violence of 1844 did not
leave a permanent and unbridgeable cleavage in the life of the
expanding and increasingly cosmopolitan city. Rather, despite its legacy of suspicion and partial social segregation,
which did not differ greatly from the caste and class divisions
among the various Protestant denominations, it permitted
cooperation and secular civic interaction between Catholics
and non-Catholics.

The social and economic advances made by the Irish Catholics in Philadelphia between 1850 and 1870 can be placed in
perspective by comparing them with those made by the Irish
Catholics in Boston. Such a comparison is made possible by
Handlin's keenly researched description of the impact of the
Irish on Boston in the period of postfamine immigration. In
1850 Boston and its environs contained 208,000 people, with
just over 35,000 Irish-born residents among them.[7] Thus, it
was about half the size of Philadelphia with about half as
many Irish-born. But, as Handlin notes, there was little heavy
industry in Boston; in 1845 the city had only 952 manufacturing establishments, while Philadelphia by 1850 contained
several thousand and by 1860 had 6,400.[8] Philadelphia far
outpaced Boston in population growth from 1850 to 1860,
with Boston increasing by 29.9 percent, Philadelphia by 65.4
percent.[9] Philadelphia was not only larger, with a more varie-
gated economic base, but it was growing more rapidly.

The Irish immigrants entering the Quaker City came into
a labor force where there was more need for them, more varied
opportunities for them, and greater prospects for their advancement. While Handlin found that 48 percent of the Boston Irish were laborers in the 1850s, in Philadelphia laborers
constituted a 34.4 percent of the Irish in 1850, and 25 percent
in 1870, according to the samples cited in this study.[10] In
addition, occupational diversification was already a trend
among the Philadelphia Irish between 1850 and 1870. Hand-

lin found that the Irish in Boston had few opportunities to
enter business, whereas in Philadelphia there were numerous
Irishmen in the grocery, dry-goods, tailoring, shoemaking, and
real-estate businesses, and a number of larger manufacturing
enterprises were conducted by Irishmen.[11]

These greater economic opportunities made housing improvement more accessible to the Irish immigrants in Philadelphia than to those in Boston, whose housing and chances
for residential betterment were rather circumscribed.[12] This
is reflected in the dispersion of Philadelphia's Catholic parishes, and in the lower death rates and the greater progress
in expanding Catholic school and institutional life of the immigrants in Philadelphia. While from 1850 to 1870 Boston's
Catholic parishes approximately doubled in number, increasing from nine to twenty, Philadelphia's trebled, increasing
from twelve to thirty-six. In Boston, there were only four
parish schools in existence before 1860; in Philadelphia,
nineteen.[13]

The Philadelphia Irish did not, in the long run, solidify
into an Irish-Catholic political bloc, but distributed themselves between the Democratic and the Republican parties. In
contrast, Boston's Irish Catholics remained overwhelmingly
Democratic until recent decades.[14] The long Yankee-Irish political duel in Boston does not have a parallel in Philadelphia,
where some of the Irish became Republicans before the nineteenth century ended. In Boston the constriction of social and
economic opportunities for the Irish left a legacy of enduring
hostility, whereas in Philadelphia the hostility was obscured
and tempered, and the expansion of opportunities for a portion of the Irish population led to the emergence of a stable
bourgeois community.

What was at work in Philadelphia was a process of differ-
entiated development that was one feature of a broader dynamic of social and economic expansion. As some men were
moving upward toward a better life, others were losing advantages or remaining immobile in the slums.[15] The multi-

plicity of choices available in the city prompted a diversity of reactions, from broad mobility in some spheres to relatively static conditions in others. This process was ambiguous and contradictory in many ways, but it was a process appropriate to the heterogeneous nature of the great city. There was differentiation among the areas in which mobility could occur, such as housing, jobs, education, and politics, and the levels that the immigrants could reach were varied. Some would become respectable skilled workers, others "lace curtain" bourgeoisie, others wealthy men. And the rate of social mobility would differ also, depending on a number of variables such as aspirations, talent, economic climate, education, and chance.[16]

Stephan Thernstrom states that the differences between a small and a large city are of kind as well as of scale that is, the nature and the quality of life vary with the size of the city.[17] Philadelphia's heterogeneity was partly a result of its size. Its industrial complexity and its varied population induced a response from the immigrants that was as checkered and irregular as the city itself. Within this context of differentiation, the Irish constructed a subcultural system that cushioned them amid urban misfortunes, preserved their identity, and served as a medium for mutual support and advancement. For the city itself, this subculture created not so much a cleavage as a discontinuous set of segregating and polarizing influences. Within the social structure of the city, the Irish subculture acted sometimes as a magnet, sometimes as a centrifuge, sometimes as a protective shell. The Irish Catholic churches, schools, and organizations functioned within a nineteenth-century system of social segregation that operated for all groups in the city. Hence, Nathaniel Burt's allegation that the Irish were "more wilfully separatist than the Jews" must be evaluated in the light of the pervasive system of ethnic, religious, and social segregation that existed in the city and that continued for generations.[18] Digby Baltzell and Sam Bass Warner have described the "privatization" and withdrawal of the Philadelphia Anglo-Saxon upper class during the Victorian period.[19] If this was the example of the city's old leadership, the preoccupation of the Irish with their own needs and affairs is hardly surprising.

The question of the adjustment of the immigrants to American conditions, especially to urban conditions, has been a subject of interest to historians who have dealt with immigration. Not only the human drama of immigrant arrival and struggle was involved in the question, but also the social experience of an America in which immigration was a central historical influence. With respect to the latter consideration, historical writing has been superficial. The primacy of the Irish in length of time and in numbers in the nineteenth century endows their immigration experience with a special interest. As the precursors of other great waves of immigrants, and as the prototypes of new urbanites in the industrial cities, their reaction to the urban world set certain precedents and institutional patterns.

Oscar Handlin has written that the immigrants "escaped into a way of life completely foreign and completely unfavorable to them." Ralph Turner saw the peasant immigrant in the city unable to cope with changes required by its labor market, machine technology, and problems of urban association. William Forbes Adams, however, stated that emigration did not change life for the immigrants greatly, for the urban slums of America were not much different from the rural slums of Ireland. George Potter is more sanguine, asserting that the immigrants bridged in "one evolutionary leap" the gap between lonely villages on the outermost edge of Europe and the gaudy cities of the New World.[20]

What does the Philadelphia experience of the Irish immigrants indicate with respect to these contrasting opinions? Handlin's statement that the urban way of life was "completely" unfavorable to the immigrants may have seemed justified by his study of the Irish in Boston, but it hardly holds true for Philadelphia. Aside from the fact that American conditions were generally more favorable than those in Ireland, the immigrants in Philadelphia demonstrated an effective capacity to make adjustments in their residential, occupational, and organizational lives. Turner's generalization that immigrants were unable to cope with the waves of social change generated by urban conditions seems only partially true in the light of the Philadelphia Irish activities in the fields of education and social development. It is true that in retrospect the positive institutional responses are more evident than the myriad failures and sufferings experienced by obscure people striving for coherence and stability in the turbulent city. But the positive achievements testify to a partial success in constructing institutions and behavior patterns to deal with urban conditions.

Adams's assertion that American slums were little different from impoverished Irish villages, and that the immigrants' lives altered little between one and the other, fails to recognize the larger environment. The Irish situation was imminently disastrous for those who lived in the rural environment's stricken extremity, as did most of the emigrants prior to emigration. In the American city, though the immigrants' lot might be hard, at least there was more security, opportunity, and freedom in a dynamic urban environment characterized by gradually increasing standards of living.[21] Potter's judgment that the immigrants made the transition from Ireland to the urban world in "one evolutionary leap" oversimplifies the process. Actually, as the Philadelphia experience shows, the transition from the old identity to the new, from the old values and associations to American behavior and social patterns, was partial, ambivalent, and uneven. Assimilation was far from complete, and the process of social adjustment was protracted and subtle. But their moderately successful adjustment in housing, employment, education, and organizational activity in the city enabled the Irish to transcend their rural experience and to construct a framework for an urban subculture that was a viable mechanism for their development.

If the absorption of the immigrants remained incomplete,

the system of accommodation worked out through the Protestant tolerance of parallel institutions, and the fact that partial segregation did not threaten the city with disruption or partition. The adumbration of Irish political strength by the weakness of the Democrats and by the partial adherence of the Irish to the Republicans helped to foster a one-party rule that probably worked to the city's long-range disadvantage by breeding irresponsibility and inefficiency in municipal affairs. The upper-class caste of "Philadelphia Gentlemen" remained unchallenged in its casual exercise of social leadership, and the politicos of the Republican machine took effective control of the city's public life. A concerted Irish Catholic political challenge to this situation in the 1870s might have changed the political history of the city, but that concerted challenge never came. Perhaps the opportunities and amenities offered by Philadelphia sufficiently satisfied the aspirations and needs of the immigrants so that they lost the desire to contend for power. The homely conservatism of the city may have divested them of the drive for political control, since they could enjoy a modicum of patronage and political expression through the Republican machine.

The development by the Irish of their own minority culture entailed more than random urban diversity. It projected an Irish Catholic way of life that, once established, resulted in a degree of separatism that subtly estranged the Irish from many of the city's cultural institutions and advantages. Separate schools, organizations, and traditions perpetuated cultural pluralism, but the negative effects of the Irish separatism denied the city at large a reservoir of talent and leadership that could perhaps have benefited it greatly had this reservoir been freely available in public life without religious and ethnic restrictions.

Robert D. Cross has contended that the Catholic experience in urban areas has been interpreted pessimistically by the Catholics themselves. Their interpretation, emphasizing poverty and social disorganization, "does less than justice to the

resilience and adaptability of American Catholics in respond-
ing to the protean challenges of the varieties of urban life.'' [22]
What is incontrovertible is the fact that immigrant groups
like the Irish in Philadelphia built a religious establishment
that was to be a major stabilizing factor in the steady adaptation of newcomers to urban areas.

A key feature of the urban adjustment of the Irish was the
formation, under pressure, of the first large-scale ethnic ghet-
toes in American cities. These sociocultural enclaves would become one of the most persistent American urban institutions.
As areas of cultural difference and segregation, and as catch-
ment districts for the afflicted and the failures among the immigrants, the ghettos had both positive and negative aspects.
If they concentrated misery and hostility, they also provided
necessary way stations between the immigrants' arrival and
their full immersion in the mainstream of urban life. If they
segregated immigrants from some of the beneficial currents of
the mainstream, they also afforded a protective solidarity
without which the individual immigrant would have been even
more vulnerable to the exploitative forces of a society that had
scant regard for his welfare.

From their experience in the urban centers the Irish also
derived a political skill that enabled them to make extensive
contributions to the urban political machine, which was a distinctively American vehicle for the promotion of political participation and the fabrication of solutions to the problems of
government in new and unprecedented conditions. Through
this identification with urban politics, the Irish were not only
able to remedy some of their most basic social needs, but,
despite the corruption and jobbery involved, were able to
point the way toward expanded social responsibility on the
part of government. The Irish political bosses attended to the
needs of the poor for food, clothing, and shelter at a time
when other levels of municipal leadership were blind to evident need. The difficulty in evolving such ministrations into

the bureaucratized welfare, housing, and employment programs that now function in cities would have been even greater
without their representative role, and the machinery of mass
political pressure they helped bring into being.

The exertions of the immigrant Irish also helped to promote
a cult of motivation that would be a signal feature of American urban life. By proving that social and economic mobility
was attainable, if only for a small number in each generation,
the Irish propagated one of the central principles of the American creed. The cult of success and the quest for mobility helped
each individual to believe in his own dignity and future amid
the struggles against poverty and discouragement in the urban areas. The Irish, by being the first and the largest urban
minority group with which American society had to deal, and
by working, prying, and infiltrating their way into the general
society, would constitute an example for the array of other
immigrants that would follow them.[23]

The adjustment of the Irish in the city, molded in the nineteenth century, was cast in enduring form in the Victorian
years of free-enterprise exuberance. The domination of the
city by the capitalist class was accepted, since there was access, albeit limited, to its benefits, for those who could compete. The continuation of a cult of crime and wracking social
problems within the group was balanced by the broad educational advances and social improvement promoted by Catholic
facilities and steady Irish political pressures. But the Irish
were as unable as many others to change the exploitative and
wasteful nature of the city. Sweatshops, low-wage industries,
institutionalized poverty, and huge slum belts endured. An
elite, occasionally enlightened but usually indifferent, ruled
businesses and institutions that were consecrated to class gains
and inequality. The urban crisis of the mid–twentieth century
mirrored this collective failure.

The higher intellectual and artistic life of the city remained
a largely Anglo-Saxon and German preserve until the advent

of the enlarged Jewish population in the twentieth century. The original Anglo-Saxon character of the cultural elite induced in the Irish a wary reserve toward it. The city's great orchestra, its learned societies, and its artistic circles were largely without Irish imprint until recently. The Irish preoccupation with religion and educational work, the deep interest in politics, and the lack of a group tradition of discriminating artistic patronage retarded the participation in this kind of urban creativity. While John Tracy Ellis has lamented this cultural and intellectual omission, the breadth of the Irish social engagement must be kept in view. The Irish achievement in the city has been one of democratic social creativity, not one of artistic excellence. The recent data compiled by Andrew Greeley seem to indicate a trend toward greater intellectual and cultural commitment.[24]

For the Irish, an ancient people thrust into a grave social struggle in the nineteenth century, the movement from rural to urban life was a transforming experience. Their emigration introduced them, almost by accident, into two related trends of epochal significance. Industrialization and urbanization became the dynamic social processes through which the emigrants were ushered from folk society into modern life. Endowed with a plasticity of temperament and cultural outlook, and prepared for cultural adaptation by their experience in surviving foreign conquest and oppression, the Irish were in certain respects especially equipped to cope with the contradictions and the turmoil of urban life. Steeped in a tradition of religious and ethnic loyalty, they used religious and ethnic ties to promote their own organization and advancement under city conditions. Having experienced in its fullest compass the transition from rural to urban life, the Irish immigrants displayed in striking fashion the adaptability of man. Their attainment of status and sufficiency in America made it possible for them to play a critical role in the ultimately successful effort to relieve their homeland of colonial domination. Thus, a fitting climax was added to the human drama of emigration.

Irishmen, walking the cities of the New World as free men, were able to reach back, to clasp the hands of those whose past they shared, who still led the life of the soil, and to join in the fulfillment of those ideals of Irish nationhood that had for so long been denied their people.

# NOTES

## Preface

1. E. A. Gutkind, *Revolution of Environment* (London: Routledge & Kegan Paul, 1957).
2. Oscar Handlin and John Burchard, eds., *The Historian and the City* (Cambridge, Mass.: MIT Press, 1963), p. 26.
3. "The importance of immigration . . . remains as yet only dimly grasped. We shall have to disentangle the special effects of immigration from the encompassing legends; and that will require all the light that comparative history can shed" (John Higham, "Immigration," in C. Vann Woodward, ed., *The Comparative Approach to American History* [New York: Basic Books, 1968], p. 92). See also Rudolph Vecoli, "Ethnicity: A Neglected Dimension of American History" (Paper delivered at the Sixty-second Annual Meeting of the Organization of American Historians, Philadelphia, Pa., 18 April 1969).
4. E. Digby Baltzell, *The Philadelphia Gentlemen* (Glencoe, Ill.: Free Press, 1958); Nathaniel Burt, *The Perennial Philadelphians* (Boston: Little, Brown & Co., 1963); Sam Bass Warner, *The Private City: Philadelphia* (Philadelphia: University of Pennsylvania Press, 1968). The ethnic and class bias of older historians of the city is noted in Edward Pessen, "The Egalitarian Myth and the Social Reality," *American Historical Review* 76, no. 4 (October 1971): 1031.

## Chapter 1

1. Myles Dillon, "The Antiquity of Irish Tradition," *Proceedings of the British Academy,* vol. 33 (1947), J. C. Beckett, *A Short History of Ireland* (New York: Harper & Row, 1966), pp. 96–130; James

Carty, ed., *Ireland from the Flight of the Earls to Grattan's Parliament* (Dublin: C. J. Fallon, 1949), pp. 28–78.

2. Quoted in John Mitchel, *The Jail Journal* (Dublin: M. H. Gill & Sons, 1854), p. xxix.

3. Benedict Kiely, "Land without Stars," *Capuchin Annual* 16, no. 1 (November 1945) :206–22.

4. J. G. Sims, *The Williamite Confiscations in Ireland, 1690–1703* (London: Faber & Faber, 1966), p. 196.

5. Albert Cook Myers, *The Immigration of the Irish Quakers into Pennsylvania, 1682–1750* (Swarthmore, Pa.: Published by the author, 1902), p. 48.

6. E. C. Beatty, *William Penn as Social Philosopher* (New York: Columbia University Press, 1939), pp. 178, 286; William I. Bull, *William Penn: A Topical Biography* (London: Oxford University Press, 1937), pp. 88–105.

7. John W. Reps, *Town Planning in Frontier America* (Princeton, N.J.: Princeton University Press, 1969), pp. 22–23.

8. Howard Mumford Jones, *O' Strange New World: American Culture: The Formative Years* (New York: Viking Press, 1964), pp. 167–72; David B. Quinn, *The Elizabethans and the Irish* (New York: Cornell University Press, 1966).

9. Myers, *Immigration of the Irish Quakers*, pp. 45–48. The antipathy of the Catholic Irish toward the Quakers was an additional spur to emigration.

10. Charles H. Browning, "Extracts from the Journal of Charles Clinton Kept During the Voyage from Ireland to Pennsylvania, 1729," *Pennsylvania Magazine of History and Biography* 26, no. 1 (January 1902) :112–14.

11. "Obstructions to Irish Emigration," *Pennsylvania Magazine of History and Biography* 21, no. 4 (October 1897) :485–87. The traffic with Ireland was steady nevertheless. It continued into the nineteenth century. Between 1815 and 1819, for instance, sixty-two ships reached Philadelphia from Irish ports (William Forbes Adams, *Ireland and the Irish Emigration to the New World from 1815 to the Famine* [New Haven, Conn.: Yale University Press, 1932], p. 425). See also Carl Bridenbaugh, *Cities in the Wilderness: The First Century of Urban Life in America* (New York: Capricorn Books, 1964), p. 408; and Carl and Jessica Bridenbaugh, *Rebels and Gentlemen: Philadelphia in the Age of Franklin* (New York: Reynal & Hitch-

cock, 1942), pp. 4, 230. An early listing of Irish residents of the city is given in J. D. Hackett, "Philadelphia Irish," *Journal of the American Irish Historical Society* 30 (1932) :103.

12. Richard B. Morris, *Government and Labor in Early America* (New York: Harper & Row, 1946), p. 336; "List of Servants Who Sailed from Dublin, 1746," *Pennsylvania Magazine of History and Biography* 26, no. 2 (April 1902) :287.

13. Myers, *Immigration of the Irish Quakers,* p. 102.

14. Edith Abbott, *Immigration: Select Documents and Case Records* (Chicago: University of Chicago Press, 1924), p. 9; C. A. Herrick, *White Servitude in Pennsylvania* (Philadelphia: J. McVey, 1926).

15. John F. Watson, *Annals of Philadelphia and Pennsylvania,* 3 vols. (Philadelphia: Edwin S. Stuart, 1884), 2:259.

16. For a discussion of the term "Scotch-Irish" see James G. Leyburn, *The Scotch-Irish: A Social History* (Chapel Hill: University of North Carolina Press, 1962), p. 40; and for a history of the Ulster emigration from 1718 to 1775 see Robert Dickson, *Ulster Emigration to Colonial America* (London: Routledge & Kegan Paul, 1966). It would add greatly to the coherence of the history of the Irish in the United States if the fortunes of both Protestant and Catholic Irishmen could be treated as a whole. But because of differences between the two groups in cycles of emigration, cultural and religious traditions, and social position, such a unified treatment would be a false reconciliation that would contradict the reality of the antipathy that has so disastrously divided the groups since the seventeenth century. In this study I use the term "Irish" largely to denote Irish Roman Catholics, for it is the overwhelmingly Catholic migration of the mid–nineteenth century that is dealt with in the bulk of the book. It is salutary to record that, despite intense religious divisions, the Society of the Friendly Sons of St. Patrick has continued to unite Catholic and Protestant Irishmen in the city to this day.

17. Leyburn, *Scotch-Irish,* p. 317.

18. Sam Bass Warner, *Private City,* p. 11.

19. Watson, *Annals of Philadelphia,* 2:259.

20. Ibid., 2:453, 3:345; Carl Bridenbaugh, *Cities in the Wilderness,* p. 107.

21. J. Thomas Scharf and Thompson Westcott, *History of Phila-*

*delphia, 1609–1884,* 3 vols. (Philadelphia: L. H. Everts, 1884), 2:1367–71.

22. Michael J. O'Brien, *A Hidden Phase of American History: Ireland's Part in America's Struggle for Liberty* (New York: Dodd, Mead & Co., 1920), pp. 38–53.

23. Ibid., p. 364; John Tracy Ellis, *Catholics in Colonial America* (Baltimore: Helicon Press, 1965), p. 398; Charles H. Metzger, *Catholics in the American Revolution* (Chicago: Loyola University Press, 1962), pp. 220–35; C. P. Whittemore, "John Sullivan: Luckless Irishman," in G. A. Billias, ed., *George Washington's Generals* (New York: William Morrow Co., 1964), pp. 98, 137–62.

24. *The Poetical Works of Thomas Moore* (Boston: Phillips, Samson & Co., 1954), p. 151.

25. Frank McDermot, *Theobold Wolfe Tone: A Biographical Study* (London: Macmillan & Co., 1939), pp. 171–75.

26. Edward C. Carter, "Mathew Carey in Ireland, 1760–1784," *Catholic Historical Review* 51, no. 4 (January 1966):503–27; and Kenneth Rowe, *Mathew Carey: A Study in Economic Development* (Baltimore: Johns Hopkins University Press, 1933).

27. Original editions of these works are in the library of the American Philosophical Society, Philadelphia.

28. Louis Hartz, *Economic Policy and Democratic Thought in Pennsylvania, 1776–1860* (Cambridge, Mass.: Harvard University Press, 1948), p. 25.

29. Mathew Carey, *Vindiciae Hibernicae; or, Ireland Vindicated* (Philadelphia: Carey & Lea, 1823).

30. Lewis Leary, "Thomas Brannagan: An American Romantic," *Pennsylvania Magazine of History and Biography* 77, no. 3 (July 1953):332–80; Jesse L. Hartman, "John Dougherty and the Rise of the Sectional Boat System," *Pennsylvania Magazine of History and Biography* 69, no. 4 (October 1945):294–314.

31. Dumas Malone, ed., *Dictionary of American Biography,* 20 vols. (New York: Charles Scribner & Sons, 1946), 19:701.

32. The papers of the O'Conway family and the manuscript of the Gaelic dictionary are in the Archives of the American Catholic Historical Society, Saint Charles Borromeo Seminary, Overbrook, Pa.

33. Dennis Clark, "Kellyville: Immigrant Enterprise," *Pennsylvania History* 39, no. 1 (January 1972):40–49.

34. *American Catholic Historical Researches* 4, no. 2 (January 1898) :42; ibid., n.s. 3, no. 1 (January 1907) :95.

35. James Morton Smith, *Freedom's Fetters: The Alien and Sedition Laws and American Civil Liberties* (Ithaca, N.Y.: Cornell University Press, 1956), pp. 24–25.

36. Ibid., pp. 204–46; John Sartain, *Reminiscences of a Very Old Man* (New York: D. Appleton & Co., 1899), p. 193.

37. Harry Tinkcom, "Sir Augustus in Pennsylvania," *Pennsylvania Magazine of History and Biography* 75, no. 4 (October 1951) :396–97.

38. *An Account of the Proceedings of the Celebration of St. Patrick's Day, 1837* (Philadelphia: M. Fithian, 1837), Pamphlet Miscellany, vol. 2, XMDA, 950.z917, McGarrity Collection, Villanova University, Villanova, Pa.

39. Edward C. Carter, "A Wild Irishman under Every Federalist's Bed," *Pennsylvania Magazine of History and Biography* 94, no. 3 (July 1970) :342.

40. John Binns, *Recollections of the Life of John Binns* (Philadelphia: Perry & McMillan, 1854). For the effect of such leaders on ordinary Irishmen see Thomas N. Brown, "Nationalism and the Irish Peasant," *Review of Politics* 15, no. 4 (October 1953) :403–45.

41. Carey, *Vindiciae Hibernicae*, p. xi.

42. H. C. Carlisle, Jr., *American Satire in Prose and Verse* (New York: Random House, 1962), p. 70; The *Erin*, issues for 1823, Library of Congress, Washington, D.C.

43. Frederick Marryat, *A Diary in America*, ed. Sidney Jackson (New York: Alfred A. Knopf, 1962), pp. 395–96. See also Tyrone Power, *Impressions of America, 1833–1835* (Philadelphia: Carey & Blanchard, 1836), 1:115.

44. William Sullivan, *The Industrial Worker in Pennsylvania, 1800–1840* (Harrisburg: Pennsylvania Historical and Museum Commission, 1955), pp. 32, 49.

45. Marcus Lee Hansen, *The Immigrant in American History* (Cambridge, Mass.: Harvard University Press, 1940), p. 132.

46. Hugh Nolan, *The Most Reverend Francis P. Kenrick: Third Bishop of Philadelphia, 1830–1851* (Philadelphia: American Catholic Historical Society, 1948); and Francis E. Tourscher, *The Hogan Schism and Trustee Troubles, 1820–1829* (Philadelphia: Peter Reilly Co., 1930).

47. Elizabeth M. Geffen, "Violence in Philadelphia in the 1840's and 1850's," *Pennsylvania History* 36, no. 4 (October 1969) :381.

48. The only extant copy of the *Irish Republican Shield and Literary Observer* is that for 15 September 1832, in the Logan Library, Philadelphia. The meeting notice above appears in the *Philadelphia Daily Express,* 1 August 1832.

49. *Public Ledger,* 3 June 1843 (Newspapers cited throughout Notes are Philadelphia papers unless otherwise identified). One tavern on Second Street near Master, an Irish area, honored Daniel O'Connell by putting his portrait on its signboard together with the words "Hereditary bondsmen, who would be free, themselves must strike the blow!" (Watson, *Annals of Philadelphia,* 3 :360). The Repeal Fund collection is noted in Charles Gavan Duffy, *Young Ireland: A Fragment of Irish History, 1840–1850* (New York: D. Appleton & Co., 1881), p. 318.

50. The breakup of the local Repeal Association also reflects the rising strains between Catholics and Protestants. Such men as William Stokes and Samuel Hood found it impossible to deal with the wrathful Irish assemblage in the meetings of 1843 (*Public Ledger,* 5 May, 12, 23, 28 June, and 20 July 1843).

51. *Celebration of St. Patrick's Day, 1837,* McGarrity Collection.

52. Henry Steele Commager, ed., *The Era of Reform, 1830–1860* (Princeton, N.J.: Van Nostrand Co., 1960), p. 9; Geffen, "Violence in Philadelphia," pp. 381–440.

53. Ray Allen Billington, *The Protestant Crusade, 1800–1860* (Chicago, Quadrangle Books, 1964), pp. 220–37.

54. Sam Bass Warner, *Private City,* pp. 156–57.

55. Raymond F. Schmandt, ed., "A Selection of Sources Dealing with the Nativist Riots of 1844," *Records of the American Catholic Historical Society* 80, nos. 2 and 3 (June and September 1969) :68–113. See also Geffen, "Violence in Philadelphia."

56. The Orange character of the riots is noted by contemporaries (Schmandt, "Nativist Riots," pp. 84, 115–20). While the riots were under way at Saint Michael's Church, an Orange band played "The Boyne Water," an Irish Protestant march. One student traces the riots to economic origins, which again, has religious implications, since the Scotch-Irish craftsmen were in competition with the Irish Catholics in the new factories where they were employed (Michael

Feldberg, "The Philadelphia Riots of 1844" [Ph.D. diss., University of Rochester, 1970].).

57. E. Digby Baltzell, *The Protestant Establishment* (New York: Random House, 1964), p. 73.

58. J. St. John Joyce, ed., *The Story of Philadelphia* (Philadelphia: City of Philadelphia, 1919), p. 248.

59. Robert Lee Benson, *The Concept of Jacksonian Democracy* (Princeton, N.J.: Princeton University Press, 1961), p. 117; Vincent Lannie and Bernard Duthorn, "For the Honor and Glory of God: The Philadelphia Bible Riots of 1840," *History of Education Quarterly* 7, no. 1 (Spring 1968) :55, 97.

## Chapter 2

1. For the economic and social history of Ireland prior to the famine see Elié Halévy, *England in 1815*, vol 1 of *A History of the English People*, R. D. McCallum, ed., 6 vols. (New York: Barnes & Noble, 1961), pp. 205–18; R. D. Collison-Black, *Economic Thought and the Irish Question, 1817–1870* (Cambridge: Cambridge University Press, 1960), pp 6–14; R. B. McDowell, ed., *Social Life in Ireland, 1800–1845* (Dublin: Colm O'Loughlin, 1957), pp. 43–56; Radcliffe Salaman, *The History and Social Influence of the Potato* (Cambridge: Cambridge University Press, 1949), p. 279; Kenneth H. Connell, *The Population of Ireland, 1750–1845* (Oxford: Oxford University Press, 1950); John T. Noonan, "Intellectual and Demographic History," *Daedalus* 97, no. 1 (Spring 1968) :463–85.

2. W. A. Carrothers, *Emigration from the British Isles* (London: P. S. King, 1929), p. 39.

3. A. M. Sullivan, "Why Send More Irish out of Ireland?," *Nineteenth Century* 14, no. 77 (July 1883) :135.

4. R. Dudley Edwards and T. D. Williams, eds., *The Great Famine* (New York: New York University Press, 1957), p. xii; see also Cecil Woodham-Smith, *The Great Hunger* (New York: Harper & Row, 1962), pp. 69, 105. The land agent of one of the great estate holders in County Monaghan recounted how in 1843 his master, the Marquis of Bath, withstood with icy imperturbability the sight of hundreds of his suppliant tenants actually kneeling before him in a throng to

beg him to reduce their rents. Their importunings were in vain (William Stewart Trench, *Realities of Irish Life* [London: MacGibbon & Kee, 1966], pp. 222–23). Another poignant scene is given in Oscar Handlin, ed., *Immigration as a Factor in American History* (Englewood Cliffs, N.J.: Prentice-Hall, 1959), pp. 21–24.

5. Figures on land consolidation are given in E. R. R. Green, "Agriculture," in Edwards and Williams, *Great Famine*, p. 123.

6. Roger McHugh, "The Famine in Irish Oral Tradition," in Edwards and Williams, *Great Famine*, pp. 434–35. Two books on Gaelic culture are Seán de Fréine, *The Great Silence* (Dublin: Foilseacháin Náisiunta Teoranta, 1965); and Daniel Corkery, *The Hidden Ireland* (Dublin: M. H. Gill & Sons, 1925).

7. The antagonism of the times is highlighted by Nassau Senior, who quoted his brother-in-law in 1852 as saying on behalf of the land owners, "We have power enough to hang every rebel in Ireland," and quoted a priest as advising his parishioners, "I now tell you, the people, to assert your rights, and it is not in the power of the oligarchy to crush you" (Nassau William Senior, *Journals, Conversations, and Essays Relating to Ireland*, 2 vols. [London: Longmans, Green & Co., 1868], 1:20, 54). Another observer noted, "It is probable that the true cause of the savage hatred of England that animates great bodies of Irishmen on the other side of the Atlantic has little connection with the penal laws, or the rebellion or the Union. It is far more due to the great clearances and the vast unaided emigration that followed the famine" (W. E. Lecky, *Leaders of Public Opinion in Ireland*, 2 vols. [New York: Longmans, Green & Co., 1912], 2:177). See also F. S. L. Lyons, *Ireland since the Famine* (London: Weidenfeld & Nicolson, 1971), p. 4.

8. Sean O'Faolain, *The Irish* (New York: Devin-Adair Co., 1949), p. 26.

9. Arland Ussher, *The Face and Mind of Ireland* (New York: Devin-Adair Co., 1950), p. 156. Feudalism was only partially and imperfectly developed in Ireland; it was a system for an Anglo-Norman minority (F. X. Martin, "The Anglo-Norman Invasion," in T. W. Moody and F. X. Martin, eds., *The Course of Irish History* [Cork: Mercier Press, 1967], p. 135). The Celtic majority remained within a clan system until the seventeenth century, with cattle as the main measure of wealth (J. C. Beckett, *A Short History of Ireland* [New York: Harper & Row, 1952], p. 133; Stephen Gwynn, *The*

*Famous Cities of Ireland* [Dublin: Maunsel & Co., 1915], p. 3).

10. William Reeves, "On the Townland Distribution of Ireland," (Paper read before the Royal Irish Academy, 22 April 1861), Joly Collection, National Academy of Ireland, p. 8. The Gaelic term for a collection of houses or a village is *clachan*. The disparity between English and Irish reality and usage is explained in E. Estyn Evans, *Irish Heritage* (Dundalk: Dundalgen Press, 1963), pp. 47–48. Irish urban figures are given in Edward Wakefield, *An Account of Ireland: Statistical and Political,* 2 vols. (London: Longmans, Hurst, Rees, Orme & Brown, 1812), 2:684–700; and Gwynn, *Famous Cities of Ireland,* p. 39.

11. Constance Maxwell, *Country and Town in Ireland under the Georges* (Dundalk: Dundalgen Press, 1949), pp. 22–74; and Maureen Wall, "The Catholics of the Towns and the Quarterage Dispute in Eighteenth Century Ireland," *Irish Historical Studies* 8 (1952–53):91–114.

12. T. W. Freeman, *Pre-famine Ireland: A Study in Historical Geography* (Manchester: Manchester University Press, 1957), p. 25.

13. R. Montgomery-Martin, *Ireland before and after the Union* (London: Nichols & Co., 1848), unnumbered table, "A Statistical View of Ireland."

14. R. B. McDowell, "Ireland on the Eve of the Great Famine," in Edwards and Williams, *Great Famine,* p. 27.

15. Halévy, *England in 1815,* p. 409.

16. Maurice Craig, *Dublin, 1660–1860* (New York: Coward-McCann, n.d.), pp. 80–93.

17. *Times* (London), August 1845, cited in E. R. R. Green, "Agriculture," p. 113. The haphazard location of Irish towns is indicated in the case of Charlestown, County Mayo, founded in famine times as a result of a landlord's whim (John Healy, *The Death of an Irish Town* [Cork: Mercier Press, 1968]).

18. John J. Clarke, *A History of Local Government in the United Kingdom* (London: Herbert Jenkins, 1955), p. 277; and J. C. Beckett, *The Making of Modern Ireland* (New York: Alfred A. Knopf, 1966), p. 322; F. S. L. Lyons, *Ireland since the Famine* (London: Weidenfeld & Nicolson, 1971), p. 63.

19. Kenneth Connell, *Irish Peasant Society* (Oxford: Clarendon Press, 1968), p. 135; Woodham-Smith, *Great Hunger,* p. 376; Adams, *Ireland and the Irish Emigration,* p. 238; Handlin, *Boston's*

*Immigrants* (New York: Atheneum, 1969), p. 55.

20. There was only limited government-assisted emigration. The commissioners of the Treasury decided in 1847 that "having regard to the probable demands on that fund of a more pressing nature, my Lords do not feel that they should be justified in authorizing any expenditure for this purpose at the present time" (Collison-Black, *Economic Thought and the Irish Question*, p. 234). See also "State Aided Emigration Schemes, c. 1850," *Analecta Hibernica*, no. 22 (Dublin: Stationery Office, Irish Manuscripts Commission, 1960), pp. 329–85. The Atlantic traffic is covered in Edwin C. Guillet, *The Great Migration* (Toronto: University of Toronto Press, 1963), p. 64; and Terry Coleman, *Passage to America* (London: Hutchinson, 1972), pp. 1–40. Oliver MacDonough, *A Pattern of Government Growth* (London: MacGibbon & Kee, 1961), p. 29; Michael Dillon, Jr., "Irish Emigration, 1840–1855" (Ph.D. diss., University of California, 1940), p. 388. For further emigration statistics, see Adams, *Ireland and the Irish Emigration;* Handlin, *Boston's Immigrants;* Woodham-Smith, *Great Hunger;* and Hansen, *Immigrant in American History.*

21. Geoffrey G. Williamson, "Ante-bellum Urbanization in the American Northeast," *Journal of Economic History* 25, no. 4 (October 1965):598. Stuart Blumin, "Mobility and Change in Antebellum Philadelphia," in Stephan Thernstrom and Richard Sennet, eds., *Nineteenth Century Cities: Essays in the New Urban History* (New Haven, Conn.: Yale University Press, 1969), p. 208, n. 19; Simon Kuznets and Ernest Tubin, *Immigration and the Foreign Born* (New York: National Bureau of Economic Research, 1954), p. 45; Sam Bass Warner, *Private City*, pp. 49–62.

22. J. B. De Bow, *A Statistical View of the United States: Being a Compendium of the Seventh Census* (Washington, D.C.: Government Printing Office, 1866), p. lvii, gives figures for Irish-born. For immigration totals see William J. Bromwell, *History of Immigration to the United States* (New York: Redfield, 1856), pp. 121, 129, 133, 137, 141 and 145.

23. Bromwell, *Immigration to the United States*, App. A.

24. *Transactions of the Central Relief Committee of the Society of Friends* (Dublin: Hodges & Smith, 1852), pp. 476–77.

25. Arnold Schrier, *Ireland and the American Emigration* (Minneapolis: University of Minnesota, 1958), pp. 20, 33.

26. Louis Sullivan, "A People Gone Astray," in Oscar Handlin, ed., *Children of the Uprooted* (New York: George Braziller, 1966), p. 49.

27. R. A. Smith, *Philadelphia as It Is in 1852* (Philadelphia: Lindsay & Blakiston, 1852), p. 18.

28. Ibid., p. 18; De Bow, *Statistical View of the United States,* p. 339; and Joseph C. Kennedy, *Population of the United States in 1860* (Washington, D.C.: Government Printing Office, 1864), pp. 410–11.

29. This topographical and industrial description of the city is based upon R. A. Smith, *Philadelphia as It Is in 1852;* Edwin T. Freedley, *Philadelphia and Its Manufactures* (Philadelphia: Edward Young, 1859), pp. 15–43; Edgar Martin, *The Standard of Living in 1860* (Chicago: University of Chicago Press, 1942); David Van Tassel, ed., *Science and Society in the United States* (Homewood, Ill.: Dorsey Press, 1966), pp. 42–57; Sam Bass Warner, "Innovation and Industrialization in Philadelphia, 1800–1850," in Handlin and Burchard, *Historian and the City,* pp. 65–68; Robert B. Thomas, "A Study of Industry in the Falls of the Schuylkill-Manayunk Area from the Colonial Era to the Civil War" (M.B.A. thesis, Temple University, 1960); James Weston Livingood, *The Philadelphia-Baltimore Trade Rivalry, 1780–1860* (Harrisburg: Pennsylvania Historical and Museum Commission, 1947).

30. Board of Health Reports (1848–60), Archives of the City of Philadelphia, RG 37.195 (microfilm), p. 13; H. Reid, *Sketches in North America* (London: Longmans, Green & Roberts, 1861), pp. 223–25.

31. Baltzell, *Philadelphia Gentlemen.*

32. *Philadelphia North American,* 2 January 1851; *Evening Bulletin,* 30 July 1859.

33. On the persistence of names in Irish localities see Edward Mac-Lysaght, *Irish Families: Their Names, Arms, and Origins* (Dublin: Hodges, Figgis & Co., 1957), pp. 36–37. For a map showing the heavy emigration from Ulster, see Adams, *Ireland and the Irish Emigration,* p. 158. See also Schrier, *Ireland and the American Emigration,* p. 4; Maldwyn Jones, *American Immigration* (Chicago: University of Chicago Press, 1966), pp. 128–29; Handlin, *Boston's Immigrants,* pp. 49–51; Michael Dillon, "Irish Emigration," p. 449.

34. Ray Allen Billington, *The Protestant Crusade* (Chicago: Quad-

rangle Books, 1964), pp. 220–37. See also *A Full and Complete Account of the Awful Riots in Philadelphia* (Philadelphia: John B. Perry, n.d.), Archives of the American Catholic Historical Society, Overbrook, Pa.; Baltzell, *Philadelphia Gentlemen*, p. 188; Sam Bass Warner, *Private City*, p. 234; George Stephenson, *A History of American Immigration* (Boston: Guin & Co., 1926), p. 112.

35. Max Berger, "The Irish Emigrant and American Nativism as Seen by British Visitors, 1836–1860," *Pennsylvania Magazine of History and Biography* 65, no. 2 (April 1946) :150.

36. *Evening Bulletin*, 15, 16 December 1858, and 4 December 1855; *Foreign Pauperism in Philadelphia: A Memorial to the Legislature of Pennsylvania* (Philadelphia: Craig's Cheap Printing, 1851), Archives of the American Catholic Historical Society, Overbrook, Pa.

37. Earl Shinn [Edward Strahan], ed., *A Century After: Picturesque Glimpses of Philadelphia* (Philadelphia: Allen, Lane & Scott, 1875), p. 188. Services to German immigrants were praised in the *Public Ledger*, 17 January 1851. An examination of the Record of House Relief of the House of Industry (Urban Archives, Paley Library, Temple University, Philadelphia, Pa.) shows that needy persons were often referred to Scotch, Welsh, and English immigrant-aid groups, but the Irish, the largest group of clients, were given no such recommendation. This may have been because the House of Industry was not a Roman Catholic institution and Irish Catholic organizations had no dealings with it.

38. Henry C. Lea [Rufus K. Shapley], *Solid for Mulhooly* (New York: C. W. Carleton & Co., 1881); Ellis Paxson Oberholtzer, *History of the United States since the Civil War*, 5 vols. (New York: Macmillan Co., 1917–37), 5:732; Handlin, *Boston's Immigrants*, p. 176.

39. Part of the record of this lengthy Irish organizational activity is contained in John H. Campbell, *A History of the Friendly Sons of St. Patrick and of the Hibernian Society for the Relief of Emigrants from Ireland* (Philadelphia: Hibernian Society, 1890). For the militia see the *Philadelphia North American*, 3 January 1851. The separatist tendencies were rooted in Ireland (see J. A. O'Gorman, "The Irish Ghetto Originated in Ireland," *Eire-Ireland* 3, no. 4 (1968) :147–50.

40. Stephen Byrne, *Irish Emigration to the United States* (New York: Arno Press, 1969), p. 12. A typical affirmation of this Irish

view is a speech defending immigrants given by Ignatius Donnelly on 4 July 1855 (Martin Ridge, *Ignatius Donnelly: Portrait of a Politician* [Chicago: University of Chicago Press, 1962], p. 11).

41. Schrier, *Ireland and the American Emigration*, p. 33.

42. Friedrich Engels, *The Condition of the Working Class in England* (London: George Allen & Unwin, 1892), p. 60.

43. George Kitson-Clark, *An Expanding Society* (Cambridge: Cambridge University Press, 1967), p. 8.

44. Schrier, *Ireland and the American Emigration,* table 1, p. 157.

45. George Kitson-Clark, *The Making of Victorian England* (Cambridge, Mass.: Harvard University Press, 1962), p. 240.

## Chapter 3

1. *The Works of William Carleton,* 3 vols. (New York: Peter Fenelon Collier, n.d.), 2:256. See also the description of housing in T. P. O'Neill, "Rural Life," in McDowell, *Social Life,* pp. 47–49.

2. Evans, *Irish Heritage,* p. 57. Although a house could be built of mud and thatch at little cost in Ireland, a landlord assessed rent on the house according to its size, doors, windows, hearth, and outbuildings. A man might pay £70–£100 to the landlord, while his family would have to exist on one-fourth that amount (Kevin Danaher, "Old House Types," *Journal of the Royal Society of Antiquaries in Ireland* 68, pt. 2 [December 1938] :237).

3. Evans, *Irish Heritage,* pp. 56–57. For persistence of this type of house, see plans in Conrad M. Arensberg and Solon T. Kimball, *Family and Community in Ireland* (Cambridge, Mass.: Harvard University Press, 1940), pp. 34, 132–33.

4. *Statistics of the United States in 1860 of the Eighth Census* (Washington, D.C.: Government Printing Office, 1866), p. lv.

5. E. R. R. Green, "Agriculture."

6. Quoted in Margaret Digby, *Horace Plunkett* (Oxford: Basil Blackwell, 1949), p. 109.

7. Carrothers, *Emigration from the British Isles,* p. 204.

8. Edgar W. Martin, *Standard of Living in 1860,* p. 110; Charles J. Cohen, *Rittenhouse Square: Past and Present* (Philadelphia: Privately printed, 1922); Freedley, *Philadelphia and Its Manufactures,* p. 72.

9. *Philadelphia North American,* 27 January 1851.

10. Ivan D. Steen, "Philadelphia in the 1850's as Described by British Travelers," *Pennsylvania History* 33, no. 1 (January 1966) : 37; Handlin, *Boston's Immigrants,* pp. 88–111.

11. Sam Bass Warner, *Private City,* pp. 123, 139. The figures showing Irish concentration are from 1860.

12. This figure was obtained by a court of Irish-born persons enumerated on the original census schedules (*Seventh Census of the United States* (National Archives of the United States, Microcopy no. 432, roll no. 809).

13. For the most heavily Irish wards, see Sam Bass Warner, *Private City,* table 12, p. 139. *McElroy's Philadelphia Directory* for 1860 listed one-fourth of the Bradys and one-third of the O'Donnells in center city, half the Devlins in Kensington, half the Gallaghers in the Schuylkill district, and one-third of the Reillys in Southwark.

14. Tax Assessor Ledger, Moyamensing, First Ward (1849–51), Archives of the City of Philadelphia, RG. 214.5. This ledger contains listings by street for 450 properties, a 10 percent sample of which yielded the conclusions above.

15. *Catholic Herald and Visitor,* 13 March 1858.

16. Board of Health Report (1849), Archives of the City of Philadelphia, RG 37.195, microfilm, p. 13.

17. Tax Assessors Ledger, Moyamensing, First Ward (1849–51), Archives of the City of Philadelphia, RG 214.5. Property owners are listed by street on unnumbered pages.

18. Tax Assessors Ledger, Moyamensing, Fifth Ward (1849–51), pp. 12, 13, 24, 25, 33, 41. Of the 400 entries in this ledger, a sample of 78 was chosen for analysis.

19. County Tax Assessment Ledger, Kensington, First and Second Wards (1853–54), Archives of the City of Philadelphia. Property owners are listed by street. On the east side of Second Street only one of the twenty-one owners was Irish by surname, and ten of the thirty-nine tenants (pp. 88–89); on Front Street below Franklin Street, six of the thirteen owners were Irish (pp. 175–87).

20. George B. Foster, "Philadelphia in Slices," *Pennsylvania Magazine of History and Biography* 43, no. 1 (January 1969) :23–72.

21. *Philadelphia Inquirer,* 9 February 1863.

22. *Evening Star,* 18 September 1867; and *Annual Report of the*

*Society for the Employment and Instruction of the Poor, 1850–51* (Philadelphia: Merrihew & Thompson, n.d.), p. 6.

23. George Lippard, *The Quaker City* (Philadelphia: Published by the author, 1845), p. 341.

24. For municipal ordinances concerning pauper immigrants, see Frank B. Brightly, *A Digest of the Laws and Ordinances of the City of Philadelphia* (Philadelphia: Kay & Brother, 1887), pp. 456–58. For an account of early poor-relief work, see O. A. Pendleton, "Poor Relief in Philadelphia, 1790–1840," *Pennsylvania Magazine of History and Biography* 70, no. 2 (April 1946) :161–72.

25. R. A. Smith, *Philadelphia as It Is in 1852*, pp. 157–83, 249–77.

26. *Annual Report of the American Emigrants Friend Society for 1852* (Philadelphia: Mercantile Herald Printer, 1852). The report for 1848 gives the percentage of Irish served. These reports are in the collection of the Historical Society of Pennsylvania, Harrisburg, Pa.

27. For references to living conditions, see *Annual Reports of the Philadelphia Society for the Employment and Instruction of the Poor* (Philadelphia: Merrihew & Thompson, n.d.), Report for 1850–51, p. 6, Pennsylvania Library, Harrisburg, Pa.

28. Ibid., Report for 1854–55, p. 6.

29. Ibid.

30. Ibid.

31. Record of House Relief of the House of Industry, Urban Archives, Paley Library, Temple University, Philadelphia, Pa.

32. *Philadelphia North American*, 17 January 1853.

33. Charles Lawrence, *History of the Philadelphia Almshouses and Hospitals* (Philadelphia: Published by the superintendent, 1905), pp. 154–55.

34. Record of Property Deposited, Blockley Almshouse, in Records of the Guardians of the Poor, entries for 1848–53, Archives of the City of Philadelphia.

35. *Evening Bulletin*, 16 September 1859; ibid., editorial, 29 December 1855; ibid., editorial, 5 January 1858.

36. *Evening Bulletin*, case of Catherine Mulligan and a man named Casey, 22, 24 May 1858.

37. *Catholic Herald and Visitor*, 23 February 1856.

38. Ibid., speech by Rev. N. O'Brien, 27 September 1856.

39. Report of the Sanitary Committee of the Board of Health of

Philadelphia on the Subject of the Asiatic Cholera (1848), microfilm, RG 37.195, Archives of the City of Philadelphia.

40. Ibid., p. 44.

41. Board of Health Reports, 1848–60, p. 13, microfilm, Archives of the City of Philadelphia.

42. Statistics of Cholera with the Sanitary Measures Adopted by the Board of Health (1849), p. 43, microfilm, Archives of the City of Philadelphia.

43. *Evening Bulletin,* 7 January 1858.

44. Charles E. Rosenberg, *The Cholera Years* (Chicago: University of Chicago Press, 1962), pp. 121, 136.

45. Cited in *Catholic World,* vol. 6, no. 36 (March 1868), in a review of Maguire's book.

46. *Report of the Committee on Vice and Immorality of the Senate of Pennsylvania in Relation to the Manufacture and Sale of Spirituous Liquors* (Harrisburg, Pa.: A. B. Hamilton, 1855), p. 5.

47. Adams, *Ireland and the Irish Emigration,* p. 346.

48. *Philadelphia Inquirer,* case of Edward Flannery, 16 December 1860. See also U.S., Congress, House, Committee on Foreign Affairs, *Foreign Criminals and Paupers,* 67th Cong., 2d sess., 18 August 1856, H. Rept. 359, p. 9.

49. Sanitary Meteorological and Mortuary Report of the Philadelphia County Medical Society for 1855, p. 32, RG 762, Archives of the City of Philadelphia. Comparative death rates over the period 1871–1904 show a slight advantage for Philadelphia over Boston and New York, although the Irish had the highest rate of four major ethnic groups (F. L. Hoffman, "The General Death Rate of Large American Cities," *Quarterly Journal of the American Statistical Association,* n.s., no. 73 [March 1906], pp. 1–75). See also J. B. De Bow, *Mortality Statistics of the Seventh Census of the United States* (Washington, D.C.: A. O. P. Nicholson, 1855), p. 235. Percentages of the Irish in the three cities were obtained from De Bow, *The Seventh Census of the United States,* p. 399. For a local comparison of rates for 1855, also favoring Philadelphia, see the *Evening Bulletin* (Philadelphia), 5 January 1856.

50. Robert H. Wiebe, *The Search for Order, 1877–1920* (New York: Hill & Wang, 1967), p. 3.

51. Deed Book, TH 100, pp. 148, 378, 396, 471, 518, Archives of

the City of Philadelphia, shows purchases in low-density neighborhoods by Irishmen.

52. Freedley, *Philadelphia and Its Manufactures*, p. 72; John M. Murtagh, "The Philadelphia Row House," *Journal of the Society of Architectural Historians* 16 (1957) :8–13; Kenneth Ames, "Robert Mills and the Philadelphia Row House," *Journal of the Society of Architectural Historians* 27, no. 2 (May 1968) :140–46; C. Bernard, "A Hundred Thousand Homes and How They Were Paid For," *Scribner's Monthly* 11 (1875) :477–87; and A. B. Burk, "Philadelphia and Its Building Societies," *American Journal of Social Sciences* 15 (1882) :121–34. The *Philadelphia Inquirer*, 17 January 1865, had advertisements for $275 houses in Kensington.

53. *Encyclopaedia Britannica*, 11th American edition, 1943, 3:932, 16:377, 17:704. Actually, Boston proper consisted of about 1,200 square acres in 1863, some 336 having been added to the city by land fill. See George F. Weston, *Boston Ways* (Boston: Beacon Press, 1957), p. 15.

54. *North American*, 16 January 1851.

55. J. H. Perkins, *Thirty-third Annual Report of the Philadelphia Board of Trade* (Philadelphia: J. B. Chandler, 1865), p. 86.

56. Lorin Blodgett, "Building Systems of the Great Cities" (Paper read to the Philadelphia Social Science Association, 5 April 1877), Historical Society of Pennsylvania, Philadelphia, Pa.

57. Ibid., p. 13.

58. *Philadelphia Inquirer*, 1 January 1861, 2 January 1864.

59. Emerson D. Fite, *Social and Industrial Conditions in the North during the Civil War* (New York: Peter Smith, 1930), p. 216.

60. *Philadelphia North American*, 14 January 1864, 9 March 1864.

61. Frederic W. Speirs, *The Street Railway Systems of Philadelphia* (Baltimore: Johns Hopkins University Press, 1897), p. 16.

62. *Philadelphia Press*, 16 March 1864.

63. Lorin Blodgett, "Census of Industrial Employment, Wages, and Social Conditions" (Paper read before the Philadelphia Social Science Association, 25 April 1872), Historical Society of Pennsylvania, Philadelphia, Pa.; Edgar W. Martin, *Standard of Living in 1860*, p. 400.

64. Edward Young, *Special Report on Immigration* (Washington, D.C.: Government Printing Office, 1872).

65. Stephan Thernstrom, *Poverty and Progress: Social Mobility in a Nineteenth Century City* (New York: Atheneum, 1969), p. 29; Handlin, *Boston's Immigrants,* p. 109.

66. Cited in Schrier, *Ireland and the American Emigration,* p. 177.

67. *Evening Bulletin,* 14 September 1856.

68. *Public Ledger,* 14 January 1851.

69. Will of Bernard McCredy, bk. 32, no. 353 (1855), Office of the Register of Wills, Philadelphia, Pa. McCredy owned lands in Delaware County, Pa.

70. Will of Matthew McBride, bk. 32, no. 304 (1854); Will of James Murphy, bk. 25, no. 146 (1850); Will of Terence Devitt, bk. 32 no. 233 (1854); Will of Thomas Kiernan, bk. 32, no. 205 (1855); Will of Edward Gormley, bk. 32, no. 234 (1854), Office of the Register of Wills, Philadelphia, Pa. Other wills show that such bequests were not unusual.

71. County Tax Assessment Ledger, First Ward, Kensington (1853–54), pp. 156, 177.

72. Deed Book, TH 100 (1853), Archives of the City of Philadelphia. References are to pages 122 (Henry Williams to John McGinty); 128 (Jacob Dunton to Catherine Cline); 57, 124, 128, 518, 549. Other pages show numerous Irish names.

73. John McDermott is listed in *McElroy's Philadelphia Directory* in 1849, 1850, 1851, and 1852. His later moves are noted in family papers of John A. McDermott, staff member of the Community Renewal Society, Chicago, Ill.

74. August Laugel, *The United States during the Civil War* (London: H. Balliere, 1866), pp. 78–79.

75. Bernard, "Hundred Thousand Homes," p. 484.

76. Ibid.; and Blodgett, "Building Systems of the Great Cities," p. 10. See also "Dwellings for Work People of Small Incomes in Philadelphia," *Journal of Social Science and Transactions of the American Social Science Association* 4 (1871) :181.

77. Constitution of the Aramingo Building Association of the District of Richmond (1848), Collection of the Historical Society of Pennsylvania; Constitution and By-laws of the Flanagan Building Association (1855), American Catholic Historical Society, St. Charles Seminary, Overbrook, Pa.

78. *Constitution and By-Laws of the Union Land and Homestead Association* (Philadelphia: Duross, Printer, 1854); *Articles of Asso-*

*ciation of the Broad Street Homestead Association* (Philadelphia: C. Harris, 1849). These documents are in the collection of the Historical Society of Pennsylvania. For details of Bernard Rafferty, see Campbell, *Friendly Sons of St. Patrick,* p. 507.

79. Freedley, *Philadelphia and Its Manufactures,* pp. 59–60, 189.

80. In drawing this sample, the following procedure was followed: prominent professional men and businessmen whose names appeared in Campbell, *Friendly Sons of St. Patrick,* and in other sources were chosen; their names and occupations were then checked in *McElroy's Philadelphia Directory, 1860* (Philadelphia: J. and E. C. Biddle, 1860), and their addresses determined; finally, these addresses were aligned with the locations designated by Norman Johnston in his article "The Caste and Class of the Urban Form of Historic Philadelphia," *Journal of the American Institute of Planners* 32, no. 4 (November 1966):344–49. Although Johnston's classifications pertain specifically to an earlier period, they were still largely valid for 1860.

81. There is not sufficient evidence from Philadelphia property records to verify the existence of a "zone of emergence" such as that detailed by Miller for a later period for Cincinnati (Zane Miller, *Boss Cox's Cincinnati* [New York: Oxford University Press, 1968], pp. 26–30). For an example of a twentieth-century concentration of Irish in an area of improved housing, see Joseph P. Barrett, "The Life and Death of an Irish Neighborhood," *Philadelphia Magazine* 61, no. 3 (March 1970):85–87, 128–36.

# Chapter 4

1. C. E. Black, *The Dynamics of Modernization* (New York: Harper & Row, 1966), p. 24; T. S. Ashton, *The Industrial Revolution, 1760–1830* (New York: Oxford University Press, 1964), p. 3.

2. E. R. R. Green, "Industrial Decline in the Nineteenth Century," in L. M. Cullen, ed., *The Formation of the Irish Economy* (Cork: Mercier Press, 1968), pp. 89–100.

3. McHugh, "Famine in Irish Oral Tradition," p. 434. See also Kevin Danaher, *Irish Country People* (Cork: Mercier Press, 1966), pp. 106–10.

4. Thomas Mooney, *Nine Years in America* (Dublin: James

McGlashen, 1850), cited in John R. Commons et al., eds., *A Documentary History of American Industrial Society,* 10 vols. (Cleveland: Arthur H. Clark Co., 1910), 7:71–79.

5. The *Irishman* (Dublin), 12 January 1850, Files of Trinity College Library, Dublin.

6. The *Constitution; or, Cork Examiner,* 21 May 1867, Trinity Colleg Library, Dublin.

7. *Statistics of the United States in 1860 of the Eighth Census* (Washington, D.C.: Government Printing Office, 1866), p. iv.

8. This percentage was calculated from table entitled "Occupations of Passengers Arriving in the United States from Foreign Countries," in Joseph C. G. Kennedy, *Preliminary Report on the Eighth Census* (Washington, D.C.: Government Printing Office, 1862), pp. 16–17.

9. Handlin, *Boston's Immigrants,* p. 57.

10. De Bow, *Seventh Census of the United States, 1850,* table 10, p. 193.

11. R. A. Smith, *Philadelphia as It Is in 1852,* p. 15; Freedley, *Philadelphia and Its Manufactures,* p. 65.

12. De Bow, *Statistical View of the United States,* p. 301; and J. L. Bishop, *A History of American Manufactures from 1608 to 1860,* 3 vols. (Philadelphia: Edward Young, 1868), 2:17.

13. Ashton, *Industrial Revolution,* pp. 24–30.

14. Bishop, *History of American Manufactures,* 2:14–17.

15. Ibid., 3:453.

16. Clark Kerr et al., eds., *Industrialism and Industrial Man* (New York: Oxford University Press, 1964), pp. 28, 169.

17. Sam Bass Warner, *Private City,* p. 71.

18. George R. Taylor, "The National Economy before and after the Civil War," in David T. Gilchrist and W. D. Lewis, eds., *Economic Change in the Civil War Era* (Greenville, Del.: Eleutherian Mills-Hagley Foundation, 1965), p. 21.

19. Bishop, *History of American Manufactures,* 2:16.

20. George R. Taylor, "National Economy," p. 17.

21. *Evening Bulletin,* 17 March 1851.

22. *Documents Relating to the Manufacture of Iron in Pennsylvania, Published in Behalf of the Convention of Iron Masters* (Philadelphia: General Committee, 1850), p. 15.

23. This was part of a general trend. See Herbert Heaton, "Eco-

nomic Change and Growth," in J. P. T. Bury, ed., *The New Cambridge Modern History,* vol. 10, *The Zenith of European Power* (Cambridge: Cambridge University Press, 1964), pp. 28–29.

24. Sam Bass Warner, *Private City,* p. 70.

25. William B. Wilson, *History of the Pennsylvania Railroad Company,* 2 vols. (Philadelphia: Henry T. Coates Co., 1895), 1:107, 124.

26. Edward C. Kirkland, *Men, Cities, and Transportation* (Cambridge, Mass.: Harvard University Press, 1948), pp. 398–99.

27. Hubertis Cummings, "Pennsylvania's Network of Canal Ports," *Pennsylvania History* 21, no. 3 (July 1954):260–273 (see map [p. 262] for an indication of the size of the canal network).

28. George R. Taylor, *The Transportation Revolution, 1815–1860* (New York: Harper & Row, 1951), p. 292.

29. Earl F. Niehaus, *The Irish in New Orleans, 1800–1860* (Baton Rouge: Louisiana State University Press, 1965), p. 45.

30. Quoted in Irvin G. Wyllie, *The Self-made Man in America: The Myth of Rags to Riches* (New Brunswick, N.J.: Rutgers University Press, 1954), p. 42.

31. Record Group 17, Board of Canal Commissioners, Delware Division, Records of the Land Office, Box 18, 1850, Archives of the Commonwealth of Pennsylvania, Harrisburg, Pa. The names of the laborers are found on Supervisors Check Roles, vouchers 8, 9, 11, 15, and 17.

32. George R. Taylor, *Transportation Revolution,* pp. 289–90.

33. Terry Coleman, *The Railway Navvies* (London: Hutchinson of London, 1965), pp. 40, 50.

34. *Report of the Delegation of the Philadelphia Emigrant Society to Enquire into the Nature and Operation of Emigration Laws in the State of New York* (Philadelphia: Merrihew & Thompson, 1854), p. 7, Historical Society of Pennsylvania, Philadelphia, Pa.

35. Henry Thoreau, conscious of the terrible toll exacted by the exhaustion, accidents, disease, and substandard living conditions associated with railroad building, scathingly criticized the system under which the building proceeded. Every tie supporting the rails represented the body of a man, he wrote. His heart went out to the Irish diggers who suffered through the lengthening miles of construction (Irving H. Bartlett, *The American Mind in the Mid-nineteenth Century* [New York: Thomas Y. Crowell Co., 1967], p. 45).

36. Kirkland, *Men, Cities, and Transportation,* pp. 398–99.

37. Wilson, *Pennsylvania Railroad Company,* 2:185.

38. *Catholic Instructor,* 8 March 1851, American Catholic Historical Society, St. Charles Seminary, Philadelphia, Pa.

39. Walter Coleman, *The Molly Maguire Riots* (Richmond, Va.: Garrett & Massic, 1936), p. 20.

40. Freedley, *Philadelphia and Its Manufactures,* pp. 253–62. See also Adams, *Ireland and the Irish Emigration,* p. 86.

41. Sam Bass Warner, *Private City,* p. 71.

42. Freedley, *Philadelphia and Its Manufactures,* p. 71.

43. Howard Gitelman, "The Waltham System and the Coming of the Irish," *Labor History* 8, no. 3 (Fall 1967) :227–33.

44. Sam Bass Warner, *Private City,* p. 70; Freedley, *Philadelphia and Its Manufactures,* pp. 250–56; and Norman Ware, *The Industrial Worker, 1840–1860* (Chicago: Quadrangle Books, 1964), pp. 107–24.

45. Liam O'Flaherty, *Famine* (New York: Literary Guild, 1937), p. 307; Ware, *Industrial Worker,* pp. 62–63.

46. Cited in Schrier, *Ireland and the American Emigration,* p. 29.

47. Charles E. Zaretz, *The Amalgamated Clothing Workers of America* (New York: Ancon Publishing Co., 1934), pp. 18–19.

48. Sam Bass Warner, *Private City,* pp. 68–69.

49. Freedley, *Philadelphia and Its Manufactures,* p. 342.

50. *One Hundred Years of Leadership: The Story of the Stanley G. Flagg Company* (Philadelphia: Stanley G. Flagg Co., 1954), pp. 13–16.

51. R. A. Smith, *Philadelphia as It Is in 1852,* pp. 91, 360.

52. Bishop, *American Manufactures,* pp. 35–36.

53. Freedley, *Philadelphia and Its Manufactures,* pp. 454–57.

54. Ware, *Industrial Worker,* p. xviii; and Anne Bezanson, "Some Historical Aspects of Labor Turnover," Arthur H. Cole et al., eds., *Facts and Factors in Economic History* (Cambridge, Mass.: Harvard University Press, 1932), pp. 692–708.

55. Ware, *Industrial Worker,* p. 148.

56. Lorin Blodgett, "The Census of Industrial Employment and Wages and Social Conditions in Philadelphia in 1870" (Paper read to the Philadelphia Social Science Association, 25 April 1872), p. 17, Historical Society of Pennsylvania, Philadelphia, Pa.

57. See the typical advertisements for labor: "Superior Protestant Seamstress," "Good cooks. Protestant and Catholic" (*Philadelphia Inquirer,* 2 July 1862). For additional evidence of racial competition and hostility, see the *Advocate,* 21 April 1882; and the *Philadelphia Inquirer,* 11 October 1871.

58. Arthur M. Schlesinger, Jr., *The Age of Jackson* (New York: New American Library, 1949), p. 166.

59. Charlotte Erickson, *American Industry and the European Immigrant, 1860–1885* (Cambridge, Mass.: Harvard University Press, 1957), p. 7.

60. The 1857 depression was severe enough to prompt government endorsement of public work for relief of unemployment, unusual in a free-enterprise age (see Benjamin J. Klebaner, "Poor Relief and Public Works during the Depression of 1857," *Historian* 22, no. 3 [May 1960]:264–79). The *Evening Bulletin,* 31 December 1857, notes the Irish distress in depression conditions. A glimpse into the need of the working-class families whose wage earners went off to war may be had by considering the numbers of them receiving relief during the years 1861–65: 1861—11,012; 1862—10,610; 1863—9,130; 1864—8,981; 1865—8,974 (*Report of the Commission for the Relief of the Families of Philadelphia Volunteers* (Philadelphia: E. C. Markley & Son, 1865), p. 4, Collection of the Historical Society of Pennsylvania, Philadelphia, Pa.

61. An Irish immigrant in Philadelphia wrote of the inflation of 1866, noting the triple rise in clothing costs (Erickson, *American Industry and the European Immigrant,* p. 23).

62. The designation "laborer," as used in the census, includes various unskilled jobs. These percentages were obtained from 20 percent samples drawn from the seventh, eighth and ninth censuses (National Archives of the United States, micro copy no. 432, roll no. 809 [1850]; micro copy no. 653, roll no. 1153 [1860]; and micro copy 593, roll no. 1389 [1870]). For details of these and the following computations see Dennis Clark, "The Adjustment of Irish Immigrants to Urban Life: The Philadelphia Experience, 1840–1870" (Ph.D. diss., Temple University, 1970).

63. Record of House Relief, Philadelphia House of Industry, 1861–1870, Urban Archives of Temple University, Philadelphia, Pa. Only a minority of the men in the sample gave Philadelphia as their

residence, which confirms Thernstrom's statement that mobility was a characteristic of the laboring class (Thernstrom, *Poverty and Progress,* p. 17).

64. See Dennis Clark, "Adjustment of Irish Immigrants," app. B.

65. Record of House Relief, Philadelphia House of Industry, 1861–1870.

66. For a discussion of the dispersion of the labor force in the city see Sam Bass Warner, *Private City,* p. 71.

67. For industry locations see Freedley, *Philadelphia and Its Manufactures,* pp. 199–200, 246, 286–89.

68. Ibid., p. 221. The transit fare remained at five cents a ride until 1864, when it rose to six cents (Speirs, *Street Railway System of Philadelphia,* p. 49.

69. Data on street railways are given in Scharf and Westcott, *History of Philadelphia,* 3:2202–2203; Thomas Roberts, "A History and Analysis of Labor-Management Relations in the Philadelphia Transit Industry" (Ph.D. diss., University of Pennsylvania, 1959), p. 2; Speirs, *Street Railway System of Philadelphia,* pp. 10–49; and W. B. Zieber, *The Chestnut and Walnut Street Railway* (Philadelphia: W. B. Zieber, 1858).

70. Speirs, *Street Railway System of Philadelphia,* pp. 17, 49.

71. John L. Commons, *History of Labour in the United States* (New York: Macmillan Co., 1918), 1:564.

72. *Philadelphia North American,* 6 February 1851, 14 April 1853.

73. Edgar B. Cales, "The Organization of Labor in Philadelphia, 1850–1870" (Ph.D. Diss., University of Pennsylvania, 1940), pp. 15, 17, 25, 38.

74. *Public Ledger,* 13 July 1870.

75. Cales, "Organization of Labor in Philadelphia," p. 83.

76. Available in reprint edition (New York: Arno Press, 1969); for names listed, see pages 114–50.

77. The map used to locate the addresses was published by A. McElroy in 1849 and is in the map collection of Paley Library, Temple University. The second listing referred to is in Joseph Jackson, *Market Street: Philadelphia* (Philadelphia: Joseph Jackson, 1918), p. 210. Jackson lists 168 mid-city businesses on numbered streets from Tenth to Seventeenth.

78. For biographical notes on many of the 1,800 members of the

Friendly Sons of Saint Patrick whose names appear in this volume, see Campbell, *Friendly Sons of St. Patrick,* pp. 338–500.

79. *A. McElroy's Philadelphia City Directory* (Philadelphia: E. & J. Biddle, 1857, 1867), Paley Library, Temple University, Philadelphia, Pa. Of a sample composed of 38,000 of the names listed in the 1857 directory, 10 percent were recognizably Irish. The directory for 1857 was the first in which businesses were listed separately.

80. For Kelly, see Campbell, *Friendly Sons of St. Patrick,* pp. 442–43; for Fitzgerald, see Charles Morris, *Makers of Philadelphia* (Philadelphia: Hamersley Co., 1894), p. 122.

81. *Evening Bulletin,* advertisement, 2 August 1859. For tradesmen's wages see Byrne, *Irish Emigration,* p. 35. According to Byrne, mechanics made $5–$6 a day in the 1850s, but lower rates are given by Thomas Mooney in Commons et al., *A Documentary History of American Industrial Society,* 7:71. Contractors' bills are recorded in Board of Commissioners Minutes, Richmond District, 1852–54, Record Group 219.1, Archives of the City of Philadelphia. The *Philadelphia Inquirer,* 13 January 1875, lists advertisements for domestics through the Employment House, 802 Locust Street. The biographies of members of the Friendly Sons of Saint Patrick list some of these connections.

82. Bezanson, "Historical Aspects of Labor Turnover," p. 705.

83. This is attested to by such business histories as *The History of the Baldwin Locomotive Works* (Philadelphia: Edgell Co., 1907), p. 57; and Thomas C. Cochran and William Mills, *The Age of Enterprise* (New York: Harper & Row, 1942), p. 113. For scholarly works, see Gilchrist and Lewis, *Civil War Era,* p. 103; Scharf and Westcott, *History of Philadelphia,* 3:2239.

84. R. A. Smith, *Philadelphia as It Is in 1852;* and Freedley, *Philadelphia and Its Manufactures.*

85. Handlin, *Boston's Immigrants,* pp. 54–55, 57.

86. Maldwyn Jones, *American Immigration,* p. 130; Handlin, *Boston's Immigrants,* p. 57.

87. Handlin, *Boston's Immigrants,* pp. 64, 65, 319n.

88. Thernstrom, *Poverty and Progress,* p. 85; idem, "Working Class Mobility in Industrial America," Society for the Study of Labor History, Bulletin no. 17 (Autumn 1968), pp. 24–25.

89. De Bow, *Statistical View of the United States*, p. 192; and Handlin, *Boston's Immigrants*, pp. 12, 89, 91, 93, and 214. De Bow, *Mortality Statistics*, p. 41, gives figures on the foreign-born in major cities.

90. Handlin, *Boston's Immigrants*, p. 13.

91. This enumeration of manufacturing establishments is conservatively based on the tables for Philadelphia County in *The Sixth Census of the Inhabitants of the United States* (Washington, D.C.: Department of State, 1841), p. 153.

92. De Bow, *Statistical View of the United States*, p. 17.

93. Douglas C. North, *The Economic Growth of the United States, 1790–1860* (Englewood Cliffs, N.J.: Prentice-Hall, 1961), pp. 168–69.

94. Joseph C. G. Kennedy, *The Eighth Census, 1860* (Washington, D.C.: Government Printing Office, 1862), p. 117, gives the percentage increases in the populations of cities.


# Chapter 5

1. Examples of the simplicity of Irish rural life are provided in pejorative fashion in Gerald Fitzgibbon, *Ireland in 1868* (London: Longmans, Green, Reader & Dyer, 1868), pp. 150–54. The significance of literacy for urban learning and social discipline is noted in David Thomson, *Europe since Napoleon* (New York: Alfred A. Knopf, 1958), p. 339. The desire of the Irish to become literate in English is cited in Connell, *Irish Peasant Society*, p. 140.

2. For examples of immigrant impact, see Henry Nash Smith, ed., *Popular Culture and Industrialism, 1865–1890* (Garden City, N.Y.: Doubleday & Co., 1967); for the long-range impact, see John A. Garraty, *The New Commonwealth, 1877–1890* (New York: Harper & Row, 1968), pp. 203–204. The subcultures of immigrants are considered in Milton M. Gordon, *Assimilation in American Life: The Role of Race, Religion, and National Origin* (New York: Oxford University Press, 1964); and the immigrants are seen as a major factor in the development of American education in Frank Tracy Carlton, *Economic Influences upon Educational Progress in the United States,*

*1820-1850* (New York: Teacher College Press, Columbia University, 1965), pp. 144-45.

3. Angus MacIntyre, *The Liberator: Daniel O'Connell and the Irish Party, 1830-1847* (New York: Macmillan Co., 1965), pp. 28-29; Daniel Corkery, *The Fortunes of the Irish Language* (Cork: Mercier Press, 1968), pp. 105, 116-17; P. J. Dowling, *The Hedge Schools of Ireland* (Cork: Mercier Press, 1968), pp. 55-61.

4. Dowling, *Hedge Schools of Ireland*, p. 112; Seán de Fréine, *The Great Silence* (Dublin: Foilseacháin Náisiunta Teoranta, 1965), pp. 135-150; McDowell, "Eve of the Great Famine," p. 66.

5. De Bow, *Statistical View of the United States*, p. 148; Schrier, *Ireland and the American Emigration*, p. 22.

6. MacIntyre, *Liberator*, p. 29.

7. For an account of the scope of the National Schools see Thomas Wyse, "Elementary Education in Ireland," *American Journal of Education* 11 (1862):133-54; for an account of the daily schedule of the system see Francis Head, *A Fortnight in Ireland* (London: John Murray, 1852), pp. 30-40. See also Donald H. Akenson, *The Irish Education Experiment* (London: Routledge & Kegan Paul, 1969); Oliver MacDonough, *Ireland* (Englewood Cliffs, N.J.: Prentice-Hall, 1968), p. 23.

8. Marcus Bourke, *John O'Leary: A Study in Irish Separatism* (Tralee: Anvil Books, 1967), p. 7.

9. See autobiographical note on Thomas F. Tierney in Campbell, *Friendly Sons of St. Patrick*, p. 536. Educational conditions in Shercock, County Cavan, were described to the author by James McCann, master of the Shercock National School, Shercock, County Cavan, Ireland, verbally and in a letter (McCann to Clark, 28 November 1969).

10. Emmet Larkin, "Church and State in Ireland in the Nineteenth Century," *Church History* 31, no. 3 (September 1962):303; J. A. Murphy, "The Support of the Catholic Clergy in Ireland, 1750-1850," in *Historical Studies* (London: Bowes & Bowes, 1965), 5:103-21.

11. *Catholic Herald*, 20 February 1851.

12. Corkery, *Fortunes of the Irish Language*, pp. 118-19; for a discussion of the service orientation of the church see Emmet Larkin, "Economic Growth, Capital Investment, and the Roman Catholic

Church in Nineteenth Century Ireland," *American Historical Review* 72, no. 3 (April 1967) :852–75.

13. Scharf and Westcott, *History of Philadelphia*, 2 :1921–49; and Watson, *Annals of Philadelphia*, 3 :390.

14. Lannie and Duthorn, "Honor and Glory of God," p. 47; Carlton, *Economic Influences upon Educational Progress*, p. 84.

15. F. Butts and L. A. Cremin, *A History of Education in American Culture* (New York: Holt, Rinehart & Winston, 1953), p. 239.

16. John S. Brubacher, *A History of the Problems of Education* (New York: McGraw-Hill, 1966), p. 90; and Carlton, *Economic Influences upon Educational Progress*, p. 84.

17. Sam Bass Warner, *Private City*, p. 118; R. A. Smith, *Philadelphia as It Is in 1852*, pp. 136–37; John T. Custis, *The Public Schools of Philadelphia* (Philadelphia: Burke & McFetridge, 1897), p. 22; De Bow, *Statistical View of the United States*, pp. 147, 297; and *Evening Bulletin*, 15 February 1856.

18. The *Public Ledger*, 13 January 1851, quoted Governor Johnson of Pennsylvania as saying, "The school system, although still imperfect, is rapidly improving. . . . The education of the people is the great question of the age."

19. L. G. Walsh and Matthew Walsh, *History and Organization of Education in Pennsylvania* (Indiana, Pa.: Published by the authors, 1930), p. 169; Joseph P. Wickersham, *A History of Education in Pennsylvania* (Lancaster, Pa.: Inquirer Publishing Co., 1886), p. 63; R. H. Beck, *A Social History of Education* (Englewood Cliffs, N.J.: Prentice-Hall, 1965), pp. 88–89, 110.

20. For buildings and dates of construction see Frank D. Edmunds, *The Public School Buildings of the City of Philadelphia from 1853 to 1867* (Philadelphia: n.p., 1917).

21. *Pennsylvania School Journal* 2 (1853) :90.

22. Merle Curti, *The Social Ideas of American Educators* (New York: Charles Scribner's Sons, 1935), pp. 78–82; Maxine Greene, *The Public School and the Private Vision* (New York: Random House, 1965), p. 94; Ridge, *Ignatius Donnelly*, p. 5.

23. Butts and Cremin, *Education in American Culture*, p. 274. So strict were the teaching methods that some parents complained strongly of overwork of students (*Philadelphia Inquirer*, 20 November 1860, 13 December 1860).

24. These conclusions are based upon a review of textbooks in the

Pedagogical Library of the School District of Philadelphia, including: S. A. Mitchell, *Modern Geography* (Philadelphia: E. A. Butler
Co., 1864); L. B. Monroe, *Monroe Fifth Reader* (New York: L. B.
Monroe Co., 1871); R. E. Peterson, *Familiar Science* (Philadelphia:
Sower & Potts Co., 1851); Samuel Gummere, *Scholar's Progressive
and Etymological Spelling Book* (Philadelphia: Urich Hunt & Son,
1858); W. Smith, *Speller's Manual* (Philadelphia: J. W. Miller,
1852); Rembrandt Peale, *Graphics* (Philadelphia: E. C. & J. Biddle
Co., 1850); *French's Elementary Arithmetic* (New York: Harper
Bros., 1855).

25. Mitchell, *Modern Geography*, p. 243.

26. Butts and Cremin, *Education in American Culture*, p. 239;
Greene, *Public School and the Private Vision*, p. 140.

27. Lannie and Duthorn, "Honor and Glory of God," p. 97. See
also Mary Ann Meyers, "Philadelphia Catholics and the Public
Schools," *Records of the American Catholic Historical Society* 75,
no. 2 (June 1964) :103–23.

28. Brubacher, *Problems of Education*, p. 533.

29. Lannie and Duthorn, "Honor and Glory of God," p. 97. The
predominance of Protestant values and norms in the schools is traced
in Timothy Smith, "Protestant Schooling and American Nationality,
1800–1850," *Journal of American History* 53, no. 4 (March 1967):
679–95. See also Ray Allen Billington, *The Protestant Crusade* (Chicago: Quadrangle Books, 1938), p. 221.

30. These figures are taken from De Bow, Seventh Census of the
United States, pp. 62, 131, 203; *Philadelphia North American*, 17
January 1851; The Metropolitan Catholic Almanac (1850) (Balti-
more: L. Fielding, Jr., 1849); ibid. (1860) (Baltimore: John Mur-
phy, 1860), p. 167; and *Sadlier's Catholic Directory* (New York:
D. & J. Sadlier Co., 1870), pp. 127, 245. Important information on
early Catholic education in Philadelphia is given in Thomas J.
Donaghy, *Philadelphia's Finest: A History of Education in the Cath-
olic Archdiocese, 1692–1970* (Philadelphia: The American Catholic
Historical Society, 1972), pp. 32–122.

31. *Evening Bulletin,* 19 August 1859, noted Papal repression in
the Papal states; the *Philadelphia Inquirer,* 9 November 1860, gave
an example of religious qualifications for employment; the *Catholic
Herald* (Philadelphia), 30 January 1851, published anti-Catholic editorials; and Rev. Henry Mayo, a Protestant clergyman, wrote in 1859

that the only hope for Christian democracy was in the rural areas away from the immigrant influence (Anselm Strauss, *Images of the American City* [Glencoe, Ill.: Free Press, 1961], p. 146).

32. Carleton Beale, *Brass Knuckle Crusade* (New York: Hastings House Publishers, 1960), p. 44; *Evening Bulletin*, 19, 24 December 1855, 20 August 1859; James Dixon to his sister, 4 September 1855, in Schrier, *Ireland and the American Emigration*, p. 33; Timothy L. Smith, *Revivalism and Social Reform: American Protestantism on the Eve of the Civil War* (New York: Harper & Row, 1957), pp. 41, 165, 169.

33. F. E. T., ed., *The Kenrick-Frenaye Correspondence, 1830–1862* (Philadelphia: Wickersham Printing, 1920), p. 367, relates some of the problems of Bishop Francis Kenrick in recruiting priests. The full name of the author is not known.

34. William J. Boyle, *The Story of St. Michaels, 1834–1934* (Philadelphia: Jeffries & Manz, 1934), p. 8; *Philadelphia Inquirer*, 24 December 1860; *Memorial Book: Centenary of St. Stephen's Parish, 1843–1943*, p. 20; F. X. McGowan, *Historical Sketches of St. Augustine's Church* (Philadelphia: Augustinian Fathers, 1896), p. 84 (for list of pastors see appendix); *Souvenir Sketch of St. Patrick's Church, 1842–1892* (Philadelphia: Hardy & Mahony, 1892) (between 1843 and 1869 there were 1,800 marriages, and between 1843 and 1874 there were 3,758 baptisms, at Saint Patrick's).

35. For a chronological listing of parishes see Dennis Clark, "A Pattern of Urban Growth: Residential Development and Church Location in Philadelphia," *Records of the American Catholic Historical Society* 82, no. 3 (September 1971) :159–70.

36. *Philadelphia Press*, 18 March 1867.

37. Scharf and Westcott, *History of Philadelphia*, 2:1360. See also Daniel H. Mahony, *Historical Sketches of Catholic Churches and Institutions in Philadelphia* (Philadelphia: D. H. Mahony, 1895) (for chronology of parishes see appendix).

38. *Catholic Herald*, 6 January 1858; *The Philadelphia Theological Seminary* (Philadelphia: Catholic Standard & Times, 1917), pp. 117–18.

39. Sam Bass Warner, *Private City*, p. 118.

40. Handlin, *Boston's Immigrants*, pp. 168–69. In Philadelphia there were already three Catholic schools in 1808. By 1838 there were sixty-one churches in the Diocese of Philadelphia, but only

eighteen in the Boston Diocese (J. A. Burns, *The Catholic School System in the United States* [New York: Benziger Bros., 1908], pp. 256–60, 386). For Boston in the 1850s see *Metropolitan Catholic Almanac* 1850, 1860.

41. "Early Catholic Secondary Education in Philadelphia," *Records of the American Catholic Historical Society* 59, no. 3 (September 1948:158–89, and 70, no. 4 (December 1948):259–78. There were academies at Saint Augustine's and Saint Mary's parishes in the 1830s, and a number of such schools were set up in the 1850s. See also "Early Schools in Philadelphia," *Records of the American Catholic Historical Society* 22, no. 3 (September 1911):155.

42. M. H. Gowen, "The Sisters of Notre Dame de Namur: Philadelphia, 1856–1956," *Records of the American Catholic Historical Society* 68, nos. 1 and 2 (March–June 1957):32.

43. "Early Catholic Secondary Education," p. 172; F. X. Talbot, *Jesuit Education in Philadelphia* (Philadelphia: Saint Joseph's College, 1927), pp. 35–46. As early as 1847 Saint Philip's Church had in its basement what has been called Philadelphia's first "free school" (*Historical Sketch of St. Philip Neri Church, 1840–1940* [Philadelphia: Jeffries & Manz, 1940], p. 2).

44. *Souvenir Sketch of St. Patrick's Church*, p. 17; A. J. Ennis, *Old St. Augustine's Church in Philadelphia* (Philadelphia: Old St. Augustine's Church, 1965), p. 3; *St. Malachy's Souvenir Booklet* (Philadelphia: American Catholic Historical Society, n.d.), p. 5. The *Catholic Herald*, 19 January 1863, advertised a school run by Holy Child nuns but earlier had noted the Academy of the Assumption on Spring Garden Street (2 January 1858) and the Academy of the Visitation (2 January 1851).

45. Talbot, *Jesuit Education in Philadelphia*, p. 40.

46. "One Hundred Years in Philadelphia," *Records of the American Catholic Historical Society* 58, no. 1 (March 1947):1–21.

47. *Catholic Herald*, 2 January 1851. For other girls' academies see the *Catholic Instructor*, 19 August 1854 (Mrs. Holmes Seminary for Ladies), and *Evening Bulletin*, 11 August 1856 (Misses Casey and Beebe Young Ladies Day and Evening School). Textbooks from the parish schools in the Archives of the American Catholic Historical Society, St. Charles Borromeo Seminary, Philadelphia, are quite similar to those of public schools, except that catechism and Bible history are included (see S. Bartlett, *Principles of Grammar* [Al-

bany: Maunsell, 1849]; D. McKerney, *Ancient and Modern History* [Baltimore: John Murphy, 1871]; *Class Book of Nature* (New York: Hamersley, 1850]).

48. *Catholic Instructor,* 4 September 1852. The Jesuit school encountered financial difficulties that forced it to close in 1862 (Thomas J. Donaghy, *Conceived in Crisis: A History of La Salle College* [Philadelphia: La Salle College, 1966], p. 3).

49. *Catholic Herald,* 6 March 1858.

50. Ibid., 23 January 1851, 13 January 1856.

51. Edward A. Mallon, "Sisters of Charity, St. Joseph's College, 1859–1947," *Records of the American Catholic Historical Society* 58, no. 3 (June 1947) :204.

52. "History of the Society of St. Vincent de Paul in the Archdiocese of Philadelphia," *Records of the American Catholic Historical Society* 47, no. 3 (September 1963) :198–207. *Souvenir Sketch of St. Patrick's Church. Annual Report of the Superior of the Theological Seminary of St. Charles Borromeo, 1856–1860,* p. 83, Archives of the American Catholic Historical Society, St. Charles Borromeo Seminary, Philadelphia.

53. *Report of the Central Committee for Relief of Distress in Ireland, 1862–1863* (Dublin: Browne & Nolan, 1864), p. 47; Martin Griffin, "Historical Notes of St. Ann's Church," *Records of the American Catholic Historical Society* 6, no. 4 (December 1895) :438.

54. Ridge, *Ignatius Donnelly,* p. 5. The closing exercise list for Mount Vernon Grammar School includes Irish names (*Philadelphia Inquirer,* 22 December 1860), and there was opportunity for the Irish in night schools as well (*Evening Bulletin,* 28 November 1855 [Crittenden's Commercial College]; in the 1860s there were 8,000 enrolled in the city's night schools (see Edgar W. Martin, *Standard of Living in 1860,* p. 310). Various prominent Irish Catholic leaders attended public schools: William V. McGrath, Democratic state treasurer; Lewis Cassidy, Pennsylvania attorney general; and Dennis Dealy, publisher (Scharf and Westcott, *History of Philadelphia,* 3:1930).

55. Campbell, *Friendly Sons of St. Patrick,* p. 539.

56. *Biographical Catalog of the Matriculates of the College of the University of Pennsylvania* (Philadelphia: Society of the Alumni, 1894), p. 171.

57. Thomas N. Brown, *Irish-American Nationalism* (Philadelphia and New York: J. B. Lippincott Co., 1966) mentions Philadelphia

only rarely in 200 pages and accords it no listing in the index. The continuity of New York's several Irish-American newspapers and the Tammany regime, and the presence of the most notable Irish exiles in New York, placed Philadelphia in a subordinate position in Irish-American affairs.

58. *Catholic Herald,* 13 February 1851, 27 February 1858, 3 March 1858.

59. Ibid., 27 November 1851.

60. Ibid., 27 February 1851.

61. Ibid., 26 February 1856.

62. *Catholic Instructor,* 12 August 1854.

63. Foster, "Philadelphia in Slices," p. 39.

64. *North American,* 25 January 1851.

65. *Evening Bulletin,* 10 January 1856, tells of the rule of intimidation and criminal conspiracy exercised by the notorious Schuylkill Rangers gang. A note on the subscription drive for the House of Good Shepherd appears in the *Catholic Herald,* 3 January 1851, but a permanent building was not built until 1878 (*Catholic Charities and Social Welfare in the Archdiocese of Philadelphia* [Philadelphia: Catholic Children's Bureau, 1825]).

66. *Guardians of the Poor Prostitute's Register* (c. 1868), Archives of the City of Philadelphia, RG 35.167. Dr. Leonard Blumberg, Department of Sociology, Temple University, who has studied prostitution in the city, stated in an interview with the author on 16 May 1969 that some local girls may have given fictitious Irish names and nativity to secure anonymity on entry to the hospital. In his view, however, this would not account for so large a number of Irish names. Dr. Blumberg has concluded that the average life expectancy of girls entering prostitution in the mid-nineteenth century was only five years from the date of entry.

67. James J. Green, "The Organization of the Catholic Total Abstinence Union of America, 1866–1884," *Records of the American Catholic Historical Society* 61, no. 2 (June 1950) :71.

68. E. A. Grattan, "The Irish in America," *North American Review* 52, no. 110 (1841) :225.

69. Connell, *Irish Peasant Society,* p. 3; *Press,* 20 January 1867.

70. *Boston Globe,* 5 August 1888.

71. James J. Green, "Catholic Total Abstinence Union," p. 72.

72. *North American,* 21 April 1853; and *Public Ledger,* 3 January

1870. The *Evening Bulletin,* 28 December 1855, tells of Eileen Muldoon, drunk on the street, husband in prison, children at home in a cold house; and a girl's misfortune due to liquor is described in the Record of House Relief of the Philadelphia House of Industry, entry for 6 November 1870, Urban Archives, Paley Library, Temple University.

73. Dr. Leonard Blumberg of the Sociology Department, Temple University, and the Philadelphia Diagnostic and Relocation Service Corporation analyzed cases 474–965 (case book 28 June 1878–9 June 1879) and found that, of the total of 107 cases of persons with presumably Irish names, 62 involved alcohol (Blumberg to Dennis Clark, 6 March 1968).

74. James J. Green, "Catholic Total Abstinence Union," p. 82.

75. Aaron Abell, *American Catholicism and Social Action, 1865–1950* (Garden City, N.Y.: Hanover House, 1960), pp. 43–44.

76. James J. Green, "Catholic Total Abstinence Union," p. 72, notes that the same process occurred in Saint Louis.

77. *Philadelphia Times,* 16 March 1875.

78. Burt, *Perennial Philadelphians,* p. 576, states that the Irish set the pattern for ghetto social organization in the city.

## Chapter 6

1. The constitution of Irish rural life is described in Evans, *Irish Heritage,* pp. 47–56; McDowell, *Social Life in Ireland,* pp. 28–56; T. W. Freeman, *Ireland: Its Physical, Historical, Social, and Economic Geography* (London: Methuen & Co., 1950), p. 160.

2. These social customs and institutions are described in James Carty, *Ireland from Grattan's Parliament to the Great Famine: A Documentary Record* (Dublin: C. J. Fallon, 1952), pp. 141–42, 149; *Works of William Carleton,* 2:129–355; Padraic Colum, *A Treasury of Irish Folklore* (New York: Crown Publishing Co., 1954), pp. 409–11, 430, 469; Edward R. Norman, *The Catholic Church and Ireland in the Age of Rebellion, 1859–1873* (Ithaca, N.Y.: Cornell University Press, 1965), pp. 45–46.

3. Campbell, *Friendly Sons of St. Patrick,* pp. 362, 380, 441, 442, 468, 474.

4. Ibid., pp. 209–26. The size of the group's treasury indicates the scale of the charitable work (p. 219).

5. Charles Gavan Duffy, *Young Ireland: A Fragment of Irish History, 1840–1850* (New York.: D. Appleton & Co., 1881), p. 318.

6. *Irish American* (New York), 25 September 1858.

7. *Evening Bulletin,* 17 March 1857.

8. *Historical Sketches of the Catholic Church and Institutions of Philadelphia* (Philadelphia: Daniel Mahony, Publishers, 1895), p. iv. These organizations had been active among the Irish for many years. *The Constitution and By-Laws of the Charles Carroll Beneficial Society,* Archives of the American Catholic Historical Society, St. Charles Borromeo Seminary, Philadelphia, Pa., is dated 1834.

9. *Philadelphia North American,* 3 January 1853.

10. John D. Crimmins, *St. Patrick's Day: Its Celebration in New York and Other Places, 1737–1845* (New York: Published by the Author, 1902), pp. 215–35.

11. *Philadelphia Inquirer,* 20 March 1865.

12. *Philadelphia Press,* 17 March 1867.

13. *Philadelphia Press,* 18 March 1868.

14. *Public Ledger,* 14 March 1870.

15. *Evening Bulletin,* 19 February 1856; *Philadelphia North American,* 25 January 1853; *Philadelphia Press,* 17 March 1864, 17 March 1867.

16. T. W. Moody, ed., *The Fenian Movement* (Cork: Mercier Press, 1968), pp. 17, 103.

17. Desmond Ryan, *The Fenian Chief* (Coral Gables, Fla.: University of Miami Press, 1967), pp. 106–17.

18. Thomas N. Brown, *Irish-American Nationalism,* p. 37.

19. William D'Arcy, *The Fenian Movement in the United States, 1858–1886* (Washington, D.C.: Catholic University Press, 1947), p. 33. The Fenian Papers, Archives of the American Catholic Historical Society, St. Charles Borromeo Seminary, Philadelphia, Pa., contain letters to James Gibbons from Colonel William R. Roberts in 1867 from Paris. Roberts was then a leader of a Fenian faction (see Dennis Clark, "Letters from the Underground," *Records of the American Catholic Historical Society* 81, no. 2 [June 1970]: 83–87; idem, "Militants of the 1860's: The Philadelphia Fenians," *Pennsylvania Magazine of History and Biography* 95, no. 1 [January 1971]:98–108). Gibbons printed Fenian and other nationalist

works and speeches (see note on Rev. Patrick Moriarty's speech in T. C. Middleton, "Some Memories of Our Lady's Shrine," *Records of the American Catholic Historical Society* 12, no. 3 [September 1901] :271).

20. Campbell, *Friendly Sons of St. Patrick,* pp. 493–94 (for Hugh McCaffrey, see pp. 468–70). For information on Michael Kerwin see Joseph Denieffe, *A Personal Narrative of the Irish Revolutionary Brotherhood, 1855–1867* (New York: Gael Publishing Co., 1906), p. 281; for note on Dr. William Carroll see Ryan, *Fenian Chief,* Biographical Appendix, p. 305. Carroll led a meeting of the Celtic Society in 1870 (*Philadelphia Press,* 18 March 1870).

21. Denieffe, *Personal Narrative,* p. 74.

22. D'Arcy, *Fenian Movement in the United States,* p. 30.

23. As early as 3 January 1851 the *Catholic Herald* warned the faithful against secret societies. Archbishop Wood issued his circular letter on 13 February 1864 (D'Arcy, *Fenian Movement in the United States,* p. 39); for the Fenians' response, see Moody, *Fenian Movement,* p. 103.

24. For data on Moriarty see McGowan, *St. Augustine's Church,* pp. 92–111. Gibbons's reprint of Moriarty's speech is in the Archives of the American Catholic Historical Society, St. Charles Borromeo Seminary, Philadelphia, Pa. (see p. 19).

25. Denieffe, *Personal Narrative,* p. 214; D'Arcy, *Fenian Movement in the United States,* p. 145. How many Philadelphians were involved is not known. As late as 1868 a Fenian demonstration to draw attention to the execution in England of the "Manchester Martyrs" Allen, Larkin, and O'Brien, seized in a raid to free Fenian prisoners, drew fifteen separate delegations in the city. The groups are listed in a reprinted speech by John O'Byrne, *An Oration on the Occasion of the Funeral Obsequies of Allen, Larkin, and O'Brien* (Philadelphia: John R. Downes, 1868), Archives of the American Catholic Historical Society, St. Charles Borromeo Seminary, Philadelphia, Pa.

26. Report on the Canadian Invasion, Philadelphia, 1867, Fenian Papers, Archives of the American Catholic Historical Society, St. Charles Borromeo Seminary, Philadelphia, Pa. This invasion, organized by Irish Union Army veterans, had high emotional appeal. One Fenian in Ireland, John McCafferty, had appealed to Irish-Americans, citing their Civil War deeds, "Will you grudge to Ireland

what you so freely gave to America?" (William G. Chamney, *Report of the Fenian Conspiracy and Trials of Thomas F. Burke and Others for High Treason and Treason Felony* [Dublin: Alexander Thom, 1869], p. 494).

27. *Philadelphia Press*, 24, 26 October 1865, 6 December 1865; *Evening Bulletin*, 1–4 June 1866, 29 August 1866, 23 September 1866, for instance; *Catholic Standard and Times*, 10, 17 March 1866; *Philadelphia Press*, 10, 11 March 1867; *Philadelphia Inquirer*, 12 March 1867.

28. D'Arcy, *Fenian Movement in the United States*, p. 411.

29. Denieffe, *Personal Narrative*, p. 281.

30. Ryan, *Fenian Chief*, p. 305; and Marcus Bourke and John O'Leary, *A Critical Study in Irish Separatism* (Tralee: Anvil Books, 1967), p. 163. Carroll is mentioned often in the revolutionary circles described in William O'Brien and Desmond Ryan, eds., *John Devoy's Post Bag, 1871–1928*, 2 vols. (Dublin: C. J. Fallon, 1948).

31. *Report of the Delegation of the Philadelphia Emigrant Society to Enquire into the Nature and Operation of the Emigration Laws of the State of New York* (Philadelphia: Merrihew & Thompson, 1854), p. 13, Historical Society of Pennsylvania, Philadelphia, Pa. The Convict Description Docket for the Philadelphia County Prison for 1868–71, Archives of the City of Philadelphia, lists prisoners by place of birth. A sample of listings of prisoners numbered 669–869 shows 27 of 200, or 13 percent, born in Ireland; the proportion of Irish in the city at that time was about 15 percent (see William Dusinberry, *Civil War Issues in Philadelphia, 1856–1865* [Philadelphia: University of Pennsylvania Press, 1965], p. 20). This docket may not reflect criminality among the immigrants with statistical accuracy, however.

32. Foster, "Philadelphia in Slices," p. 34. The *Evening Bulletin* (Philadelphia), 5 January 1856, gave nativities of those arrested in 1855 in the Fourteenth Ward (Spring Garden) and the Eighth Ward (Schuylkill): in Spring Garden 188 of the 622 arrested were Irish; in the Schuylkill area, 558, or 50 percent, of the 1,129 arrested were Irish.

33. *Philadelphia North American*, 21 May 1851; and Foster, "Philadelphia in Slices," p. 34.

34. *Philadelphia North American*, 25 January 1851; *Evening Bulletin*, 21 January 1856.

35. *Public Ledger,* 13 February 1851; *Philadelphia North American,* 10, 11 January 1851.

36. Oscar Sprogle, *The Philadelphia Police: Past and Present* (Philadelphia: n.p., 1887). Data on the role of Lieutenant Flaherty are given in a recollection of St. Clair Mulholland (p. 148). Mayor Richard Conrad, the Nativist elected in 1854, actually set up a regulation that barred foreign-born persons from the police force (St. John Joyce, *Story of Philadelphia,* p. 248).

37. Quoted in Alexander B. Callow, *The Tweed Ring* (New York: Oxford University Press, 1966), p. 196; and Carl Wittke, *We Who Built America* (New York: Prentice-Hall, 1939), p. 165.

38. Ridge, *Ignatius Donnelly,* p. 11.

39. See the listing of fire companies in Scharf and Westcott, *History of Philadelphia,* 3:1911–12.

40. Geffen, "Violence in Philadelphia," pp. 381–410. For a typical notice of fire-company rowdyism see *Evening Bulletin* (Philadelphia), 24 May 1858.

41. Ellis Paxson Oberholtzer, *Philadelphia: A History of the City and Its People,* 4 vols. (Philadelphia: S. J. Clarke Co., 1917–37), 2:309.

42. "They are leaders in all the political rows and commotions and very powerful as a party" (Marryat, *Diary in America,* pp. 395–96). See also Grattan, "Irish in America," p. 208.

43. Robert D. Cross, *The Emergence of Liberal Catholicism in America* (Cambridge, Mass.: Harvard University Press, 1958), p. 88; Callow, *Tweed Ring,* p. 75; Eric L. McKittrick, "The Study of Corruption," in Seymour Lipset and Richard Hofstadter, eds., *Sociology and History: Methods* (New York: Basic Books, 1968), p. 362.

44. *Philadelphia North American,* 28 January 1851, listed Democratic county delegates McCloskey, Meany, Sweeney, McDonough, and Fagan among twenty-eight delegates; the *Public Ledger,* 16 January 1851, listed the forty-one Democratic City Convention nominees, seven of whom had Irish names. The *Catholic Herald,* 13 November 1851, urged immigrants to become naturalized citizens quickly.

45. Benson, *Jacksonian Democracy,* p. 172; Sam Bass Warner, *Private City,* pp. 90–91.

46. Warren F. Hewitt, "The Know Nothing Party in Pennsylvania," *Pennsylvania History* 2, no. 2 (April 1935) :73. For details on James Campbell see *The Dictionary of American Biography* (New York: Scribner & Sons, 1934), 3:454.

47. *Journal of the State Council of the Order of the United American Mechanics of the State of Pennsylvania* (Philadelphia: J. H. Jones, 1850), p. 282, Historical Society of Pennsylvania, Philadelphia, Pa.

48. Warner, *Private City*, pp. 94–95. For a more detailed legal description, see Eli K. Price, *The History of Consolidation of the City of Philadelphia* (Philadelphia: J. B. Lippincott & Co., 1873).

49. Sam Bass Warner, *Private City*, pp. 94–95.

50. *Evening Bulletin*, 16 February 1857.

51. These names appear in listings of council members in *McElroy's Philadelphia Directory*, 1850, 1858, 1864. After 1857 the party affiliations are not listed.

52. Roy F. Nichols, *The Disruption of American Democracy* (New York: Free Press, 1948), p. 210; Irwin Greenberg, "Charles Ingersoll: The Aristocrat as Copperhead," *Pennsylvania Magazine of History and Biography* 93, no. 2 (April 1969) :194.

53. *Catholic Herald*, 25 October 1857.

54. Madeleine Hook Rice, *American Catholic Opinion in the Antislavery Controversy* (New York: Columbia University Press, 1944), pp. 102–3. An incident reported in 1856 illustrates this point: An Irishman in South Carolina expressed his belief in black liberty as well as Irish liberty and barely escaped the locale (*Evening Bulletin*, 13 September 1856).

55. Nicholas B. Wainwright, "The Loyal Opposition in Civil War Philadelphia," *Pennsylvania Magazine of History and Biography* 88, no. 3 (July 1964) :295.

56. Ibid. Some idea of the intensity of the class cleavage can be gathered from such satires of upper-class leadership, with its Masonic and Yankee connections, as appear in Tartan [pseud.], *Philadelphia Malignants* (Philadelphia: Weir & Company, 1863), Library Company of Philadelphia, Philadelphia, Pa. For an illustration of the Irish ties of the Democratic populist faction see *Speech by John O'Byrne to the Democratic Association of Pennsylvania* (Philadelphia: John Campbell, 1868), espousing Ireland's cause

(Library Company of Philadelphia, Philadelphia, Pa.). The taint of "copperhead" disloyalty clung to the party also (*Evening Bulletin*, 8 August 1866).

57. W. E. B. DuBois, *The Philadelphia Negro: A Social Study* (Philadelphia: University of Pennsylvania Press, 1899), p. 39, recounts some of the violent Irish-Negro clashes coincident with elections.

58. Gilchrist and Lewis, *Civil War Era*, p. 172. See also Sam Bass Warner, *Private City*, p. 91; Lincoln Steffens, *The Shame of the Cities* (New York: McClure & Co., 1902), pp. 147–48.

59. Steffens, *Shame of the Cities*, p. 142. The careers of such men as Charles O'Neill, a member of Congress from the Second District in Philadelphia whose terms extended from 1863 to 1871 and from 1873 to 1893, indicate something about party loyalty in the city (see John H. Brown, ed., *The Cyclopaedia of American Biographies*, 7 vols. [Boston: Federal Book Company, 1903), 6:71–72]). Others, among them Francis McLaughlin, Michael J. O'Callaghan, and James P. McNichol, were Republican stalwarts (see biographies in *Prominent and Progressive Pennsylvanians in the Nineteenth Century*, 3 vols. [Philadelphia: Philadelphia Record Publishing Co., 1898]).

60. *Philadelphia Inquirer*, 14 November 1860.

61. *Irish American* (New York), 19 January 1861. Stewart was the grandfather of Charles Stewart Parnell.

62. *Biographical Encyclopaedia of Pennsylvania in the Nineteenth Century* (Philadelphia: Galaxy Publishing Co., 1874), p. 276. For an account of one of Dougherty's rousing speeches, see *Philadelphia Inquirer*, 4 October 1864.

63. *Irish American* (New York), 12 October 1861. George Morgan, *Philadelphia: The City of Firsts* (Philadelphia: Historical Publication Society, 1926), p. 165, gives a list of early volunteer groups in the Twenty-fourth Pennsylvania Regiment (Hibernia Greens, Meagher Guard, Emmet Guard, etc.)

64. John Russell Young, *Memorial History of Philadelphia*, 3 vols. (New York: New York History Co., 1898), 2:179, 181. See also Paul Jones, *The Irish Brigade* (New York: Luce Publishers, 1969); Ella Lonn, *Foreigners in the Union Army and Navy* (Baton Rouge: Louisiana State University Press, 1951), pp. 124–25, 253, 257; and D. P. Conyngham, *The Irish Brigade and Its Campaigns* (London: Burns, Oates & Washbourne, n.d.), p. 300.

65. Schrier, *Ireland and the American Emigration,* p. 178.

66. Conyngham, *Irish Brigade and Its Campaigns,* pp. 261–301; Thomas J. Mullen, "The Irish Brigades in the Union Army," *Irish Sword* 9, no. 34 (Summer 1969) :50–58; *Catholic Herald,* 21 February 1863.

67. James M. Swank, *Notes and Comments on Industrial, Political, and Historical Subjects.* (Philadelphia: American Iron & Steel Assoc., 1897), p. 180. Hansen, *Immigrant in American History* (New York: Harper & Row, 1964), p. 143, notes the strategic position this war service won for the Irish in American opinion. For a Philadelphia reflection of more tolerant attitudes toward immigrants see the *Philadelphia Inquirer,* 19 March 1867. For details on Mulholland see Campbell, *Friendly Sons of St. Patrick,* pp. 465–66.

68. Alexander K. McClure, *Old Time Notes of Pennsylvania,* 2 vols. (Philadelphia: n.p., 1905), p. 371. For information about Philadelphia war industry see Young, *Memorial History of Philadelphia,* 1:535. Erwin S. Bradley, *Triumph of Militant Conservatism: A Study of Pennsylvania and Presidential Politics, 1860–1872* (Philadelphia: University of Pennsylvania Press, 1964), p. 134, notes the favoritism Pennsylvania contractors enjoyed. See also Fite, *North During the Civil War,* p. 216; and Frank R. Taylor, *Philadelphia in the Civil War, 1861–1865* (Philadelphia: City of Philadelphia, 1913), pp. 44–45.

69. Stephen N. Winslow, *Biographies of Successful Philadelphia Merchants* (Philadelphia: James K. Simon, 1864), pp. x, 166. See also *Biographical Encyclopaedia of Pennsylvania in the Nineteenth Century,* pp. 25, 39; and Campbell, *Friendly Sons of St. Patrick,* pp. 396 (Charles Dougherty), 414–15 (James S. Gibbons); Oberholtzer, *Philadelphia,* 3:21.

70. Such satires of the Irish as Lea's [Rufus K. Shapley] *Solid for Mulhooly* were so popular they continued to be printed into the 1890s.

71. Charles C. Tansill, *America and the Fight for Irish Freedom* (New York: Devin-Adair Co., 1957); Alan J. Ward, *Ireland and Anglo-American Relations, 1899–1921* (Toronto: Toronto University Press, 1969).

72. "Even the most superficial acquaintance with the American party structure reveals the prominent part played by Irish-Americans in the great city machines" (Eric Strauss, *Irish Nationalism*

*and British Democracy* [London: Methuen & Co., 1951], pp. v–vi).
The process by which this development took place is described well
in Edward M. Levine, *The Irish and Irish Politicians* (Notre Dame,
Ind.: University of Notre Dame Press, 1966), pp. 8, 53–68.

73. Callow, *Tweed Ring,* p. 4.

74. Sean O'Faolain in his *King of the Beggars* (New York: Viking
Press, 1938), a life of Daniel O'Connell, gives a full depiction of
this political emergence and its ethnic and cultural basis. Robert
McDowell notes that the close relationship between local government and poor-relief in Ireland in the nineteenth century provided a
basis in experience for the political-machine reward system (Mc-
Dowell, "Eve of the Great Famine," pp. 19–55).

75. Adams, *Ireland and the Irish Emigration,* p. 381.

76. James Bryce, *The American Commonwealth,* 2 vols. (New
York: Macmillan Co., 1895), 2:99; address by Daniel Dougherty
to the Literary Society, Lafayette College, 26 July 1859, vol. 2208,
no. 21, Halliday Collection, Royal Irish Academy, Dublin, Ireland.

## Chapter 7

1. *Evening Bulletin,* 17 March 1872.

2. *Philadelphia Times,* 16 March 1875.

3. The famous Philadelphia Mummers parade got much of its
original impetus as a city event from the Irish. Although mumming
was a custom throughout the British Isles and elsewhere, the Philadelphia festivities were stimulated in the southern part of the city,
a heavily Irish area in the nineteenth century. The costumes and
strutting frolic are strikingly similar to those of the "Wren boys"
of rural Ireland (see Lisa Stephens, "The Gaeltacht of West Kerry,"
*Natural History* 79, no. 7 [August–September 1970]:86–89; and
Dennis Clark, "The Mummers and the Mardi Gras: From Folk Fun
to Urban Spectacle" [Master's thesis, Temple University, 1966]).

4. Lorin Blodgett, "The Social Conditions of the Industrial Classes
in Philadelphia" (Paper read at a meeting of the Philadelphia Social
Science Association, 8 November 1883), pp. 7–13, Historical Society
of Pennsylvania, Philadelphia, Pa.

5. *Philadelphia Times,* 16 March 1875.

6. McClure, *Old Time Notes of Pennsylvania,* p. 371.

7. For biographical notes on McLaughlin and Fahy see Leland Williamson, ed., *Prominent and Progressive Pennsylvanians of the Nineteenth Century*, 3 vols. (Philadelphia: Record Publishing Co., 1898); for notes on O'Brien, Gallagher, and Powers see *Philadelphia and Popular Philadelphians* (Philadelphia: North American, 1891).

8. *Dictionary of American Biography*, s.v. "Campbell, James," 3:454.

9. For notes on Sullivan, see Morgan, *City of Firsts*, p. 537; on Dolan, see Cohen, *Rittenhouse Square*, pp. 329–31; on Cahill, Fitzgerald, and Colahan, see Morris, *Makers of Philadelphia*.

10. *Proceedings of the Fourteenth Annual Convention of the Irish Catholic Beneficial Association* (Philadelphia: Kildare Publishing House, 1882), p. 18, Historical Society of Pennsylvania; Goldwin Smith, "Why Send More Irish to America?" *Nineteenth Century* 13 (June 1883):913; Edward O'Meagher Condon, *The Irish Race in America* (New York: A. E. Ford Co., 1887).

11. Joseph L. Kirlin, *Catholicity in Philadelphia* (Philadelphia: James McVey, 1909), pp. 370–510.

12. J. F. Loughlin, "St. Patrick: The Father of a Sacred Nation" (Address given in Philadelphia, 1889), p. 46, Archives of the American Catholic Historical Society, St. Charles Seminary, Overbrook, Pa.; Edward C. Howland, ed., *Henry C. Lea's Minor Historical Writings* (Philadelphia: University of Pennsylvania Press, 1942), p. 313.

13. Donald Kinzer, *An Episode in Anti-Catholicism: The American Protestant Association* (Seattle: University of Washington Press, 1964), Appendix, "Honor Roll."

14. Shinn [Strahan], *A Century After*, pp. 188–90.

15. The *Annual Report of the Chief of Police of the City of Philadelphia for 1876* (Philadelphia: E. C. Markeley, 1877), pp. 100–190, lists the names of arresting officers for a force of 1,200 men; only 72 of the 1,350 arrests were made by men with recognizably Irish names. *The Annual Report of the Chief of Police of the City of Philadelphia for 1885* (Philadelphia: Dunlap & Clarke, 1886), pp. 97–220, lists 100 Irish names among those of 1,800 arresting officers on a force of 1,456 men.

16. Frank M. Goodchild, "Social Evil in Philadelphia," *Arena* 15 (1896):577.

17. *Evening Bulletin*, 15, 19, 24, 25, 26 April 1872; for arrests

see *Second Annual Message of Mayor William B. Smith* (Philadelphia: Dunlap & Clarke, 1886), p. 63; for a Fenian murder, see Henry M. Hunt, *The Crime of the Century; or, The Assassination of Dr. Patrick Cronin* (Chicago: H. L. Kochersberger, 1889).

18. Robert D. Cross, ed., *The Church in the City* (New York: Bobbs-Merrill Co., 1967), pp. 3, 24–28.

19. See Carroll's letters in O'Brien and Ryan, *John Devoy's Post Bag.* Carroll's letters show his deep involvement with the Fenians.

20. Michael Davitt, *The Fall of Feudalism in Ireland* (London: Harper & Bros., 1904), pp. 121, 309.

21. *Philadelphia Record,* 5 April 1887; *Philadelphia Press,* 5 April 1887, 27 February 1889.

22. Davitt, *Fall of Feudalism,* p. 195. A key figure in the organizing of this movement was Martin I. J. Griffin, historian and publisher of *Griffin's Journal.* The tireless Griffin combined modest success in American life with continued concern for Irish affairs.

23. Ibid. p. 432.

24. O'Brien and Ryan, *John Devoy's Post Bag,* 2:369.

25. For Michael J. Ryan see Campbell, *Friendly Sons of St. Patrick,* p. 515; for Maurice Wilhere see Morgan, *City of Firsts,* p. 284; for Timothy Daily see *Philadelphia and Popular Philadelphians,* p. 48.

26. The dour view of American city government and politics held by Bryce is now seen to have been strongly biased (see Robert C. Brooke, ed., *Bryce's American Commonwealth* [New York: Macmillan Co., 1939], pp. 56, 95). Zane Miller sees the machine as performing crucial functions (Miller, *Boss Cox's Cincinnati*). For a discussion of the differing interpretations of boss rule, see Lyle Dorsett, *The Pendergast Machine* (New York: Oxford University Press, 1968), Introduction; for a discussion of the role of the Irish leaders in urban politics see Levine, *Irish and Irish Politicians.* Lloyd Warner elevates the Irish boss to the status of an American archetypal figure, entitling him "Biggy Muldoon" (Warner, *The Living and the Dead: A Study of the Symbolic Life of Americans* [New Haven, Conn.: Yale University Press, 1959], p. 99).

27. Edward P. Hutchinson, *Immigrants and Their Children* (New York: John Wiley & Sons, 1956), tables 21, 25a, 29a, pp. 83, 103, 126.

28. Ibid., p. 95; Maldwyn Jones, *American Immigration,* p. 21;

Geoffrey G. Williamson, "Ante-bellum Urbanization," p. 589.

29. Board of Commissioners Minutes, Richmond District (1852–54), RG 219.1, Archives of the City of Philadelphia; Deed Book TH 100 (1853), p. 549, Archives of the City of Philadelphia; *Evening Bulletin,* 14 September 1856; Wittke, *Irish in America,* p. 231.

30. For a sketch of the politics of these years see St. George Joyce, *Story of Philadelphia,* pp. 273–320; for biographical notes on McAleer, Tobin, and O'Callaghan see Morris, *Makers of Philadelphia,* and *Philadelphia and Popular Philadelphians.* For Harrity, see L. Hamersley, ed., *Who's Who in Pennsylvania* (New York: L. Hamersley Co., 1904), pp. 307–8.

31. Wittke, *Irish in America,* p. 228. For McManus and Nead see Campbell, *Friendly Sons of St. Patrick,* pp. 486, 489.

32. St. George Joyce, *Story of Philadelphia,* pp. 436–37.

33. Campbell, *Friendly Sons of St. Patrick,* p. 449; and Wittke, *Irish in America,* p. 231.

34. Seymour Mandelbaum, *Boss Tweed's New York* (New York: John Wiley & Sons, 1965), p. 58.

35. Edward C. Kirkland, *Industry Comes of Age* (Chicago: Quadrangle Books, 1961), p. 238.

36. Asa Briggs, *Victorian Cities* (New York: Harper & Row, 1970), pp. 16–17.

37. Eric Lampard, "Historical Contours of Contemporary Urban Society," *Journal of Contemporary History* 4, no. 3 (July 1969) :20.

38. The Irish Catholics in Philadelphia did not elect a mayor from their group until the 1960s, but in other cities the Irish were dominant in politics and elected mayors in the late nineteenth century (Robert H. Wiebe, *The Search for Order* [New York: Hill & Wang, 1967], p. 50]).

39. Edward C. Banfield and James Q. Wilson, *City Politics* (Cambridge, Mass.: Harvard University Press, 1963), p. 39; Milton L. Barron, "Intermediacy: Conceptualization of Irish Status in America," *Social Forces* 27, no. 3 (March 1949) :256–63.

40. St. George Joyce, *Story of Philadelphia,* p. 474.

41. Reports of McNichol's activities can be seen in the *Philadelphia North American,* the *Public Ledger,* and the *Philadelphia Inquirer* throughout 1908; and in Morgan, *City of Firsts,* p. 291.

42. *Philadelphia North American,* 9 January 1908.

43. St. George Joyce, *Story of Philadelphia,* p. 474.

44. Allen Davis and Mark Haller, eds., *The Peoples of Philadelphia* (Philadelphia: Temple University Press, 1973).

45. For the position of the church in Ireland see Lyons, *Ireland since the Famine;* and Larkin, "Church and State in Ireland." For the character of Irish Catholicism in the United States, see Patrick K. Eagan, "The Influence of the Irish on the Catholic Church in America in the Nineteenth Century" (O'Donnell Lecture, National University of Ireland, 14 June 1968). The qualities of Victorian religion are discussed in David Daiches, *Some Late Victorian Attitudes* (New York: W. W. Norton Co., 1969), pp. 17–19; James Laver, *Manners and Morals in the Age of Optimism, 1848–1914* (New York: Harper & Row, 1966), pp. 40–43; Irving Bartlett, *The American Mind in the Mid-nineteenth Century* (New York: Thomas Y. Crowell, 1967), pp. 38–40.

46. Dennis Clark, "Philadelphia: Still Closed," *Commonweal,* 1 May 1964, pp. 167–70. By 1900 there were 73 parishes in the city. By 1972 the archdiocese encompassed 316 parishes, 11 colleges and universities, 31 high schools under the archdiocese, 21 private Catholic high schools, 293 elementary parish schools, and 21 private Catholic elementary schools. This structure, with more than a quarter-million students, was the outgrowth of the diligent Irish commitment of the century after 1850 (figures are taken from the *Catholic Directory, 1972* [Philadelphia: Catholic Standard & Times, 1971]).

## Chapter 8

1. Harlan B. Phillips, "The War on Philadelphia's Slums," *Pennsylvania Magazine of History and Biography* 76, no. 1 (January 1952):54.

2. Morgan, *City of Firsts,* pp. 443–44.

3. Eddie McLean was known to the author, as was Monsignor John Keogh.

4. *City Club Bulletin,* vol. 2, no. 1 (13 January 1910), and vol. 2, no. 9 (8 March 1910).

5. Constance O'Hara, *Heaven Was Not Enough* (Philadelphia: J. B. Lippincott Co., 1955), p. 109.

6. Dennis Clark, "Muted Heritage: Gaelic in an American City," *Eire-Ireland* 6, no. 1 (Spring 1971):3–7.

7. Peter Kavanaugh, *The Abbey Theatre* (New York: Devin-Adair Co., 1950), p. 95.

8. I am indebted for material on Joseph McGarrity to Catherine McGinley; to the late Monsignor Peter J. McGarrity, brother of Joseph McGarrity and my former pastor at St. Francis of Assisi parish in Philadelphia; and to John J. Reilly, a co-worker in Irish circles with McGarrity.

9. Catherine McGinley, "Irish-Americans in Philadelphia and Their Involvement with the Irish Independence Movement" (Paper presented to a seminar in the History Department, Temple University, 1966).

10. Ward, *Ireland and Anglo-American Relations*, p. 76; *Evening Bulletin*, 27 March 1960; Dennis Gwynn, *Traitor or Patriot: The Life of Roger Casement* (New York: Jonathan Cape, 1931), pp. 241–43, 328, 405. McGarrity and the Clan-na-Gael were supplying Padraic Pearse, one of the Sinn Fein leaders, with money (O'Brien and Ryan, *John Devoy's Post-Bag*, 2:430. Material on McGarrity appears in Tim Pat Coogan, *The I.R.A.* (New York: Praeger Publishers, 1970), pp. 105–7, 225–66.

11. Quoted in Emmet Larkin, *James Larkin: Irish Labor Leader* (Cambridge, Mass.: MIT Press, 1965), p. 192.

12. The role of the Clan-na-Gael in America in promoting the Easter Rising in 1916 was direct and aggressive (see Leon O'Broin, *The Chief Secretary: Augustus Birrell in Ireland* [London: Chatto & Windus, 1969], p. 193).

13. *Public Ledger*, 1 May 1916.

14. McGinley, "Irish-Americans in Philadelphia," p. 29, gives a list of over 150 organizations supporting Irish independence in Philadelphia alone.

15. *Philadelphia Inquirer*, 23 January 1918. Copies of the *Irish Press* are in the McGarrity Collection in the Villanova University Library, Villanova, Pa.

16. *An Poblacht* (Dublin), Historical Supplement, December 1971; also see Sean Cronin, *The McGarrity Papers* (Tralee: Anvil Press, 1972).

17. John Devoy, *Recollections of an Irish Rebel* (New York: Charles P. Young, 1929), p. 420.

18. The late Dr. Maire Condon of San Jose State College, California, collected archive materials of Irish groups from this period,

and the list of contributors makes clear the value of small dona-
tions. For other helpful material see Sally E. Fawcus, "The Irish in
America and the Struggle for Irish Independence" (Masters thesis,
Bryn Mawr College, 1971).

19. Tansill, in his *America and the Fight for Irish Freedom,* is
highly partisan in favor of Cohalan. Ward, *Ireland and Anglo-
American Relations,* give a more objective view of the role of De
Valera, and of McGarrity's service.

20. Arthur H. Lewis, *The Worlds of Chippie Patterson* (New
York: Harcourt, Brace & Co., 1960).

21. At the turn of the century major Irish meetings took place
in center city. By the 1930s they were held in halls on North Broad
Street, some sixteen blocks north of City Hall. Later the Commodore
Barry Irish Center was opened in Germantown, while Irish dances
were frequently held in the Sixty-ninth Street area at the western
edge of the city, in the district built by contractor John McClatchy.

22. Materials in the collection of the author list McNelis and
Fenerty leading a fund drive in 1944 for the families of I.R.A.
prisoners held by the British, while John J. Reilly gave a radio
talk on 17 March 1945 refuting Winston Churchill's allegation of
Irish "cowardice" in World War II.

23. *Evening Bulletin,* 29 October 1934.

24. Ibid.

25. James Reichley, *The Art of Reform* (New York: Fund for the
Republic, 1959), p. 6.

26. Baltzell has written of the upper-class constriction of Philadelphia (*Protestant Establishment,* p. 122). See also Burt, *Perennial Philadelphians.*

27. *Evening Bulletin,* 10 March 1936, 10 June 1962, 25 February
1968. See also Greg Walter, "Sure, It's Matt McCloskey," *Philadelphia Magazine* 60, no. 2 (February 1969) :63–66.

28. *Evening Bulletin,* 25 February 1968.

29. Ibid., 29 May 1963; and Thomas O'Malley, "John McShain,
Builder," *Columbia,* February 1955.

30. *Evening Bulletin,* 29 May 1963, 3 October 1962.

31. Reichley, *Art of Reform,* pp. 9, 20.

32. Dennis Clark, "Post-Kennedy Irish: The American Decline,"
*Hibernia* (Dublin), March 1967.

33. The largest banks and industrial firms are listed in *Greater Philadelphia Facts* (Philadelphia: Philadelphia Chamber of Commerce, 1960), pp. 14, 71. Firms are ranked by number of employees, value of assets, and volume of business. A check of officers and executives listed in annual reports for these firms revealed the data above.

34. Tom McHale, *Farragan's Retreat* (New York: Bantam Books, 1972).

35. Tate's troubled rule was attributed by some to his inability as an Irishman of modest background to harmonize with the city's elite old family leaders (*Evening Bulletin,* 21 January 1970).

36. The long social estrangement of most Blacks and Irishmen in the city is discussed in Dennis Clark, "Urban Blacks and Irishmen," in Joseph Zikmund and Miriam Ershkowitz, eds., *Black Politics in Philadelphia* (New York: Free Press, 1972).

37. John Guinther, "Has Anybody Here Seen Paddy," *Philadelphia Magazine* 63, no. 3 (March 1972) :150–63.

38. *Philadelphia Daily News,* 10 January 1972; *Evening Bulletin,* 7 February 1972. The columns of Jack McKinney in the *Philadelphia Daily News* during this period cover these activities, as does Dennis Clark's "Irish-American Presence," in *Ethnic Philadelphia* (3, no. 1 [Spring 1972] :3–4), a newsletter published by the Ethnic Heritage Affairs Center, Philadelphia. A composite newspaper entitled *Irish News* was put out during this period and circulated by the Northern Irish Aid Committee.

## Chapter 9

1. Alexis de Tocqueville, *Journeys to England and Ireland,* ed. J. P. Mayer (Garden City, N.Y.: Doubleday & Co., 1968), p. 150.

2. Constance McLaughlin Green, "Sources for Cultural History," in Caroline F. Ware, ed., *The Cultural Approach to History* (Port Washington, N.Y.: Kennikat Press, 1940), p. 277.

3. Analysis of the statistical basis for a more general social history of the city will be gradually forthcoming from the extensive tabulations of the United States census materials for Philadelphia being carried out by Dr. Theodore Hershberg of the University of Penn-

sylvania. The need for such work is stressed in Stephan Thernstrom, "Reflections on the New Urban History," *Daedalus* 100, no. 2 (Spring 1971) :p. 364.

4. Sam Bass Warner, *Private City,* p. 139.

5. Levine, *Irish and Irish Politicians,* pp. 188–89.

6. The early rise of the Irish to political power in other cities is detailed in Geoffrey Blodgett, *The Gentle Reformers: Massachusetts Democrats in the Cleveland Era* (Cambridge, Mass.: Harvard University Press, 1966), pp. 53–63; Alfred Connable and Edward Silberfarb, *Tigers of Tammany* (New York: Holt, Rinehart & Winston, 1967), pp. 149–50; Lyle Dorsett, *The Pendergast Machine* (New York: Oxford University Press, 1968).

7. Handlin, *Boston's Immigrants,* table 2, p. 239, and table 5, p. 242.

8. Ibid., p. 13, and table 1, p. 238. For the number of Philadelphia industries see J. B. De Bow, *The Industrial Resources and Statistics of the United States,* 3 vols. (New York: D. Appleton & Co., 1854), p. 374.

9. See chapter 3.

10. Chapter 4; Handlin, *Boston's Immigrants,* p. 57.

11. Handlin, *Boston's Immigrants,* table 13, pp. 350–51.

12. Ibid., pp. 89–96.

13. Chapter 5 and ibid., pp. 168–69.

14. Blodgett, *Gentle Reformers,* pp. 53–55; Michael Hennessey, *Massachusetts Politics, 1890–1935* (Norwood, Mass.: Norwood Press, 1935), p. 49; Murray Levin, *The Compleat Politician* (Indianapolis, Ind.: Bobbs-Merrill Co., 1962), pp. 32, 42–43.

15. Various works emphasize the multiplicity of factors involved in urbanization and cultural assimilation: Gorden, *Assimilation in American Life,* pp. 70–71; S. N. Eisenstadt, *The Absorption of Immigrants* (London: Routledge & Kegan Paul, 1954), p. 15; Bert F. Hoselitz, "The City, The Factory, and Economic Growth," *American Economic Review* 45, no. 2 (May 1955) :183; Black, *Dynamics of Modernization;* Herbert Gans, "Urbanism and Suburbanism as Ways of Life," in Arnold Rose, ed., *Human Behavior and Social Process* (Boston: Houghton-Mifflin Co., 1962), pp. 625–48; William Mangin, ed., *Peasants in Cities* (Boston: Houghton-Mifflin Co., 1970); Brinley Thomas, *Migration and Urban Development* (London: Methuen, 1972).

16. Lyle and Magdaline Shannon present a selection of theories about assimilation and migrant adjustment and conclude that the closest approach to a satisfactory theory would be one based upon conditions of differential association. Shannon and Shannon, "The Assimilation of Migrants to Cities," in Leo F. Schnore and Henry Fagin, eds., *Urban Research and Policy Planning* (Beverly Hills, Calif.: Sage Publications, 1967), 1:49–75, and esp. 1:69–70. This conclusion and the reasoning supporting it adequately explain the social process described in this book.

17. Thernstrom, *Poverty and Progress*, p. 204.

18. Burt, *Perennial Philadelphians*, p. 577. The comment apparently assumes that Jews are somehow "wilfully" separatist to an ultimate degree.

19. Baltzell, *Protestant Establishment*, p. 122; Sam Bass Warner, *Private City*, pp. 99–123.

20. Handlin, *Boston's Immigrants*, p. 55. Stuart Blumin makes the even stronger statement that the Irish were "absolutely unequipped for urban life" (Blumin, "Mobility and Change in Philadelphia," in Thernstrom and Sennett, *Nineteenth-Century Cities*, p. 200. See also Ralph Turner, "The Industrial City: Center of Cultural Change" in Ware, *Cultural Approach to History*, pp. 228–42; Adams, *Ireland and the Irish Emigration*, p. 346; and George Potter, *To the Golden Door* (Boston: Little, Brown & Co., 1960), p. 171.

21. In 1860 the United States offered its working class better food, housing, and clothing than any nation in Europe, though they were still often inadequate (Egdar W. Martin, *Standard of Living in 1860*, p. 400).

22. Robert D. Cross, "The Changing Image of the City among American Catholics," *Catholic Historical Review* 48, no. 1 (April 1962):51.

23. Milton L. Barron accords the Irish a central status in American life, assigning them a mediating role in the cultural and demographic process of social mobility (Barron, "Intermediacy," pp. 256–63. The distinctiveness of their position with respect to urbanization is pointed up by the fact that later immigration was not so heavily urban as was once believed (Lowell Galloway and Richard Vedder, "The Increasing Urbanization Thesis," *Explorations in Entrepreneurial History* 8, no. 3 (Spring 1971):305–19.

24. John Tracy Ellis, *American Catholics and the Intellectual Life*

(Chicago: Heritage Foundation, 1956); and Andrew Greeley, "Occupational Choice among the American Irish," *Eire-Ireland* 7, no. 1 (Spring 1972) :3–9. In Philadelphia the art exhibits, lectures, and theatrical events of the Irish American Cultural Institute aided by Austin McGreal, Frank Moran, Harry Halloran, Jr., and Hon. James Cavanaugh point toward a new Irish cultural orientation.

# NOTE ON
# SOURCES

Some especially helpful works on the Irish background of this book were *Irish Life in the Seventeenth Century,* by Edward MacLysaght (New York: Barnes & Noble, 1969); *The Great Famine,* edited by R. Dudley Edwards and T. D. Williams (New York: New York University Press, 1957) (for rural life in the mid-nineteenth century); *The History and Social Influence of the Potato,* by Radcliffe Salaman (Cambridge: Cambridge University Press, 1949) (for data on social conditions); Sean O'Faolain's *King of the Beggars* (New York: Viking Press, 1938) and *The Irish* (New York: Devin-Adair Co., 1949) (for perceptive political and social commentary); *The Fortunes of the Irish Language,* by Daniel Corkery (Cork: Mercier Press, 1968) (for linguistic background); F. S. L. Lyons's *Ireland since the Famine* (London: Weidenfeld & Nicolson, 1971) (for a wealth of factual material—a work of major stature); and Lewis Perry Curtis's *Coercion and Conciliation in Ireland, 1880–1892: A Study of Conservative Unionism* (Princeton, N.J.: Princeton University Press, 1963) (for a brilliant summary of conditions in the second half of the nineteenth century).

For demographic study of the Irish background to emigration, *The Population of Ireland, 1750–1845,* by Kenneth Connell (Oxford: Oxford University Press, 1950) is essential. *The Formation of the Irish Economy,* edited by L. M. Cullen (Cork: Mercier Press, 1968), gives a general picture of that field, but *The Economic History of Ireland from the Union to the Famine,* by George O'Brien (London: Longmans, 1921) is still a standard work.

Books formally dealing with Irish social history include the small volume *Social Life in Ireland, 1800–1845,* edited by R. B. McDowell (Dublin: Colm O'Loughlin, 1957) and Kenneth H. Connell's *Irish Peasant Society* (Oxford: Clarendon Press, 1968). T. W. Freeman's *Ireland: Its Physical, Historical, Social, and Economic Geography* (London: Methuen & Co., 1950) gives social data. One of the best works describing the details of daily life is E. Estyn Evans's *Irish Heritage* (Dundalk: Dundalgan Press, 1963). The work of Conrad Arensberg and Solon T. Kimball, *Family and Community in Ireland* (Cambridge, Mass.: Harvard University Press, 1940), is an anthropological landmark. An important tool for research of all kinds on Ireland is *Irish Historiography*, edited by T. W. Moody (Dublin: Carraig Books, 1972). The quarterly journal *Irish Historical Studies* is an excellent source for scholarly articles, but unfortunately, complete files of it are not common in the United States.

Four works by contemporary observers of the great migration are important for the reactions and details they give: John F. Maguire, *The Irish in America* (New York: D. & J. Sadlier Co., 1868); Stephen Byrne, *Irish Emigration to the United States* (New York: Catholic Publishing Society, 1874); Jeremiah O'Donovan, *A Brief Account of the Author's Interview with His Countrymen together with a Direct Reference to Their Present Location* (Pittsburgh: Published by the author, 1864); and Thomas D'Arcy McGee, *A History of the Irish Settlers in North America* (Boston: Patrick Donahoe, 1852).

Several works treating the Irish in the United States in broad survey are important for source material and a general understanding of the group. The two most helpful of these are William V. Shannon, *The American Irish* (New York: Macmillan Co., 1963), and Carl Wittke, *The Irish in America* (Baton Rouge: University of Louisiana Press, 1956). A more recent book that attempts to analyze the social position of the Irish sociologically is Andrew Greeley's *That Most Distressful Nation* (Chicago: Quadrangle, 1972), but because the work is personalized and overemphasizes contemporary social changes, it fails to give sufficient weight to the continuity of Irish-American experience.

The books most relevant to the American phases of this study are those social histories that analyze conditions in given communities during periods of immigrant adjustment. Foremost among such works is Oscar Handlin's classic study *Boston's Immigrants* (New York: Atheneum, 1969). First published in 1941, and twice reissued since then, the book is the prototype in its field. A work of similar substance and quality is Stephan Thernstrom's *Poverty and Progress: Social Mobility in a Nineteenth Century City* (Cambridge, Mass.: Harvard University Press, 1964). A work of smaller scope, but valuable for its skillful use of sources, is Donald B. Cole's *Immigrant*

*City: Lawrence, Massachusetts, 1841–1921* (Chapel Hill: University of North Carolina Press, 1963). David Ward's *Cities and Immigrants: A Geography of Change in Nineteenth Century America* (New York: Oxford University Press, 1971) is a demographic study of immigrant distribution.

Studies of immigrants other than the Irish also throw light on the process of adjustment to urban life. Barbara M. Solomon's *Ancestors and Immigrants* (New York: John Wiley & Sons, 1956) and Robert Ernst's *Immigrant Life in New York City, 1825–1863* (New York: Kings Crown Press, Columbia University, 1949) explore degrees of cohesion among ethnic groups. *The Irish in New Orleans, 1800–1860*, by Earl F. Niehaus (Baton Rouge: Louisiana State University Press, 1965) is very helpful because of its attention to conditions of local history. A penetrating and appreciative study of New York's immigrant Jews, *The Promised City*, by Moses Rischin (New York: Corinth Books, 1964) is one of the few books on immigrants pervaded by a consciousness of the novelty and the power of modern urban conditions. A realistic depiction of ethnic difference and conflict that contrasts with the older "Melting Pot" theme dominating studies of immigrants for a long period is given in Nathan Glazer and Daniel Patrick Moynihan's *Beyond the Melting Pot* (rev. ed. [Cambridge, Mass.: MIT Press, 1970]).

Works on urban history, which have been increasing rapidly in number in recent years, provide the framework within which immigrant experiences must be set. "The Diverging Paths of American History," by Dwight Hoover, in *Urban America in Historical Perspective*, edited by Raymond Mohl and Neil Betten (New York: Weybright & Talley, 1970) summarizes this literature. *A History of Urban America*, by Charles Glaab and A. Theodore Brown (New York: Macmillan Co., 1967) gives a summary view of city development.

The burden of historical work dealing with Philadelphia has been concentrated upon the colonial period when Philadelphia was first a distinctive Quaker enterprise and then the city in which the hopes of nascent nationhood were centered. Carl Bridenbaugh's *Cities in the Wilderness: The First Century of Urban Life in America* (1938) and *Rebels and Gentlemen: Philadelphia in the Age of Franklin* (1942)—both published in New York by Alfred A. Knopf—mention problems occasioned by immigrants from Ireland.

The venerable *History of Philadelphia, 1609–1884,* in three volumes by Thomas Scharf and Thompson Westcott (Philadelphia: L. H. Everts Co., 1884) devotes a few pages to the Native American riots and summarizes the growth of the Catholic church, but Irish immigrants as such are barely treated. In the four volumes of Ellis Paxson Oberholtzer's *Philadelphia: A History of the City and Its People* (Philadelphia: S. J. Clarke & Co., 1921) notice of the Irish is confined to the 1844 riots. The strong bias of such works is documented in "The Egalitarian Myth and American Social Reality," by Edward Passen, in the *American Historical Review* (76, no. 4 [October 1971]:989–1034). John Russell Young, in his *Memorial History of the City of Philadelphia* (New York: New York History Co., 1898), written at the end of the century in which hundreds of thousands of Irishmen had settled in the city, stated only that it would be futile to try to trace the history of the Irish in the city.

Twentieth-century works hardly improve on those of the nineteenth in attention to the Irish immigrants. It was not until *The Perennial Philadelphians: Anatomy of an American Aristocracy,* by Nathaniel Burt (Boston: Little, Brown & Co., 1963), and E. Digby Baltzell's *Philadelphia Gentlemen: The Making of a National Upper Class* (Glencoe, Ill.: Free Press, 1958), that the group's relationship to the upper-class elite of the city was analyzed. Historians of Pennsylvania who include brief histories of Philadelphia add little to this scanty treatment. Sam Bass Warner, in his book *The Private City: Philadelphia* (Philadelphia: University of Pennsylvania Press, 1968), uses population tabulations, city directories, and occupational data to pose an array of social factors that set forth a framework for the history of the city, and for the mass of its population.

It is amazing that the history of education in Philadelphia is so sparsely treated. One dated book, *The Public Schools of Philadelphia* by John T. Curtis (Philadelphia: Burke & McFetridge, 1897), yields some relevant data, but references to immigrant educational experiences are rare. The religious and educational roles of the Catholic church are chronicled in Joseph Kirlin's *Catholicity in Philadelphia* (Philadelphia: John J. McVey, 1909). The files of the *Catholic Herald and Visitor* (Philadelphia), the local Catholic newspapers succeeded by the *Catholic Standard and Times,* contain valuable information, as does the collection of manuscripts, pamphlets, parish histories, and other materials in the Archives of the American Catholic Historical Society, St. Charles Seminary, Overbrook, Pennsylvania.

Computations dealing with employment and housing conditions are explained more fully in "The Adjustment of Irish Immigrants to Urban Life: The Philadelphia Experience, 1840–1870," by Dennis Clark (Ph.D. diss., Temple University, 1970).

The *Pennsylvania Magazine of History and Biography* contains articles dealing with social and political conditions in the city in the mid–nineteenth century that refer to the immigrants, but few of its articles touch directly on the Irish; and less than 10 percent of its material deals with immigrant groups. Articles in the *Records of the American Catholic Historical Society* provide a considerable amount of material on immigrant education and concerns.

In order to estimate the extent to which the Irish who entered Philadelphia in the generation after the famine became subject to social and cultural change under urban influences, some definition of urbanization had to be posited. A succinct definition is hardly attainable in the face of the diversity of social scientists' views on the subject. Works that make possible a composite definition, however, are: Scott Greer, "Urbanization, Parochialism, and Foreign Policy," in James N. Rosenau, ed., *Domestic Sources of Foreign Policy* (New York: Free Press, 1967), p. 260; Richard Dewey, "The Rural-Urban Continuum: Real But Relatively Unimportant," *American Journal of Sociology* 66, no. 1 (July 1960) :126; Kingsley Davis, "The Origin and Growth of Urbanization in the World," *American Journal of Sociology* 60, no. 5 (March 1955) :429–437; Herbert Gans, "Urbanism and Suburbanism as Ways of Life," in Arnold Rose, ed., *Human Behavior and Social Processes* (Boston: Houghton-Mifflin Co., 1962); and Leonard Reissman, *The Urban Process: Cities in Industrial Societies* (Glencoe, Ill.: Free Press, 1964). A description of urbanization by two anthropologists forms a satisfactory definition for the present study: urbanization is the "process by which physical communities emerge with large populations that are concentrated in a small, continuous, compact area and are characterized by intense internal differentiation based on variations in wealth, economic specialization and power" (William T. Sanders and Barbara Price, *Mezoamerica: The Evolution of Civilization* [New York: Random House, 1968], p. 46). An essential addition to the definition above for the purpose of this study is that urbanization, or urban experience, for groups and individuals include presence in a city, livelihood bound to the city, and particular experience in the city not attainable in another social milieu.

Throughout this book there are numerous references to individuals, derived from various sources. Of these, *A History of the Friendly Sons of St. Patrick and of the Hibernian Society,* by John H. Campbell (Philadelphia: Hibernian Society, 1892), which contains much Victorian information, was of special aid.

The Irish newspapers that existed in the city for different periods of time were: The *Irishman and Weekly Review* (1823) and The *Catholic Advocate and Irishman's Journal* (1823), no copies of which are known to exist; *Erin* (1823), available at the U.S. Library of Congress; the *Irish Republican Shield and Literary Observer* (1827–1833), one issue of which is in the Logan Library in Philadelphia; the *Sunday Leader* (1878) and the *Irish Standard* (1879) (no copies extant); the *Free Man and Irish American Review* (1889–1891), the *Irish American News* (1892), The *Philadelphia Hibernian* (1893), the *Irish-American Review and Celtic Literary Advocate* (1898), all represented in the Archives of the American Catholic Historical Society; and The *Irish Press,* in the McGarrity Collection, Villanova University Library, Villanova, Pennsylvania.

# INDEX